OVER 100 NEW UFO PHOTOS! DEEMED TO BE REAL!

UFO REPEATERS!
Seeing Is Believing
The Camera Doesn't Lie!

Timothy Green Beckley And Sean Casteel

With Scott Corrales And Tim R. Swartz

Warminster Intuitive Art By Carol Ann Rodriguez

Inner Light/Global Communications

**UFO REPEATERS!
SEEING IS BELIEVING
THE CAMERA DOESN'T LIE!**

UFO Repeaters! Seeing Is Believing - The Camera Doesn't Lie!

By Timothy Green Beckley, Sean Casteel, Scott Corrales and Tim R. Swartz

Copyright © 2015- by Timothy G Beckley
dba Inner Light - Global Communications
All Rights Reserved

Printed in the United States of America
Inner Light/Global Communications, P.O. Box 753,
New Brunswick, NJ 08903

No part of this book may be reproduced, stored in retrieval system or transmitted in any form by any means, electronic, mechanical, photocopying, recording or otherwise without the express permission of the publisher. Please address any questions about this book to:
mrufo8@hotmail.com

Timothy Green Beckley: Editorial Director
Carol Ann Rodriguez: Publishers Assistant
Tim R. Swartz: Editor
Sean Casteel: Associate Editor
William Kern: Associate Editor
Cover Graphics: Tim R. Swartz

For Free Subscription To The Conspiracy Journal Write:
Tim Beckley/Global Communications
Box 753, New Brunswick, NJ 08903

Email: mrufo8@hotmail.com

www.ConspiracyJournal.Com
www.TeslasSecretLab.Com

Contents

1. IS IT THE MEAT OR THE MOTION? - 7

2. ARE THE ALIENS BEING OVERTLY FRIENDLY? - 10

3. UFOS: IGNITING THE COSMIC FIRE WITHIN - 13

4. ELLEN CRYSTALL – FAR AFIELD IN PINE BUSH - 44

5. CRYSTALL-CORNET UFO PHOTOS - 61

6. ELIZABETH KLARER OF SOUTH AFRICA - 64

7. WHEN UFOS GO BREEZING THROUGH - 70

8. THE FASCINATING ELECTRIC UNIVERSE OF THE LATE HOWARD MENGER - 85

9. JOSEPH FERRIERE – A SMOKING CIGAR AND A TOP-SHAPED SHIP - 125

10. VIVA MEXICO! - 138

11. UP WARMINSTER'S CRADLE HILL WITH SKY-WATCHERS BOB STRONG AND ARTHUR SHUTTLEWOOD - 162

12. UFO REPEATERS STILE ITALIANO - 177

13. THE GALACTIC MISSION OF MARC BRINKERHOFF - EXTRAORDINARY PHOTOGRAPHER OF SPACECRAFT AND ALIEN BEINGS - 194

14. TOM DONGO, SEDONA AND THE BRADSHAW RANCH - 217

15. STRANGE CRAFT WITH OCCUPANTS PHOTOGRAPHED OVER TURKEY - 241

16. ROB HARTLAND OF AUSTRALIA - 256

17. THE UFOS POSE FOR PAUL VILLA - 261

18. WHERE HAVE ALL THE SPACEMEN GONE? - 275

UFO Repeaters! Seeing Is Believing - The Camera Doesn't Lie!

IS IT THE MEAT OR THE MOTION?

By Timothy Green Beckley and Sean Casteel

TO cop some lyrics from the song "Some Guys Have All the Luck," sung by our favorite British rocker Rod Stewart . . .

Some guys have all the luck
Some guys have all the pain
Some guys get all the breaks
Some guys do nothing but complain

Certainly these words are very appropriate to start out this book on UFO Repeaters. Because some observers, like Joseph Ferriere, Marc Brinkerhoff and Ed Walters, seem to possess "all the luck" necessary to take repeated UFO photos.

While some people like Paul Villa "have all the pain," finding themselves harassed after going public and even their homes being burned to the ground.

Some guys "get all the breaks." Take, for example, Turkish security guard Yalcin Yalman, the late Betty Hill, and Mexican journalist Carlos Diaz, whose plasma balls seem to almost land in his lap every time he is out with a camera.

UFO Repeaters! Seeing Is Believing - The Camera Doesn't Lie!

And, certainly, nobody does more to "complain" than the skeptics of the world who are, as physicist Stanton Friedman would say, nothing but "noisy negativists."

This book could be called nothing but phenomenal. Not since the likes of the late Wendelle Steven's UFO Archives have more reputable UFO photos been published in one place. Yes, folks, step right up, for they are all here for you to gawk at and to try to explain – if that is to your liking.

After all, we were not there when these photos were taken so we only have the reliability of the observers and those that claim to be experts at analyzing UFO photos. It's up to each of you to make the ultimate decision.

There are several other areas of interest here that fascinate us but about which we can only ponder.

Is it the individual – the UFO Repeater – who is solely responsible for the images on the film or video? Do they possess some sort of tracking device – an implant? – that the aliens use as a homing apparatus to keep in touch with their representatives?

Are some of the images "psychic" in nature? Are they manifested by the Repeaters themselves? Sort of like a poltergeist event? Perhaps some of the case histories recounted in this book are not really representative of alien visitors but are paranormal in nature? Stella Lansing's case can certainly be placed in this category.

Or perhaps it's that the locale is a "hotspot" that draws the UFOs in, and anyone could be standing in this location and capture weird images which are indisputably NOT anything within the realm of the "normal."

Perhaps it is a combination of all of the above . . . that would be my thinking on the subject, but it doesn't have to coincide with yours.

Regardless of your empirical attitude, I think this is a book you will get a lot out of. It certainly is a photo album like no other, and it's probably something you could use as an ice break to show your friends.

And who knows – you could be the NEXT UFO Repeater!

Timothy Beckley
mrufo8@hotmail.com

UFO Repeaters! Seeing Is Believing - The Camera Doesn't Lie!

Tim Beckley, left, and Sean Casteel at the National UFO Conference in Hollywood, California, in 2004.

ARE THE ALIENS BEING OVERTLY FRIENDLY?

AS I was doing the research and writing for this book, I found myself greatly encouraged by all of the examples of pleasant and agreeable UFO contact reported here. Over and over, I was struck by the fact that the aliens seem to be quite overtly "making friends" with certain people, people whom the aliens regarded as worthy candidates for a trusting relationship with the unknown.

For example, the story of Howard Menger. As a young boy Howard encountered a beautiful space woman who told him there was a benevolently-planned lifetime ahead of him. The woman said human history was entering a phase in which her "alien" race would be reaching out to certain chosen individuals as part of a larger plan to save "their" portion of humanity. Menger did indeed have a lifelong relationship with the Space Brothers and was apparently chosen to spread the truth of their existence by repeatedly photographing their spacecraft and other manifestations.

Also, in the case of Joe Ferriere, we again see that the initial contact was made in childhood and that there followed a gradual opening up to a form of cosmic love as the experiencer moved on to adulthood. And Joe, like nearly everyone in this book, has the photos to prove it.

Why are these Repeaters granted this kind of privileged relationship with some UFO occupants? Why do the aliens seem to cancel the "terror factor" in some cases and instead establish a loving bond with some experiencers that continues throughout the mortal's entire life?

I know that you, the reader, realize that this is obviously an unanswerable question. The vagaries by which the Space Brothers pick and choose among us remain unknown, and this situation will likely persist until the aliens reveal the whys and wherefores of their selection process themselves. We are not likely to somehow find that out in some way independent of direct revelation on their part.

But, in the meantime, we at Inner Light/Global Communications can offer you this, a book that takes the stories of these photographs and the people who took them basically at face value. We have no reason to doubt the photos' authenticity, and many have long ago passed muster with photo analysis experts who were forced to concede that, whether or not there really IS an alien presence, the photos themselves were not the result of tampering or tricks.

The aliens have chosen to reveal their existence in many ways since Kenneth Arnold's 1947 sighting started the ball rolling into the modern UFO era. If this is so, why would occasional genuine photos not be part of that overall mix? Why would the UFO occupants withhold that kind of verification if they were willing to offer so many other forms of proof and confirmation?

I can't think of any reason. Can you?

Sean Casteel

UFO Repeaters! Seeing Is Believing - The Camera Doesn't Lie!

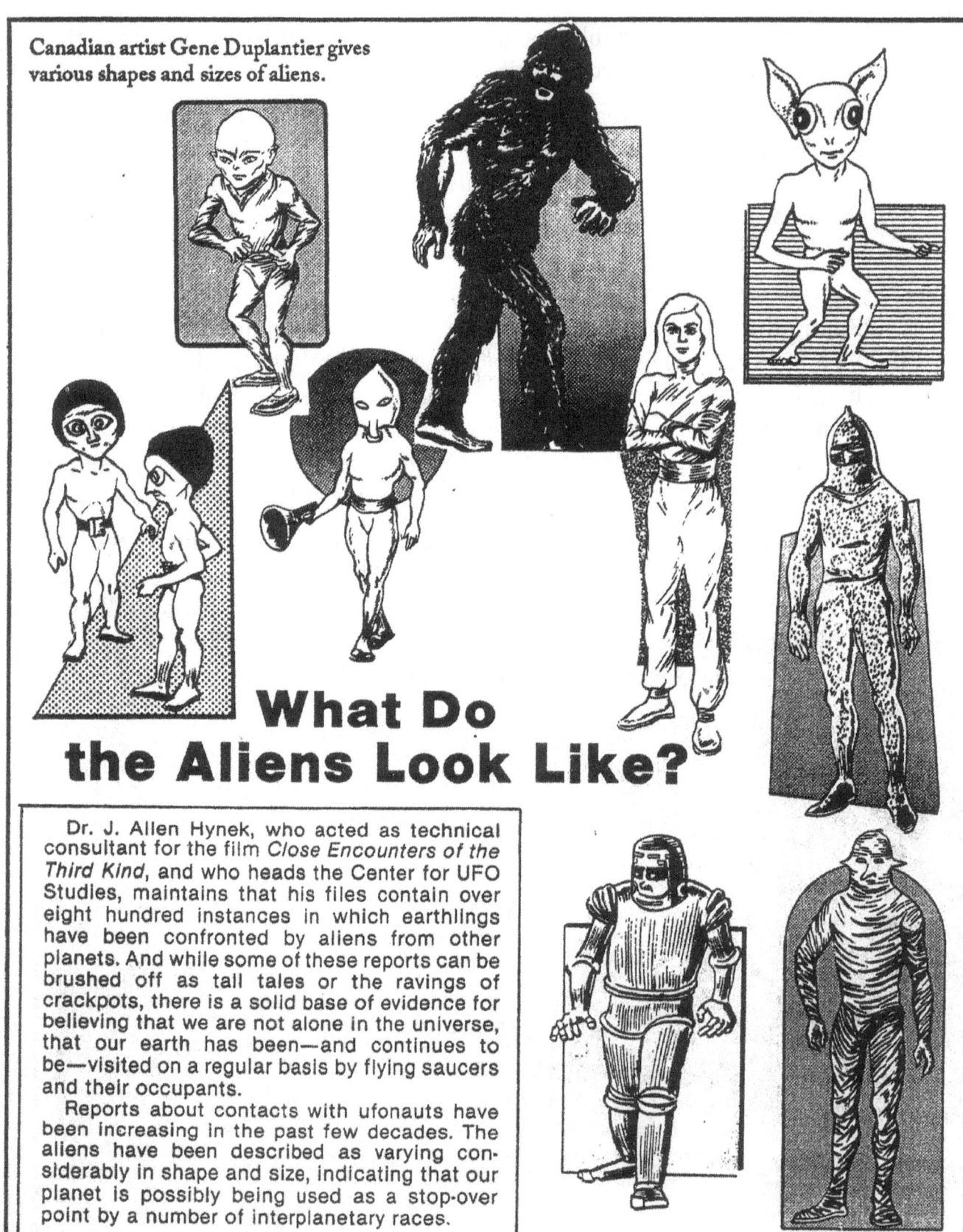

Canadian artist Gene Duplantier gives various shapes and sizes of aliens.

What Do the Aliens Look Like?

Dr. J. Allen Hynek, who acted as technical consultant for the film *Close Encounters of the Third Kind*, and who heads the Center for UFO Studies, maintains that his files contain over eight hundred instances in which earthlings have been confronted by aliens from other planets. And while some of these reports can be brushed off as tall tales or the ravings of crackpots, there is a solid base of evidence for believing that we are not alone in the universe, that our earth has been—and continues to be—visited on a regular basis by flying saucers and their occupants.

Reports about contacts with ufonauts have been increasing in the past few decades. The aliens have been described as varying considerably in shape and size, indicating that our planet is possibly being used as a stop-over point by a number of interplanetary races.

UFOS: IGNITING THE COSMIC FIRE WITHIN
By Tim R. Swartz

UFOs confound us with a number of different mysteries. First, we have the mystery of UFOs themselves: unknown, seemingly solid objects that fly around our skies with impunity. Next, there are the UFO occupants that seem to come in as many unusual shapes and sizes as the vehicles they allegedly pilot. And last are the strange aftereffects that are suffered by some people who have had contact of one form or another with a UFO. These aftereffects can be referred to as meta-consciousness.

The reactions that some people have after a UFO encounter indicate a connection between the eyewitness and the phenomenon that may go beyond the physical and into the realms of the mind and even the spirit. It also has to be taken into consideration that often UFO encounters for many people do not just happen once, but are an ongoing experience throughout a person's life.

The questions we have to ask are: Why would visitors from other planets go out of their way to continuously maintain contact with an individual, and why would these contacts also induce paranormal or mystic responses from the human contactees? Perhaps we are making some broad assumptions about the true nature of UFOs. Or maybe we are asking the wrong questions altogether.

BEYOND THE HUMAN MIND AND SPIRIT

Jerome Clark and Loren Coleman, in their book "**The Unidentified**," state as their "First Law of Paraufology" that the UFO mystery is primarily subjective and symbolic. While they admit that the phenomenon is not without objective aspects, they maintain that such manifestations are only "subsidiary" displays "whose cause can be traced to certain extrasensory functions of the brain."

Their "Second Law of Paraufology" says that the objective manifestations associated with UFOs are "psychokinetically-generated byproducts of those unconscious processes which shape a culture's vision of the Otherworld. Existing only temporarily, they are at best only quasi-physical."

There are numerous theories regarding the UFOs' place of origin and their true identity. Practically every investigator has a favorite source for the UFO phenomena, whether physical or ethereal. Generally, these arguments are distilled to the central issue of whether the UFO intelligences are essentially physical beings from some other physical planet or nonphysical beings from an invisible realm in our own world. Conceivably, both theories may be correct.

RENDEZVOUS WITH THE UNKNOWN

Author Regan Lee says that the psychic aspect of UFOs seems to be too often ignored or dismissed by many researchers who perceive it as a "New Agey" element that is an embarrassment to "serious" UFO researchers. However, Lee suggests that there is a psychic thread within the UFO experience, and it is dishonest to ignore it since UFO lore is full of stories of people who have had psychic or telepathic experiences in the context of their UFO encounter.

Gail Mangas of Toledo, Ohio, had no interest in UFOs or the paranormal. She was a divorced mother of two children and a waitress at a local restaurant with little time to do anything else except care for her family – that is, until she had a rendezvous with the unknown.

One night as she drove home from work, Gail noticed a strange light in the sky that seemed to be following her car. The light was reddish in color and about the size of a half-dollar held at arm's length.

When Gail was about a mile from her home, driving along a particularly deserted stretch of road, the light suddenly zoomed out of the sky and positioned itself directly in front of the car.

UFO Repeaters! Seeing Is Believing - The Camera Doesn't Lie!

"I was absolutely terrified," she remembered. "The object blocked the road so I had to stop or risk running into it. Its light was so bright that I had to shield my eyes with my hand."

Before Gail had a chance to react, the weird light disappeared just as suddenly as it had appeared. Shaken, Gail drove the rest of the way home without further incident. She might have forgotten about her unusual experience if it wasn't for what occurred to her afterwards.

"That was the point where my life changed completely," she said. "I became interested in science and math and read everything I could get my hands on. This was so unlike me; I had barely graduated from high school and now I was reading books that were written for scientists. And the really weird thing was that I understood them."

Gail also noticed that, along with her increased intelligence, she had also developed the power to heal and to tell what others were thinking.

"It was as if the UFO awakened some part of me that had laid dormant all of my life," she said. "I can't explain it, but I know deep inside that I have been chosen somehow."

Gail also said that she has the feeling that some other intelligence is guiding her to develop both mentally and spiritually. She feels that she has some mission to fulfill for mankind in the future.

"I don't know what my mission will be – I only know that I am not the only one to be contacted this way. There are thousands, maybe millions of others on this planet that are being prepared for something truly great in the future."

ENHANCED EVOLUTION

Gail Mangas's experience is not unique. Throughout history there have been others who have touched the unknown and returned changed somehow. They have achieved meta-consciousness. Perhaps these individuals are experiencing a sort of enhanced evolution, intended to carry humankind quickly beyond this point in our development when our passions often outweigh our intelligence.

Jacques Vallee, in his book **"*Dimensions*,"** writes that the UFO phenomenon is one of the ways through which an alien form of intelligence of incredible complexity is communicating with us symbolically, and that certain paranormal phenomena associated with UFOs are one of the manifestations of a "spiritual control system for human consciousness."

For a UFO-enhanced spiritual experience, the term "Cosmic Consciousness," coined by the Canadian psychiatrist Richard Maurice Bucke in 1899 to denote a higher state of spiritual awareness, has been used by some researchers as an explanation for what has occurred. Bucke writes in his book, **"Cosmic Consciousness,"** "The prime characteristic of cosmic consciousness is a consciousness of the cosmos, the life and order of the universe." It has been demonstrated that, under certain circumstances, the result of UFO experiences has been the transformation of human consciousness. This transformation often results in the form of changes in personal and social interactions as well as an explosive development of mental abilities and awareness that goes beyond the recipient's previous mental capabilities.

Through quantum science, researchers have been delving into the human brain as a path toward understanding human consciousness. Gerald Edelman, 1972 Nobel Prize winning neuroscientist, uses magneto encephalography to explain the workings of our brain. In his book, **"Wider than the Sky: The Phenomenal Gift of Consciousness**," he wrote how he measured tiny electromagnetic currents in small groups of neurons to develop neurological correlates of consciousness. Edelman determined that there is a wide variation in neural response among individuals responding to the same stimulus or scene. He also found that there is no command center, no single location in the brain where consciousness takes place.

Edelman's discovery ties in with the research of anesthesiologist Stuart Hameroff and mathematician Roger Penrose. The pair suggest that quantum computation occurs in cytoskeletal microtubules within the brain's neurons. They base their research on a quantum view of the brain that assumes consciousness self-organizes and forms patterns of reality. "The brain simulates reality based on sensory input and is also intimately connected to that reality at the quantum level."

If the human brain, and subsequently the human mind, actually operates on a quantum level, what is it that really takes place during a UFO experience that can cause such a drastic change in a person's mental faculties and personality? The model proposed by Hameroff and Penrose suggests that a UFO encounter affects the experiencer beyond the physical parameters of the brain to a level that is poorly understood by science. However, centuries of explorers in the realms of philosophy and the psychic sciences have a better understanding of the deeper levels of human consciousness.

Scholars, such as philosopher and scientist Michael Polanyi, assert that the sudden appearance of what seem to be extraordinary abilities (psychic powers, sudden and rapid increase in intelligence, etc.) demonstrates that human consciousness has a hierarchy of levels and that our lives evolve as we climb to higher levels, successfully integrating each stage as we progress. Cosmic Consciousness is not something that has to evolve or be artificially implanted; it is already there.

LEVELS OF CONSCIOUSNESS

The late author Colin Wilson suggests that there are at least six degrees of consciousness. Level 0—deep sleep; Level 1—dreaming or hypnagogic; Level 2—mere awareness or unresponsive waking state; Level 3—self awareness that is dull and meaningless; Level 4—passive and reactive, normal consciousness that regards life 'as a grim battle'; Level 5—an active, spontaneous, happy consciousness in which life is exciting and interesting; Level 6—a transcendent level where time ceases to exist. Wilson speculates that there are probably additional levels of consciousness that go beyond our ability to comprehend and express.

Indian yogis and mystics classify the states of consciousness differently. They point out that human beings normally experience only three states: sleeping, dreaming and waking. In meditation, you fleetingly experience Turya, literally the fourth state, or transcendental consciousness, commonly known as Samadhi. When this state coexists and stabilizes with the other three, that is the fifth state, Cosmic Consciousness. The sixth state is God Consciousness, whereby you see God everywhere and in everything. The last is Unity Consciousness, what is within is also outside—pure consciousness.

Spiritually, consciousness is as vast as the universe, both known and unknown. Consciousness at this elevated level becomes capable of magical powers, defying accepted scientific physical laws and giving us a glimpse of probable future developments. This sounds very similar to the meta-consciousness that is achieved by some UFO experiencers.

William S. English, in his article, *"Paranormal Activity and Its Relationship to the UFO Abduction Phenomenon,"* writes that the trauma of a

UFO experience may cause the brains of the experiencers to shut down in order to be able to assimilate the data necessary to cope with the incident in their lives.

"In many cases these incidents are ongoing occurrences which then would require some sort of mental manipulation on the part of the abductors to keep control of their subject," writes English.

"Because of the ingrained human survival instinct, the human brain begins to increase its bio-electrical activity, thereby causing paranormal activity in its surrounding vicinity, whether it manifests itself as uncommonly clear memories that cause the abductee/contactee to relive the physical sensations that they were subjected to during the course of their abduction or other physical manipulations in their surroundings, i.e., poltergeist, telepathy, psychokinesis.

"The second possibility we must consider is the physical modification or manipulation of the human brain on the part of the abductors, i.e., implants, bio-genetic engineering or modifications, etc. We know that it is possible to control the human mind or at least certain areas of the brain that will cause pleasure and pain, anger and apathy. Therefore, why is it not possible for a possibly more advanced culture to have carried this further and be able to control all aspects of the brain, making possible such things as channeling (communications) and all of the previously mentioned paranormal phenomena?"

In regards to the central idea of this chapter, English's thesis can be taken a step further. If the intelligence behind the UFO phenomenon can control ALL aspects of the human brain, then it is feasible that ALL aspects of human consciousness could also be controlled and advanced. What is still open to debate is whether or not the rapid advancement of consciousness is deliberately initiated or if it is a symptom/byproduct of contact with unknown energies associated with UFOs. The other question is why are only certain people affected?

THE CONTINUING UFO EXPERIENCE

One of the great mysteries of the whole UFO phenomenon is why certain people have continued UFO sightings and experiences. Debunkers insist that all repeat experiencers are perpetuating a hoax for the sake of publicity and money. However, using UFOs to gain fame and fortune is decidedly a foolish venture as there have been no millionaires made rich by claiming contact with extraterrestrials. In fact, the opposite usually occurs. UFO witnesses, especially those who go public with their encounters, often find their lives have been changed for the worse. Their friends and family may abandon them. They may experience long periods of depression and anxiety. Some have even had unexplained incidents of extremely bad luck that have resulted in horrendous injuries and even premature death.

Seeing a UFO is certainly not all fun and games.

So why would someone admit to having repeat UFO encounters? Many Repeaters never step forward, and it is only by chance that their encounters are ever discovered by researchers.

Unlike their earlier counterparts, a majority of UFO contactees after the 1960s have remained quiet about their experiences. They have avoided publicity and fame, and often not even their family or closest friends are aware of what they have been going through.

The late John Keel attempted to find a common factor in the thousands of "silent contactee" events. Originally a skeptic, Keel eventually became convinced of the existence of powerful but unpredictable beings. He found a mysterious, ultimately destructive predictive force emerging from the contactees' ongoing reports.

"What astonished me most were the predictions coming in from a wide variety of sources: mediums, automatic writers, spirit world communications – they all were coming up with the same information as the UFO contactees. Often the prophecies were phrased identically but coming in from different sections of the country. It was so beyond coincidence that I could not overlook the peculiar set of correlative factors."

STELLA LANSING

The peculiar emergence of paranormal abilities among those who have come into contact with UFO intelligences has perplexed UFO researchers and alienated many of the "nuts-and-bolts" believers in the phenomenon. One such controversial person was Stella Lansing, from Palmer, Massachusetts. Lansing had the strange ability to apparently "call down" UFOs and photograph them using both still and film cameras. Many of the images produced were not apparent when Stella took the pictures but instead seemed to spontaneously appear on film.

Unfortunately, there is scant information about Lansing's early experiences involving UFOs, but she claimed to have experienced seeing strange little men,

UFO Repeaters! Seeing Is Believing - The Camera Doesn't Lie!

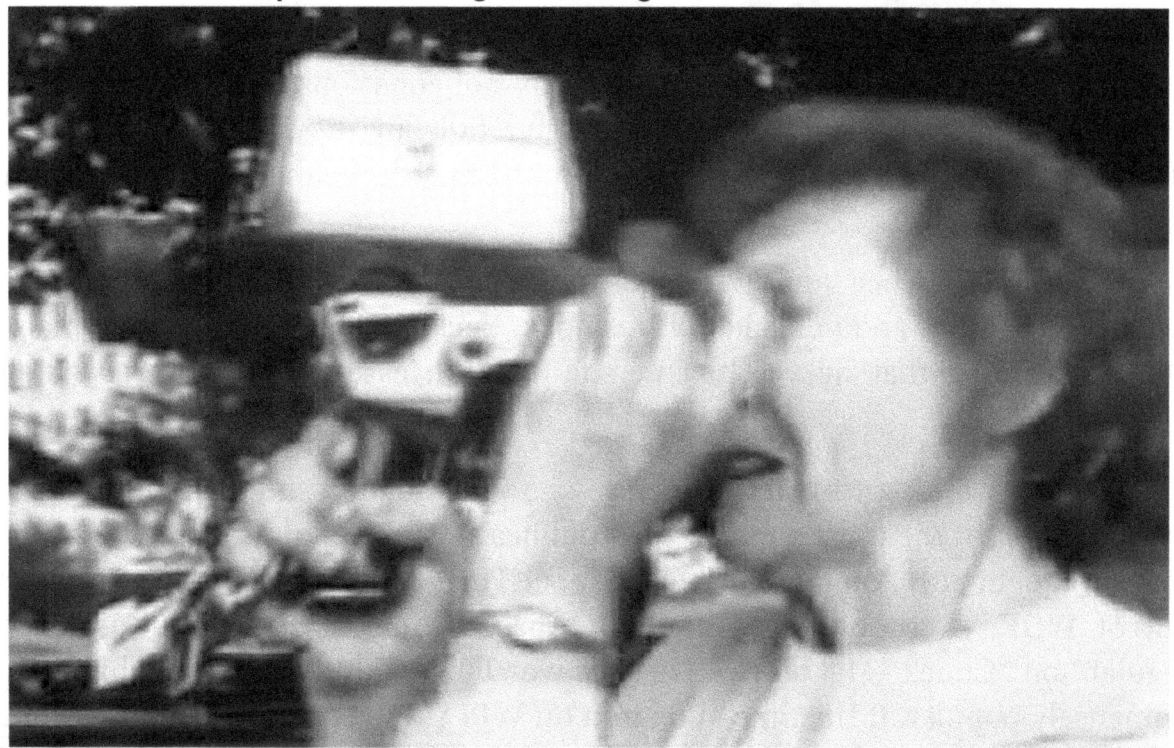

Above: Stella Lansing photographed a wide variety of unusual images on film ranging from "UFO" type objects to human figures.

Below: While filming UFOs in 1973, Lansing captured on 8MM film what appeared to be four men through a "window" of the craft.

voices speaking out of nowhere, creatures, loss of consciousness, "electric shock" from a shimmering figure, a gaping, round hole in the ice, a craft possibly surfacing from underwater, miniscule footprints, religious symbols, bizarre harassments, etc.

UFO researcher and writer Sean Casteel spoke with Timothy Green Beckley, co-author and publisher of this book. Beckley said that he has no qualms about admitting that he was the person who, in essence, "discovered" Stella Lansing.

"I was working with Jim Moseley, who was the publisher of 'Saucer News,' without a doubt the most popular UFO publication of the mid to late-1960s. Jim was a frequent guest on the Long John Nebel 'Party Line' show, broadcast nightly out of WOR, a 50,000-watt, Manhattan-based radio station. Jim was also a regular on Chuck McCann's 'Let's Have Fun' kiddie program, which was immensely popular at the time and aired on WPIX-TV. Chuck, for some peculiar reason best known to himself, brought Jim on several times to hype his semi-glossy UFO publication, although the show was aimed at a ten to fourteen-year-old audience that Chuck kept entertained by using a Charlie McCarthy-like dummy as well as other child-appropriate routines.

"As far as New York City went, Jim was most definitely 'king of the flying saucer hill.' For several years, he organized monthly UFO meetings at a number of midtown hotels, presenting lectures by some of the top names in the UFOlogical field. The average audience grew from a mere 50 people to culminate in 1967 with a crowd of over ten thousand who attended the largest indeed UFO convention ever held. I had worked with Jim helping coordinate both his giant expos as well as the meetings he held in the Times Square area.

"Since Jim was always rather busy running around like a mad man giving interviews or even just putting out folding chairs for SRO crowds that might materialize from time to time, I sort of became his eyes and ears. People would approach me when they couldn't get his attention, often wanting some sort of 'favor' or even trying to get booked to speak at one of these programs.

"One such individual came up to me one evening and introduced herself as Stella Lansing. She had driven down from New England and wanted Jim to view a series of home movies she had taken which showed, or so she said, some really weird things – from UFOs in the sky to spooky figures and faces which were not visible to the naked eye but would show up when the 8mm film strips were

UFO Repeaters! Seeing Is Believing - The Camera Doesn't Lie!

Some of Lansing's films show strange clock-like formations of lights that overlap the frames. Even more bizarre, some of the lights appear to be saucer-shaped UFOs. These unusual images appeared on six different cameras and two different types of film.

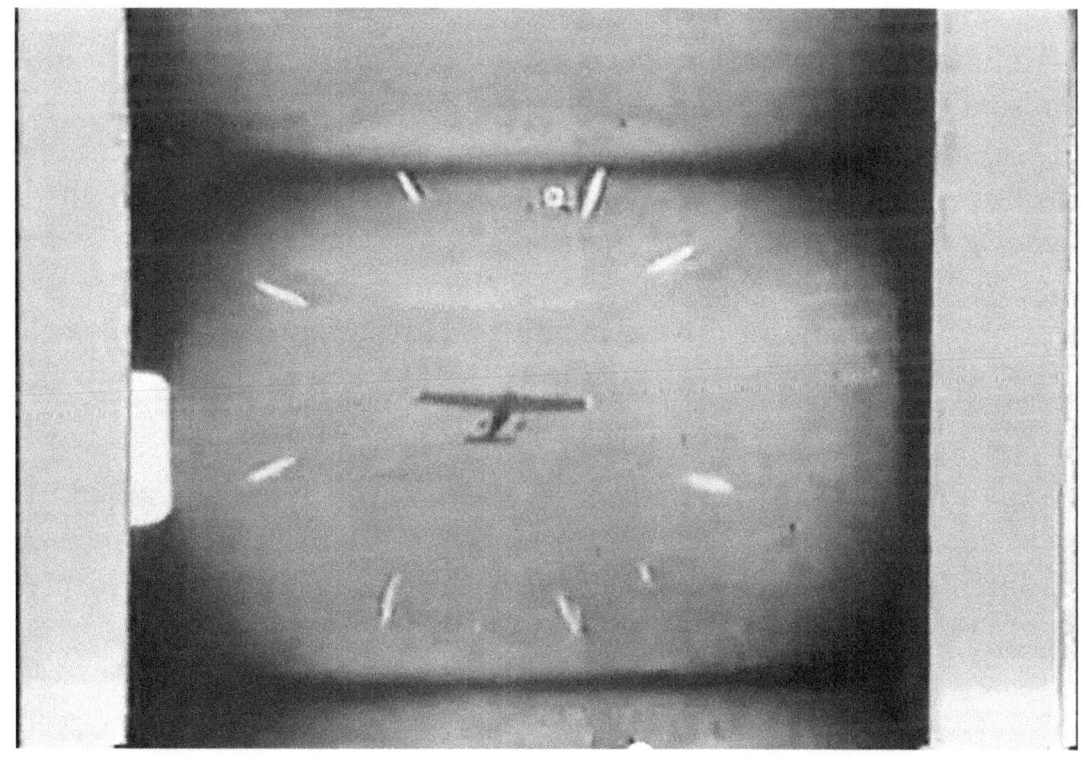

developed. Frankly, Jim was a more nuts-and-bolts sort of guy and had expressed his opinion – at least at first – that Stella was 'a bit of a flake,' or something to that effect. He didn't think that anyone would be interested in hearing what she had to say. He more or less put her in the crackpot category. Which is not to say that some of his regular speakers couldn't also be relegated to this classification, including the Mystic Barber, who walked around with an antenna on his head to ward off mental bombardment from aliens.

"But, to me, Stella Lansing seemed pretty sane, and so I offered to step in for Jimbo and view her presentation. Though skeptical about the things she had caught with her home camera, I was also impressed and thought she deserved to have her findings viewed. So, after a bit of arm twisting, I managed to get Stella a booking at one of Moseley's Friday night soirees.

"Stella talked about her experiences and showed her home movies, and those in attendance craned their necks forward to get a better view of what was being projected on the screen in front of the hall.

"After the meeting, I remember Jim saying he, too, was puzzled by what this nice enough lady had managed to photograph. At this point, I think we both realized that the camera doesn't lie, though we weren't willing to offer any suggestions as to what was causing all these eerie, phantom-like phenomena to appear on Stella's film."

Tim says there must have been a number of important researchers in the field present as she gave her talk because soon Stella Lansing was getting asked to speak elsewhere and to share her photographic data with some important investigators, including Jim and Coral Lorenzen, who headed up the Aerial Phenomena Research Organization. In fact, APRO was putting on a public symposium in Baltimore and had asked Stella to make an appearance with her photographic material at a private meeting – Invitation Only, VIP – held in a suite somewhere in the hotel.

"Jim Moseley, Gray Barker (who had written the first book on the UFO terrorists known as the Men-In-Black) as well as myself had attempted to crash the event and were quickly escorted to the door . . . sort of funny, since we had, for all intents and purposes, 'discovered' Stella Lansing and presented her findings to the world."

Lansing's photos and films of UFOs were definitely odd; one film seemed to show four occupants through a window on the object. Other 8mm films contained clock-like patterns of light that would overlap the frames, something that under normal circumstances should not happen. Those critical of the veracity of Lansing's claims point out that this is proof she was hoaxing her pictures. However, no one could ever come up with a method to duplicate her photos with the overlapping images.

Psychiatrist Dr. Berthold E. Schwarz, author of the book "***UFO-Dynamics: Psychiatric and Psychic Dimensions of the UFO Syndrome***," worked extensively with Lansing and witnessed firsthand the paranormal activity that occurred around her.

"I was with her many times when she was filming and also saw many of her films. The UFO pictures sometimes overlapped the film frames . . . an optical impossibility. She also, with beginner's luck, separately filmed a UFO-like craft and its four occupants. And once, while with Stella, it was I who filmed, and, apparently out of nowhere, there came a nocturnal mystery auto with strange alternating signaling headlights."

The nocturnal mystery car that Dr. Schwarz referred to was seen on April 15, 1971, when Dr. Schwarz accompanied Lansing and a friend to an isolated rural area to try and photograph UFOs. Not long after they arrived at the location, the area was suddenly illuminated by two brightly glowing discs in the sky. Both Lansing and Dr. Schwarz successfully captured the UFOs on film as they merged into one disc and then split back into two.

"While Mrs. Lansing and I were filming these strange lights, an automobile suddenly seemed to appear out of nowhere. It stopped approximately one to two hundred feet ahead of our car. We were shocked to see its headlights illuminate our dark area and flicker alternately left and right (and vice versa) in a manner reminiscent of semaphore signals and then dim out and come on again. Fortunately, I photographed most of this bizarre incident, and for several film frames the flaming disc can be seen gliding in the background, above and then just over the glaring headlights.

"The mystery car then suddenly turned up its lights, started its engine and barreled past us at great speed. Because of the blinding headlights, we could not make out the license plate, but the auto seemed to be a rather large, nondescript GM model of several years ago. The mystery car was noisy and sounded as if its

UFO Repeaters! Seeing Is Believing - The Camera Doesn't Lie!

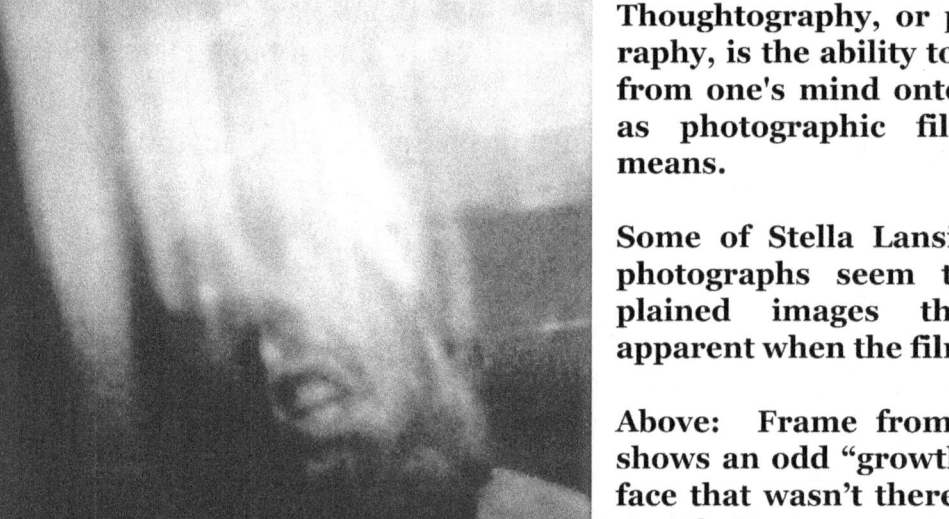

Thoughtography, or psychic photography, is the ability to "burn" images from one's mind onto surfaces such as photographic film by psychic means.

Some of Stella Lansing's films and photographs seem to show unexplained images that were not apparent when the film was exposed.

Above: Frame from an 8MM film shows an odd "growth" on Lansing's face that wasn't there when the film was shot.

Left: When Lansing took a picture of her television, this figure of a man with a beard and turban appeared, separate from the image on the TV.

muffler was defective. It was impossible to see if there were any occupants in the car. Mrs. Lansing, her friend and I were completely surprised by this weird incident."

Strange lights in the sky, mysterious cars that appear out of nowhere with headlights that seem to be flashing some sort of secret message – Dr. Schwarz's account defies any logical explanation or meaning. There have been similar situations where UFO witnesses have reported being hypnotized by flashing lights from the occupants of mysterious dark cars. Was the car in Dr. Schwarz's report attempting some sort of mental control with its use of flickering headlights?

The fact that Stella Lansing's UFO hunts often included friends who testified that they also saw and experienced UFOs and paranormal phenomena indicates that whatever was going on was not entirely a subjective experience for Lansing. Nevertheless, one is left to wonder if these unusual events would have occurred at all without the presence of Lansing. Was she somehow creating the UFOs using an as yet unknown paranormal ability? Or was she acting as a conduit for unknown intelligences that for some reason needed someone like her to make an appearance in our reality?

Psychiatrist Carl Jung noted that the UFO phenomena must be of great importance: "If UFOs are a case of psychological projection, there must be a psychic cause for it. One can hardly suppose that anything of such worldwide incidence of the UFO legend is purely fortuitous and of no importance whatever."

Lansing told Brad Steiger, in his book "**Gods of Aquarius**," that she doesn't feel like she is special in any way. In fact, she insists that everyone sometime in his lifetime has seen a UFO. The average person perhaps just does not recognize a UFO when he sees one.

"I don't know if they come from another planet, if they live right within our dimension, or if they're interdimensional – or maybe they're living somewhere on Earth that we haven't discovered yet. But whatever it is that I do, it's as if I'm programmed in some way to sense the need to take pictures of UFOs. I feel a sudden compulsion to pick up my camera, a sudden urgency to really grab that camera. I sensed that maybe I am being told, but I don't even know – I'm not consciously aware. When I snap the camera shutter, that's when I get the pictures of UFOs or entities. Something is making me do it without my being aware of it. I'm only aware of it after it's happened."

Stella Lansing continued to see and photograph UFOs as well as keeping detailed notes, but interest in what she was doing had long since faded. She was always willing to talk about her experiences, but, right up to her death on September 20, 2012, was still mystified by her strange abilities.

IMAGES FROM THE MIND

Thought photography (thoughtography), also known as "nensha" or projected thermography, is the ability to imprint an image from one's mind onto film or digitally. Stella Lansing's ability to produce unusual photographs has also been documented with people such as Chicago resident Ted Serios, who was extensively studied for his ability to produce photographs with the power of his mind. Psychiatrist Jule Eisenbud, who wrote a book called ***"The World of Ted Serios: 'Thoughtographic' Studies of an Extraordinary Mind"*** (1967), believed that Serios's abilities were genuine.

The roots of thought photography go back to the 1850s and the Spiritualist Movement. Photographs produced during some séances showed what were said to be apparitions of the dead, but these images were produced using conventional methods. However, some early experiments had spirit mediums try to capture their thoughts by placing their fingers or foreheads directly onto the photographic plates. The results were intriguing, but little scientific attention was paid to these experiments.

One of the earliest academic researchers in thought photography was Dr. Tomokichi Fukurai, an assistant professor of psychology at Tokyo University and President of the Psychical Institute of Japan. In 1910, Fukurai worked with a woman named Ikuko Nagao, who had taken up devout worship of the Shinto sun goddess, Amaterasu, as well as the Buddhist god of mercy, Kwanjeon. Supposedly, these practices opened her eyes to her own innate clairvoyant powers and resulted in her accurately predicting future tragedies for several years.

Initially, the thought photography experiments came about by accident as Nagao was being tested to determine if she could "see" writing which had been previously applied to photographic plates but left undeveloped, thus rendering it effectively invisible to the naked eye and existing only "in potentia." However, when some of the plates in question were later found to be partially or fully-developed despite remaining completely covered and unexposed to light, Fukurai was convinced that Nagao had essentially developed them with her mind and he adjusted his experiments to confirm or deny this.

Amazingly, these experiments proved successful and were continued for quite some time, becoming progressively more complex as shapes, images and eventually complex kanji characters were clearly projected onto the undeveloped plates. Each of the tests Fukurai and his research partner Imamura conducted with Nagao have been meticulously documented, complete with photographs, in Fukurai's book, **"*Clairvoyance and Thoughtography*."**

Unfortunately, Fukurai's research was deliberately sabotaged by Noriatsu Fuji, a notable physics lecturer and skeptic, who prepared an experiment for Nagao on January 4, 1911. Fuji's job was to scrutinize both the location and all the materials that were to be used in the test. As it happens, Fuji was also responsible for preparing the experimental materials but omitted the plate upon which the thoughtographs were to be projected that day, either by accident or with intent to sabotage the proceedings.

Fuji had basically crafted this experiment as a trap, hiding numerous leaden crosses, lines of manganese and "the smoke of shouldering oil" on the bag to ensure that any tampering by a third party would be made readily apparent. And, sure enough, in addition to the lack of the much-needed photographic plate, there was indeed evidence that someone had tampered with the bag – though it was all very inconclusive and questionable. This led Nagao to distrust Fuji's methods and Fuji likewise to distrust Nagao's abilities. As such, Nagao absolutely refused to conduct any further experiments with Fuji ever again, and Fuji's article, published on February 15, publicly denounced Nagao's thought photography as little more than sleight-of-hand.

Questions of fraud have surfaced time and again with thought photography experiments. Ted Serios, whose "thoughtographs" were extensively studied, produced his photos using nothing but a Polaroid camera. Later on, Serios started to insist on using a rolled up tube of paper or cardboard that he dubbed "The Gizmo." Critics claimed Serios may have used the gizmo to conceal a small marble with a photograph attached to it or a piece of previously exposed film.

There were occasions, however, on which Serios did not hold the camera or the gizmo, both of which were in the hands of an investigator. He could produce an image on a camera that was some distance away from him, as far as 66 feet in one instance, and he even produced images when the camera was in another room altogether.

Serios even agreed to being strip-searched and on one occasion was dressed in a rubber suit to rule out any photographic trick using magnetism. Nevertheless, skeptics decided that the gizmo was rigged to fake the experiments and any evidence to the contrary was dismissed.

Ted Serios never showed any interest in the UFO phenomena, nor did any of his thoughtographs show anything that looked remotely like a UFO or "extraterrestrial" beings. Nevertheless, UFOs certainly have the curious ability at times to produce "supernatural" events.

According to Dr. Berthold E. Schwarz, author of **"Psychiatric and Paranormal Aspects of Ufology"** (White Buffalo Press, 1999), UFOs and the paranormal are two sides of the same coin.

"In my experience, study of UFO contactees-abductees in many cases reveals high quality macro-psychic episodes before as well as surrounding the incident and aftermath. Almost all forms of psychic phenomena are represented: synchronicity, telepathy, clairvoyance, precognition, telekinesis, teleportation, materialization, dematerialization, bilocation, thoughtography, dowsing and reincarnation."

It has been suggested that Stella Lansing was not only psychically responsible for the images that appeared on her photos and films but that she was also able to create the UFOs in a form that could be physically seen by her and other witnesses on their UFO hunts.

In an interview for *"New Dawn Magazine,"* author and researcher John White suggests that some UFOs may be the creation of our own minds. In the 1970s, Dr. Gertrude Schmeidler, a parapsychologist at City College of New York, conducted research with Ingo Swann, known for his government remote viewing projects.

"In a completely darkened laboratory, Dr. Schmeidler photographed Swann as he used mental intention and his psychokinetic power of mind over matter to envision light streaming from his outstretched arms. The photos showed a visible glow around Swann's hands. So if one person's mental intention can produce a physical effect such as that, what might the collective intention and unconscious psychic ability which everyone seems to have in some degree produce?"

White feels that the interaction between mind and matter, between the physical brain and the metaphysical mind, points towards a category of the UFO phenomenon that originates outside the ordinary three-dimensional space-time framework. But, is this interaction between mind and matter solely the work of the individual, or are there other intelligences at work that intercede to help manifest in our physical reality?

DOROTHY IZATT

Stella Lansing is not alone in her ability to have not only repeat UFO experiences but also to produce unusual images that seem to go beyond the normal bounds of three-dimensional reality.

Since 1974, Dorothy Izatt of Richmond, British Columbia, has seen and photographed an amazing array of UFOs that almost boggle the mind. What is so incredible about Izatt's films is the "one-frame" images that pop up unexpectedly, showing streaks of light and other luminous objects.

It all started when she saw a bright object hovering in the sky above her house. Izatt went out onto her balcony with a flashlight and tried signaling the UFO, which, to her amazement, signaled back. When she told her friends about her experience, no one believed her, so she went out and bought a Keystone XL 200 Super-8 movie camera and started filming. The results were more than 600 reels of film that skeptics, right from the very beginning, have said were faked. But, if she is faking them, photo experts have yet to figure out how.

Izatt's UFO films have brought her worldwide renown among those who believe we are not alone in this universe. She's been featured on TV shows like "Unsolved Mysteries," "Sightings," "Strange Universe," and "Hard Copy" and has written a book called "***Contacts with Beings of Light***."

"I call them Light Beings. I don't call them aliens, because we are aliens, too," says Izatt.

Izatt said that from the very beginning she could tell when a UFO was near and that she was compelled to get her camera and attempt to film them. She later learned that it was a telepathic communication with the extraterrestrials onboard the ships that was directing her.

"You talk mind-to-mind," she said. "They can pick up your thoughts, and I have the ability to pick theirs up, too.

UFO Repeaters! Seeing Is Believing - The Camera Doesn't Lie!

After her first UFO encounter, housewife Dorothy Izatt discovered that she had a "special sense" to communicate with extraterrestrial visitors and to capture their craft on film.

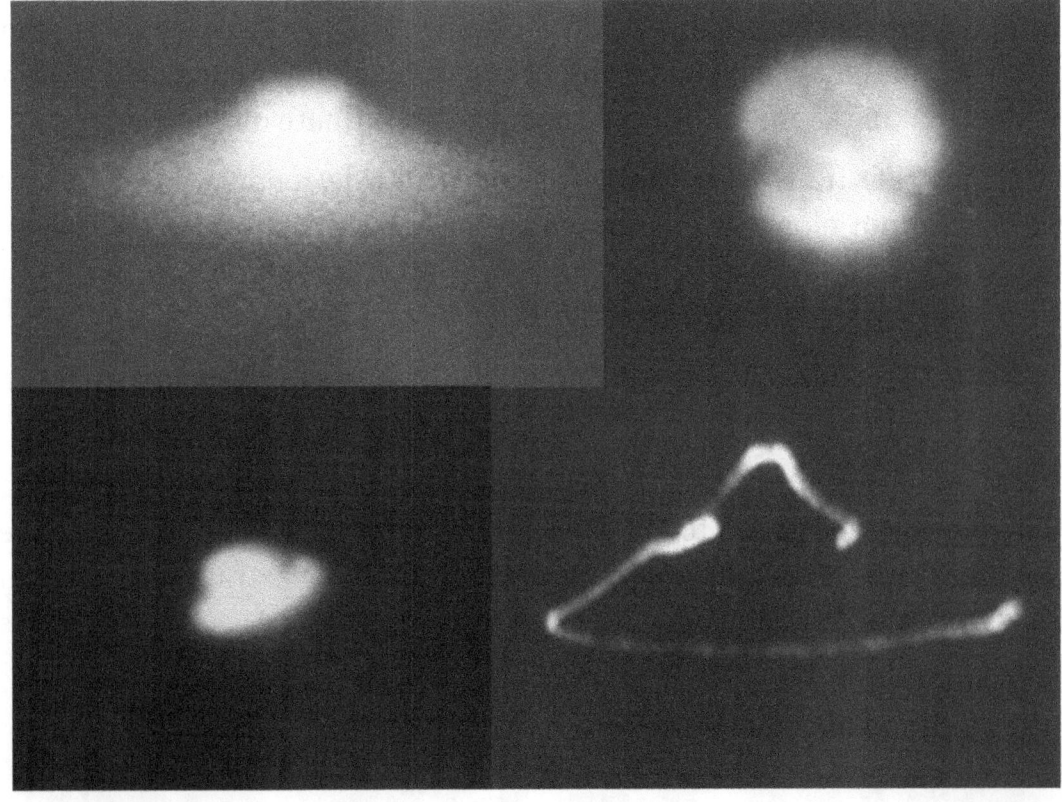

"There are all different types of beings," she explained. "Some are like us. You wouldn't be able to tell the difference if they walked among us. Some are different, but down here on this Earth we are all different, too. It all depends on where you come from and where you are born.

"With them, it's the same. I guess it depends on which planet or dimension they come from. Their skin color, hair, everything is different. I've met many, many different ones. The Light Beings don't come from other planets like ETs; they are more like angels and don't have a physical body like we do.

"ETs have been aware of what we do here since the beginning of our history. Space and time don't exist for them, or the Light Beings either, since none of them are of this Earth. The ETs from planets out there don't travel through space; they just pop in and out instantly. Of course all of this is from my own experience, or from what I've learned from the Light Beings.

"The Light Beings, like some high order ETs, want to help us. But they can only help in subtle ways because human beings have to pull themselves up by their own merits. We've got to want to do it ourselves. It's no good if somebody does it for us; there's no permanent growth in that."

Oddly, some people can see the aliens when she points them out, others can't. She feels her own ability to see them is the result of having a special sense she possesses. When she wants to make contact, all she has to do is concentrate, and they appear.

"I was born with it," she said. "My parents have it, and my family all has it. My aunts and uncles all seem to have this second sight. People call it the sixth sense. To me everyone has it. We're born with it, it's just some of us don't make use of it, and you lose it."

Dorothy Izatt's statement that she and her family have some sort of "special sense" that enables her to establish communication with the UFO intelligences is indicative of "Repeaters," people who have multiple UFO sightings and experiences. One of the key factors of repeat experiences is that the witnesses, their families and even friends and acquaintances often have "supernatural" occurrences before and after their initial UFO encounter. Of course the word "supernatural" is a sort of catch all term referring to events that are completely outside of our current understanding. But, because of these unusual, e.g. "psychic" events associated with some UFO cases, the "extraterrestrial hypothesis" needs to be reevaluated.

UFO Repeaters! Seeing Is Believing - The Camera Doesn't Lie!

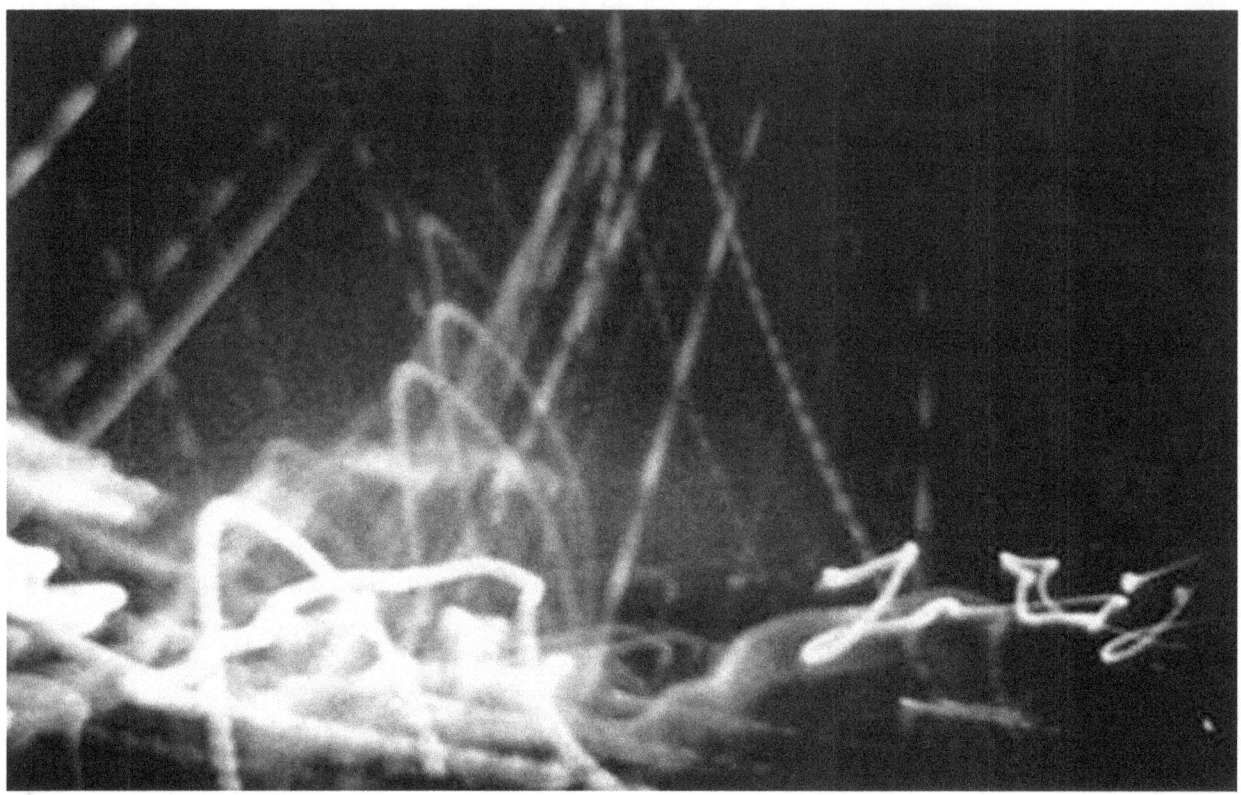

Single frames taken from Izatt's 8MM films show an amazing explosion of lights, shapes and colors that have defied explanation from photographic experts.

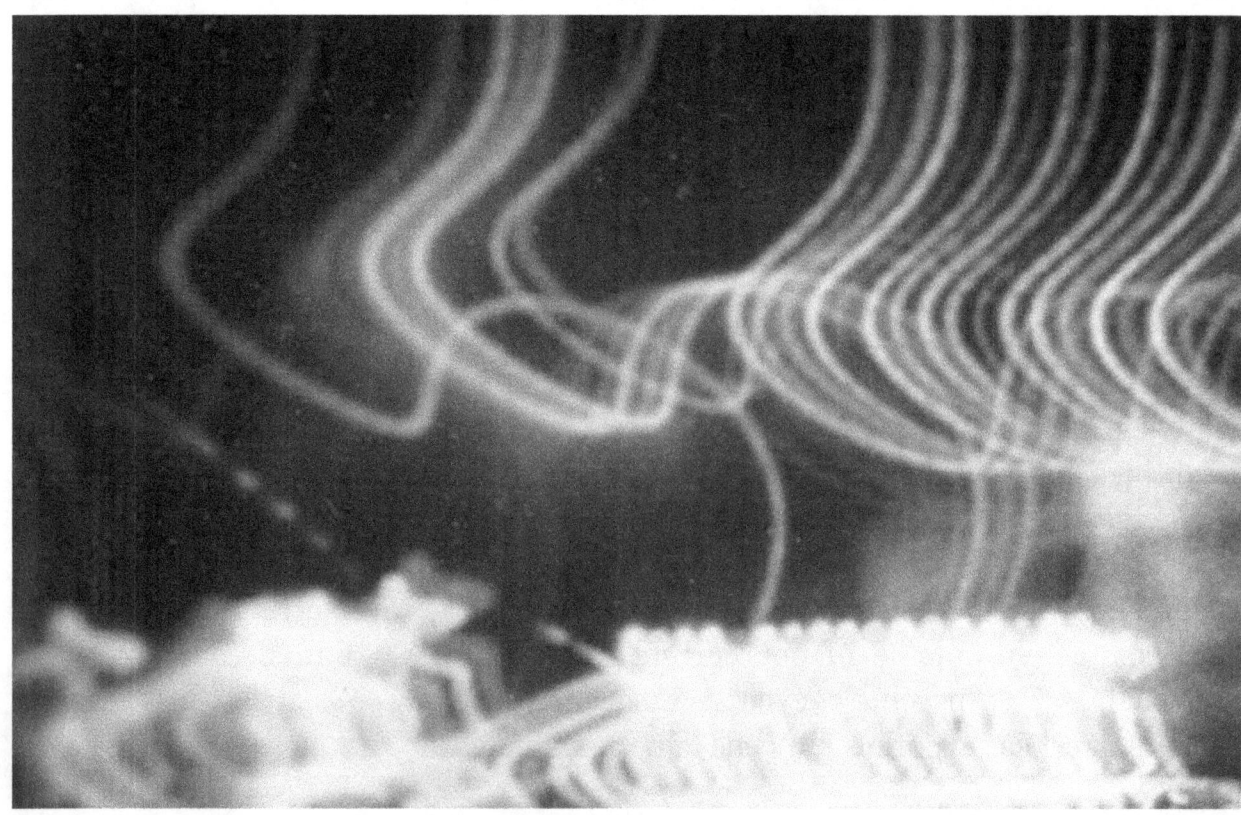

UFO Repeaters! Seeing Is Believing - The Camera Doesn't Lie!

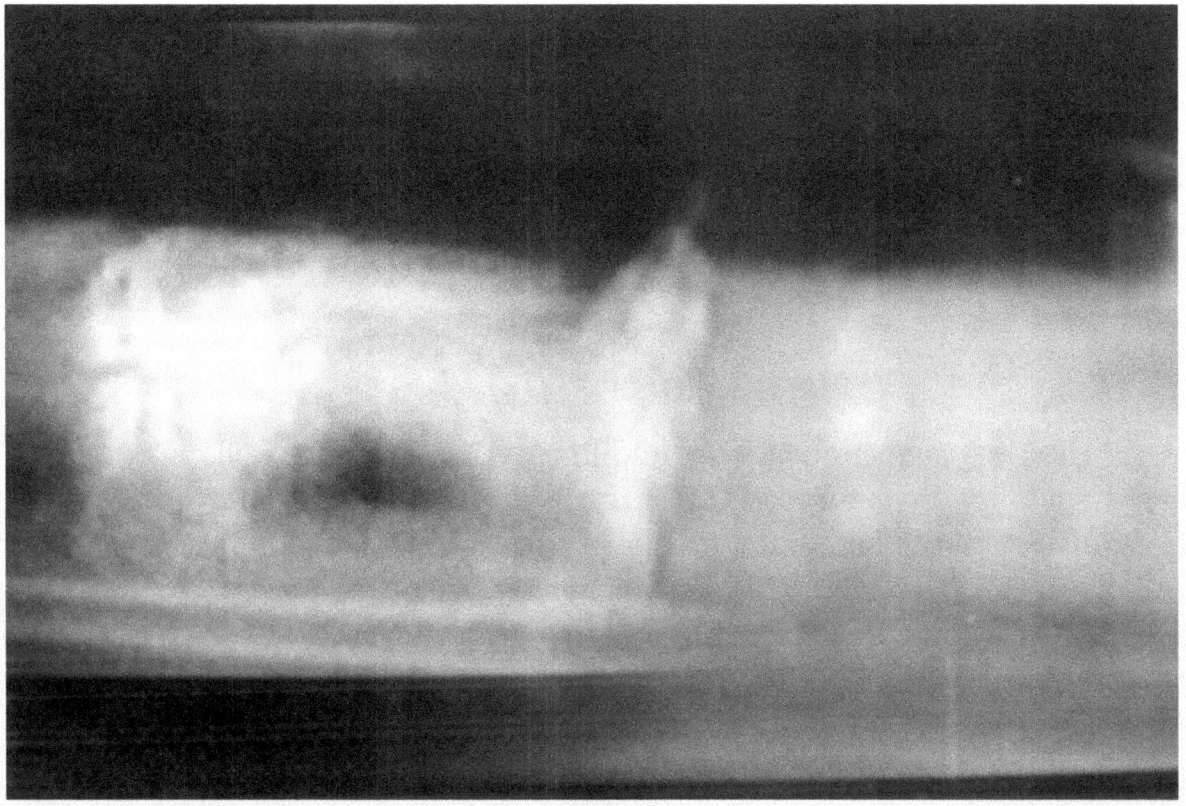

Some of Izatt's more controversial photos seem to show humanoid figures that have been interpreted as the extraterrestrial occupants of UFOs.

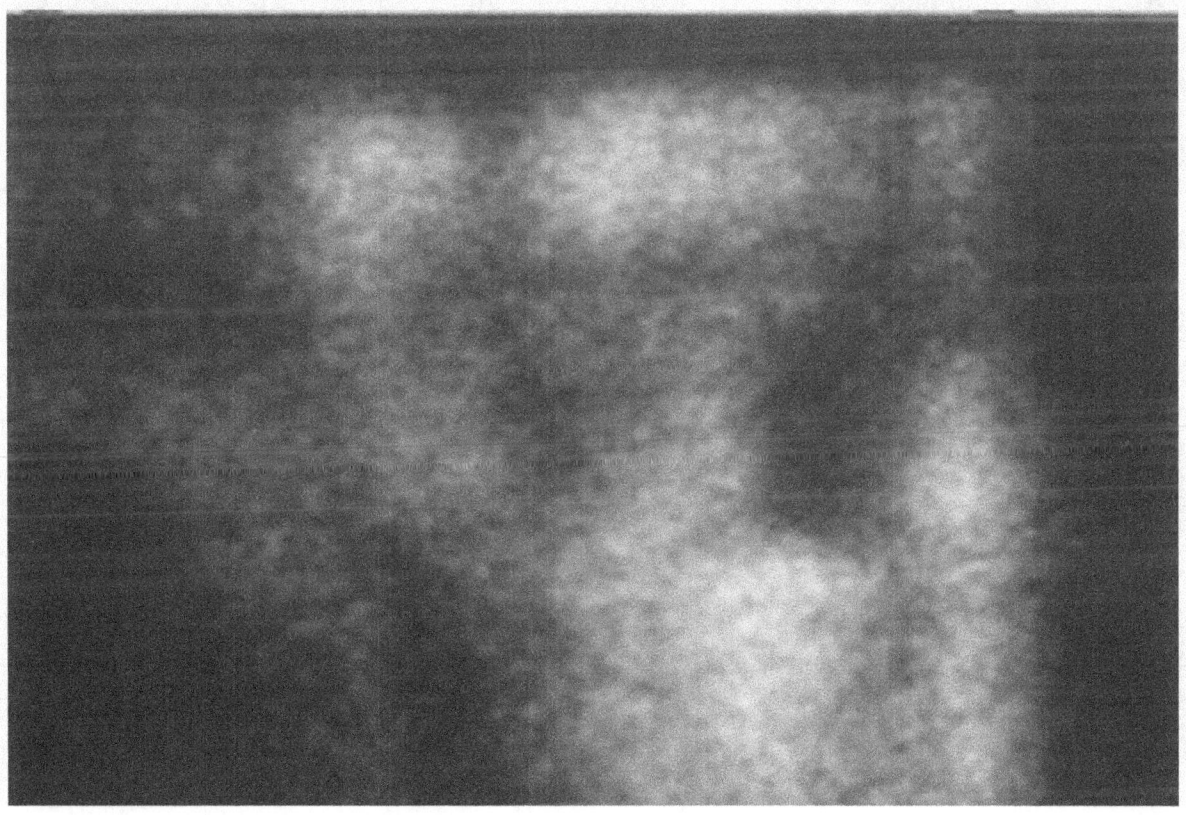

Even though many UFO researchers try to ignore the psychic component of UFOs, the rejection of this key element will only contribute to the continuing confusion that surrounds the phenomenon. Since the 1940s, UFOs have become synonymous with spaceships and extraterrestrials. However, this interpretation is far too simplistic and probably reflects modern social belief structures more than science fact.

BETTY HILL

The UFO abduction of Betty and Barney Hill has been well documented in books such as "***Interrupted Journey***" and the television movie "***The UFO Incident***." Even though there had been earlier UFO abduction cases, the Betty and Barney Hill abduction ended up being widely publicized and was better documented, both in popular entertainment media and the news, than most others.

What is not widely known is that, after their initial 1961 encounter, the Hills, especially Betty and her side of the family, experienced not only additional UFO sightings but also unusual harassments in the form of house break-ins, weird telephone calls and paranormal activity. This is a familiar, repeating pattern that has also occurred to numerous others who are involved in the UFO field.

Betty's niece, Kathleen Marden, who co-wrote the book "***Captured! The Betty and Barney Hill UFO Experience***" with veteran UFO researcher Stanton Friedman, comments on her website (http://www.kathleen-marden.com) that she first noticed psychic phenomena after a scientific research team convinced Betty to participate in a series of telepathic experiments. The experiments involved what the team termed "psychophysical" communication between Betty and the ETs. Initially, Betty attempted to reestablish contact with her captors by placing the star map she had drawn under posthypnotic suggestion, as well as some of the materials that were present in her vehicle during the Hills' initial contact in September of 1961, in her car.

"The goal was to vector in a craft to land on my grandparents' farm across the street from my childhood home," Kathleen writes. "Night after night, Betty attempted to communicate with the ETs via verbal and telepathic messages. Finally, UFOs began to show up. One early evening, in the mid-1960s, I was on my front porch setting up my telescope for an evening astronomy lesson when I

UFO Repeaters! Seeing Is Believing - The Camera Doesn't Lie!

Betty and Barney Hill shortly after the publication of John G. Fuller's book "The Interrupted Journey" which thrust the Hill's into the public spotlight.

observed a disc-shaped object with a row of windows suspended in the air over my grandparent's barn. You can imagine my excitement!"

In 1966, a commercial pilot on his way home from work in the middle of the night sighted a lighted UFO over the woods across the street from Kathleen's childhood home. Her grandmother said that she had been awakened by a loud noise that shook the house followed by measured knocks on her front door.

"My grandmother had jokingly told Betty that if she could vector a craft to land on the family farm, they should knock on the door and she'd serve them coffee."

But Kathleen's grandmother panicked and would not budge from her bed until the knocks finally ceased.

The next day, Kathleen and her two brothers found a circular area of wilted vegetation in the woods along with three triangle shaped depressions inside a circular 15 to 18 foot area. The tops of three nearby birch trees had been sheared off about 10 feet above the ground. Others had been scraped and were bent over.

Soon thereafter, Kathleen's family became aware of paranormal activity in their home.

"I grew up in a normal, stable family, and this had never occurred in the past," Kathleen says. "But suddenly family members reported seeing items fly off shelves, doors open and close on their own and light orbs darting through the air. I was incredulous when I heard these stories and refused to believe what my eyes observed when a knickknack flew off a shelf near me."

As part of the experiment, Betty and Barney had been instructed to report any and all unusual occurrences regardless of how insignificant they seemed. In a letter dated January 14, 1966, Betty described her family as hard-headed, practical realists who were beginning to feel "on edge" over the intrusion of paranormal activities into their homes.

She wrote, "These things are happening to Barney and me as well as to most of my relatives, but they have been witnessed by other people who were present. We do not believe in ghosts but we do believe in space travel and life on other planets, so we wonder if these space travelers might have the ability to be unseen to us."

According to Betty, it was more than coincidence that her Portsmouth home was entered, and uncanny events transpired almost immediately after she

UFO Repeaters! Seeing Is Believing - The Camera Doesn't Lie!

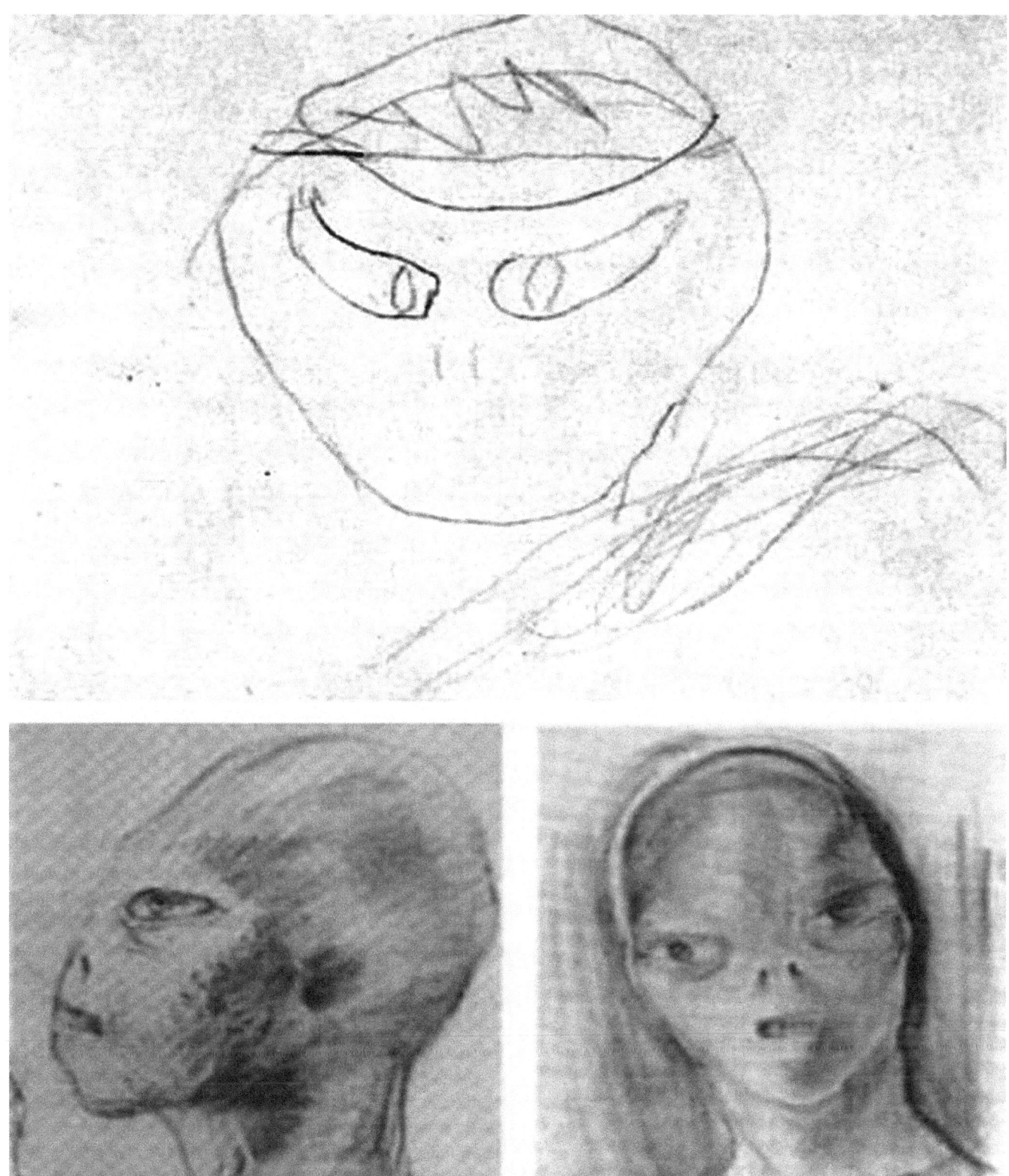

Barney Hill, under hypnosis, drew the above (top) sketch of the "leader" of the UFO occupants. Bottom: Two sketches by David Baker are based on two interviews Baker had with Barney, one under hypnosis. (credit: NICAP 1972)

began her contact attempts. In the January 14 letter, Betty wrote, "Recently Barney and I heard the front door open, someone stamp his feet and walk upstairs. We checked and found no one, and the door was still locked. This happened in the middle of the night and it awoke both of us."

Betty also noted that at that time the other apartments in their home were unoccupied, yet she could hear the sliding door on a closet in one apartment going back and forth; in another apartment, there was the sound of water running in one of the bathrooms.

"On three occasions we found a light turned on in one of the apartments. On Christmas week, as we were going into the apartment to turn the light off and were unlocking the door, it went off by itself."

Betty reported that these strange occurrences were also taking place in the homes of her family members. In one inexplicable incident, a vehicle seemed to have entered a family driveway at night, and a man with indistinguishable features exited the car and seemingly lit a cigarette. When no one appeared at the door, the eight witnesses went to look for him. They could not locate the man or his car but they observed a large ball of light traveling about 10 to 20 feet above the ground. They watched in bewilderment as the ball of light traveled across the street, through the adjacent yard and then disappeared behind a garage located approximately 100 feet from the witnesses.

There was speculation on Betty's part that these seemingly mundane events could have been signals from the UFO occupants that she and Barney failed to comprehend. However, despite continued attempts to reestablish contact with the UFO occupants, nothing definitive happened and the experiment was ended.

After Barney passed away in 1969, Betty continued on with her UFO research. People were reporting their own sightings to her, and she sometimes went out with them to areas where they were observing unconventional lights in the sky. She began to document their reports, and this resulted in an extensive database, but the sightings, often without directional data, estimated size, time reference or detailed description, were never investigated.

Betty was beginning to accept the mere description of lights in the sky as evidence that a UFO had been observed, without the careful, sometimes tedious, investigation and documentation required as acceptable standards of evidence.

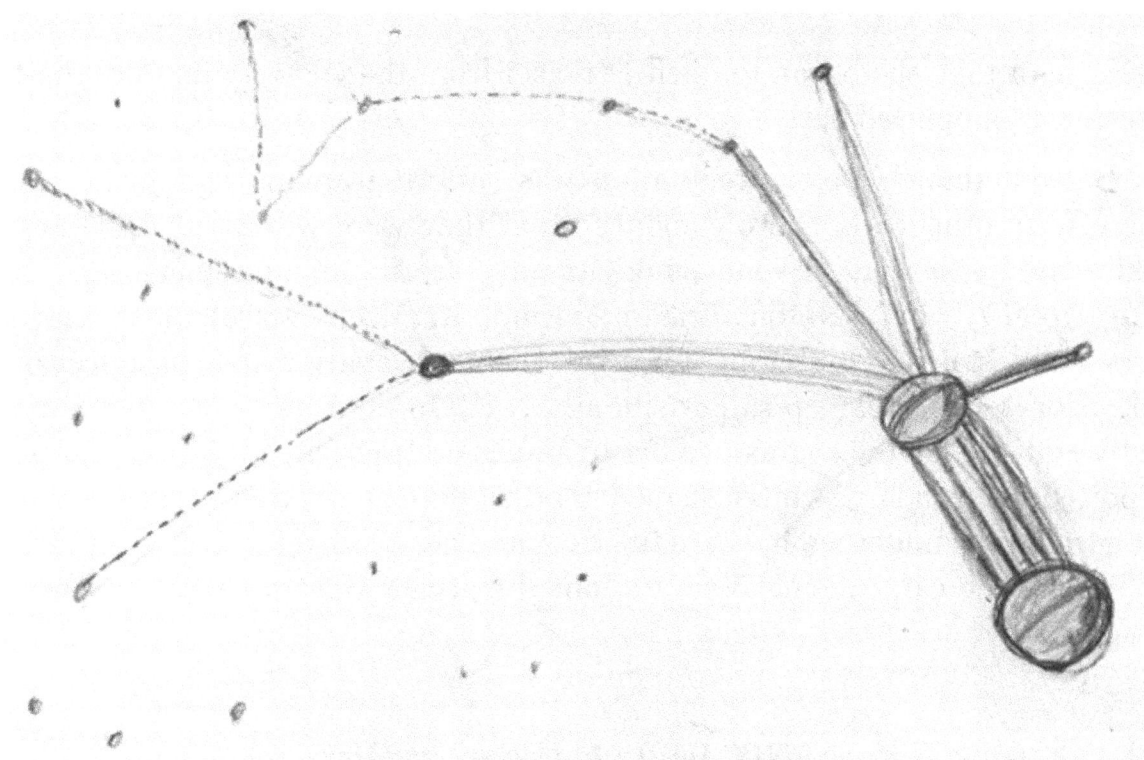

Above: Betty Hill's original "star map" that she was able to draw after hypnotic regression.

Below: Timothy Green Beckley and Betty Hill.

Because of this, she began to illicit criticism from the UFO community that had previously supported her.

Even though Betty's reputation was suffering among her former peers, there were others who were convinced that they were witness to UFO activity while out with her. In one such account, from the aforementioned book "***Captured!***," by Stanton Friedman and Kathleen Marden, a television personality states: "On October 23, 1979, [name deleted], who is producer of my television series, went up to Portsmouth, N.H., to do a preshow interview with Betty Hill and later accompanied her to a railroad track site in East Kingston. He reported seeing a large saucer-shaped 'mother ship' on the tracks, saw it lift off to let a train pass underneath, heard it 'beep,' and claims that it directed a red beam of light at the car, causing Betty to floor the accelerator and take off down the road."

ANOTHER FORCE AT WORK

Betty Hill's experiences, as well as the stories in this chapter and throughout this book, show that sighting UFOs can go way beyond simply seeing "strange lights in the sky" and into realms that defy common and even uncommon explanations. Remote viewer Ingo Swan said in the October 1996 issue of the *"Stargate Newsletter"* that all abductees and many who have sighted UFOs insist that ETs communicate with them by telepathy – via an outright, undeniably psychic method.

"Using an outmoded description of telepathy, they are the psychic senders while we are the psychic receivers. This form of communication makes it patently clear that they possess psychic abilities and communicate to us through ours. The ETs psychically 'read' or 'scan' human mind contents, and abductees report their own awareness of this. Psychic communicating and scanning is reported in all abductee stories. Yet human UFO-ET researchers have not followed up on it. Researchers avoid the psychic issues altogether, and few of them are willing to become involved with psychic research. Mainstream resistance to their mission is difficult enough without incorporating psychic research, the other topic which the mainstream resists vigorously."

Swan also says that if the UFO occupants possess developed psychic capabilities and we undeveloped ones, it is feasible to assume that, if we developed ours, we could achieve some measure of penetration into ET motives, activities, and purposes. It is clear they will continue to have immeasurable psychic and other real advantages over us as long as we do not develop psychic capabilities and permit the issue to be completely ignored.

In his book, "***Aliens Above, Ghosts Below: Explorations of the Unknown,***" Dr. Barry Taff says that there is a rather fascinating, yet obscure, interrelationship between paranormal experiences and UFO encounters. "Why is it that many close encounters of the third kind have paranormal fallout following the event?" Dr. Taff asks. "Why is it that certain people who have frequent paranormal experiences are more likely to experience a UFO encounter?"

Taff says that these unusual events point to the hypothesis in which there is a fifth force operating both here and out there. This is a force that is not electromagnetic, nuclear or gravitational. It is a force that does its work without heat (endothermic). A force that could be at the root of both paranormal as well as UFO-related events. A force many of us refer to as Zero Point Energy (ZPE).

"I have this sneaking suspicion that UFOs use this ZPE force the same way we interpret paranormal events and use electromagnetism (to a point) wherein one can be linked to the other in as yet unknown ways to produce seemingly impossible events. The cumulative data from many decades of UFO research strongly suggests that whatever these things and their occupants are, they can affect matter, energy and mind (consciousness) with the ease with which we affect water."

Perhaps, somewhere, there is an intelligence that can see our potential as an enlightened species and has made it their mission to see us through these difficult times by awakening our hidden, spiritual capabilities. We may have an important role to play on the universal stage. Maybe UFOs are here to show us the hidden meaning between the lines of our lives.

UFO Repeaters! Seeing Is Believing - The Camera Doesn't Lie!

ELLEN CRYSTALL – FAR AFIELD IN PINE BUSH

By Timothy Green Beckley and Sean Casteel

TIM BECKLEY RECALLS ELLEN CRYSTALL

THOUGH she is no longer with us, Ms. Ellen Crystall was a remarkable lady – at least as far as photographing UFOs goes. She was a controversial UFO Repeater, more so than most of the others, because she was not photographing metallic, disc-shaped craft piloted by the friendly Space Brothers. Ellen seems to have tapped into another realm, another dimension. The beings that showed up, whom she believed were connected with the objects she photographed, were more or less "creatures," I guess you could say. She at one time described them to me as "giant grasshoppers," kind of along the same line as the UFOnaunts PK man Ted Owens cavorted with. This is the stuff that science fiction movies are made of, and Ellen Crystall's contacts were something out of a Sci-Fi thriller from the 1950s in which bug-eyed monsters seemed to be overwhelming the Earth's population.

And while it was not until many years later that the town of Pine Bush, New York, became a recognized UFO "hotspot," this tiny upstate community has had a huge number of sightings over the years. Starting in the time of the early settlers, people would see these wickedly bizarre orbs nestling down in the open fields. By the 1950s, residents had come to think of these bizarre intruders as visitors from the ghostly realms . . . perhaps signifying the return of the Native-

UFO Repeaters! Seeing Is Believing - The Camera Doesn't Lie!

Above: After years of "fly-by"-type sightings, Ellen Crystall found herself in Pine Bush, New York, in 1980, where she began taking pictures not only of the ships but of the UFO occupants as well.

Below: It was not unusual for Ellen to interact with a variety of UFOs on any given night. She admitted that you almost had to be there to decipher their shapes and sizes. Some of the craft were immense. In addition to the ships, which materialized in split seconds, the occupants were also photographed. "You have to study the photos to make all of this out," Ms. Crystall explained.

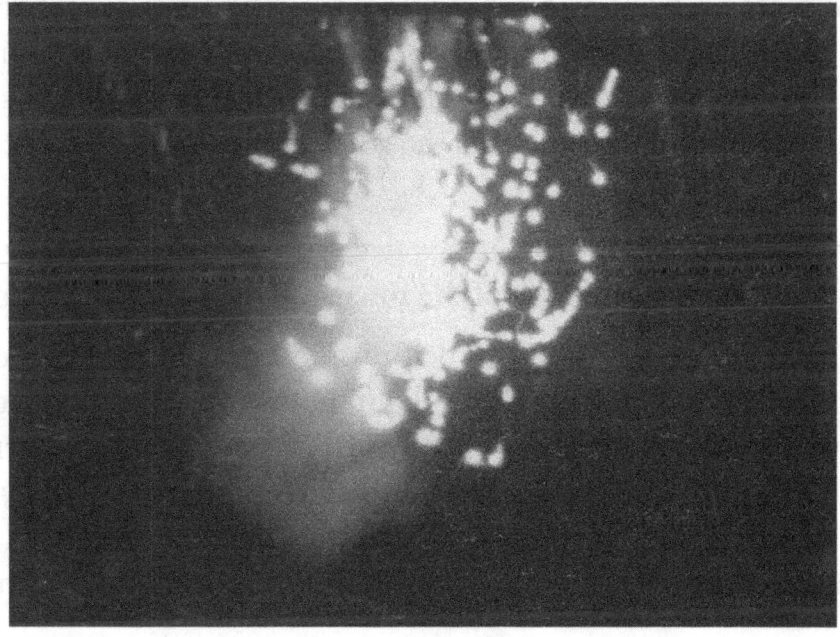

Americans who had died in generations past. It wasn't until the mid-1960s that UFOlogists started picking up on a "UFO threat" in the area. Astronomer Dr. J. Allen Hynek and educator Philip Imbrogno found themselves immersed in a wave of sightings of a massive boomerang which was said to hover low over homes in towns bordering on Pine Bush in nearby Putnam and Westchester counties.

I first heard of Ellen Crystal via my friend Harry Lebelson, who was both freelance writer and UFO staffer for the very high gloss magazine "OMNI," published by Bob Guccione. Guccione put out the far less respected – but much more widely circulated – *"Penthouse Magazine."* It was definitely a case of skin versus sky. During our frequent phone conversations, Harry would tell me the cases he was planning to write something on, be they phantoms of the night or Ultra-terrestrial visitors – which he firmly accepted were coming here regularly – though in the magazine officially he had to play down the legitimacy of the stuff he believed so strongly in.

It was during one of our gab fests that Harry first bought up the subject of Pine Bush and how the number of sightings in this quiet rural town in Orange County, New York, with a population that hovered around two thousand, were nothing but phenomenal. He said if I wanted to perhaps have a sighting of my own that I should gather my team of researchers together and follow them up to Pine Bush in a caravan of two. At the time I was running the New York School of Occult Arts and Sciences, one of the first, if not the first, metaphysical centers in the country. Someone had donated "to the cause" a rather threadbare van, the type with two seats up front and a door that opens in the back where you might put cargo. I think there were four of us. We were somewhat excited because Harry said he would be traveling to Pine Bush with this mysterious lady, Ellen, who could call down the space ships so that they could be seen by everyone in our party.

A good portion of the sightings were being made, Harry explained, amongst the fields, on the outskirts of the town and over a Jewish cemetery.

Never having been to Pine Bush before, and not being able to read a map in the dark – the van had no overhead light naturally (what do you want for nothing?) – we found ourselves way behind Harry and Ellen and arrived just as they were pulling out of one of the side roads. Apparently, they had had a monumental sighting. After being introduced to Ellen, we were told that a giant cross had appeared and hovered over their heads (hopefully not in the Jewish cemetery). Now, we were a bit skeptical to say the least, because why hadn't we seen this humungous ship as we pulled up?

As it turns out, Ellen's sightings were more psychic than substantial, in the physical sense. My memory is cloudy from too much wine, too much rock music and the passing of time. True, my name is enshrined on a plaque hanging on the restroom wall of the Pine Bush barber shop along with all the other major researchers who have sky-watched there, but I can't tell you too much else about my visit(s) there.

But here is the funny part (I'm not laughing): one of those who had accompanied us there in our hippie van, an ex-girlfriend, Jean, who I hadn't seen in maybe 15 years, told me later on that she was surprised that I didn't recall actually looking at the sky and pointing out several passing lights that seemed to be – at least in our excitement – unexplainable. On top of this, I had apparently started to channel and began identifying the occupants who were meandering around overhead. One was Ashtar, who is seemingly always nearby and ready to focus his attention on any New Agers who appear to need him. I can't remember who Jean said the rest were.

While I have no reason to contradict what Jean told me, I can't remember consciously speaking with Ashtar on this occasion, but if he was there and I failed to say "Hello" properly I apologize. Although I am not sure what good that would do at this late date as the sightings around Pine Bush have died down, mainly due to a local ordinance which says you will be ticketed if you lounge about for the purposes of sky-watching. Talk about f---ing censorship and the New World Order! Furthermore, this doesn't seem to fit in with the fact that the town annually throws a UFO day where the locals paint themselves green, parade along "Main Street" and eat Mars burgers from the town's diner, which calls itself the Cup and Saucers Restaurant (menu at UrbanSpoon.com – we hear their French toast is great!). Kooky, perhaps, but it gives the tourists something to do besides loitering for the purpose of committing a criminal offense, i.e. waiting for the cosmic express to pull through.

But enough of my trivializing the matter. The truth is that hundreds of other individuals besides Ellen Crystall have encountered the entities here, be they friend or foe. Ellen seems to have given her "contacts" a negative spin, mainly I guess because they are far from human and keep hidden in the darkness of other dimensions and realms from which they can "pop out" and appear to her camera.

UFO Repeaters! Seeing Is Believing - The Camera Doesn't Lie!

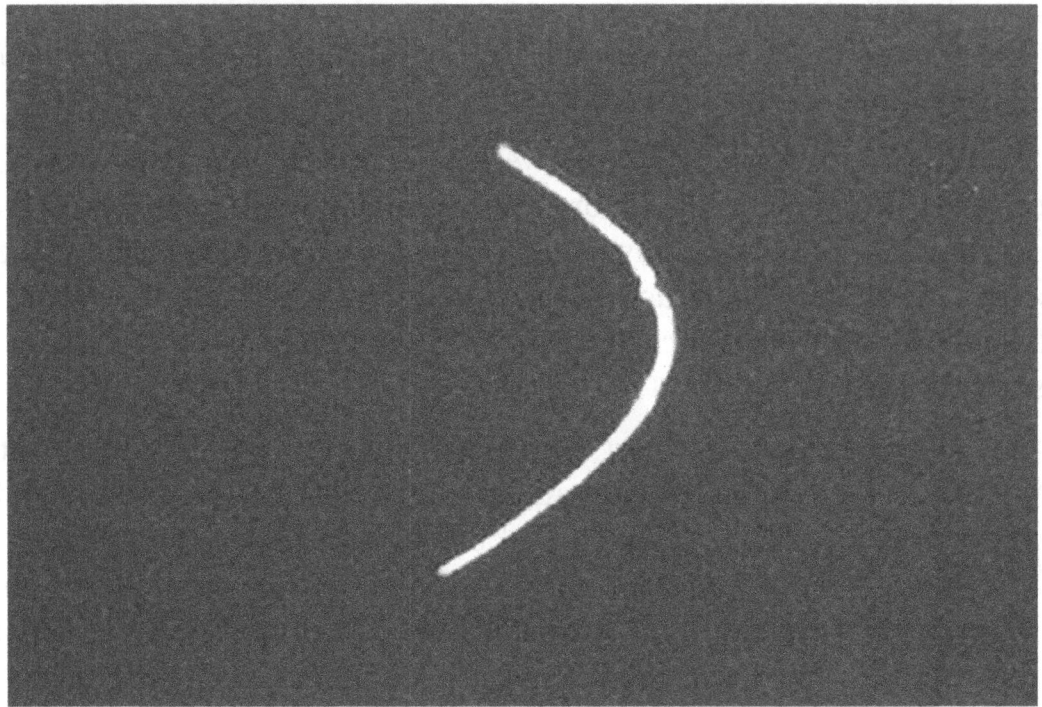

Above: A boomerang headed east over Chapel Hill Road. It apparently materialized out of "thin air."

Below: High tension and telephone lines seem to attract a variety of objects, including what Ellen identified as "Tesla Orbs" because of the energy they generated.

Since Ellen is no longer residing on the Earth plane – she passed in 2002 – we will have to dig deep into what she wrote at the time to try and unravel the mystery of the Pine Bush UFO sightings and their true meaning. And, like I said, though the sightings have decreased, there are still others that continue to evoke the "madness" of UFO sightings around this rural community, including Bruce Cornet, who is known to carry a camera with him most of the time and has taken some rather controversial scans of the night sky showing . . . only God and the heavenly hosts above Pine Bush, New York, know what.

* * * * * *

THE LIGHTS OF HOLLYWOOD

Ellen Crystall's initial experience with UFOs happened in 1971, shortly after she had moved from her native New Jersey to Hollywood, California, to begin a career in music. On her very first day in her new garden apartment, some of the other residents told her about the nightly appearances of UFOs, which they had made a habit of sitting outside to watch. Though Crystall considered herself to be a nominal believer in the phenomenon, she was nevertheless surprised to hear this from her neighbors.

That night, she and 20 or so of the other tenants gathered around a center courtyard and looked at the sky. The others pointed at stationary objects and warned Crystall that they would soon start to move. Crystall protested that the objects looked like ordinary stars, but soon they did in fact start to move, noiselessly and in no discernible pattern.

As Crystall would later write in her book, ***Invasion: They Come In Silence***, "At any given moment, there seemed to be as many as 30 objects moving in the sky. The atmosphere above the Los Angeles basin is, of course, filled with commercial and private aircraft. The moving objects I'm talking about were clearly not that sort. These objects made right angle turns, had no noise associated with them, and seemed to be going nowhere. The activity also appeared to be centered over our area, which wasn't far from the downtown section of Hollywood."

The appearances of the UFOs went on night after night, as did the gathering of sky-watchers. The group believed the ships were of extraterrestrial

UFO Repeaters! Seeing Is Believing - The Camera Doesn't Lie!

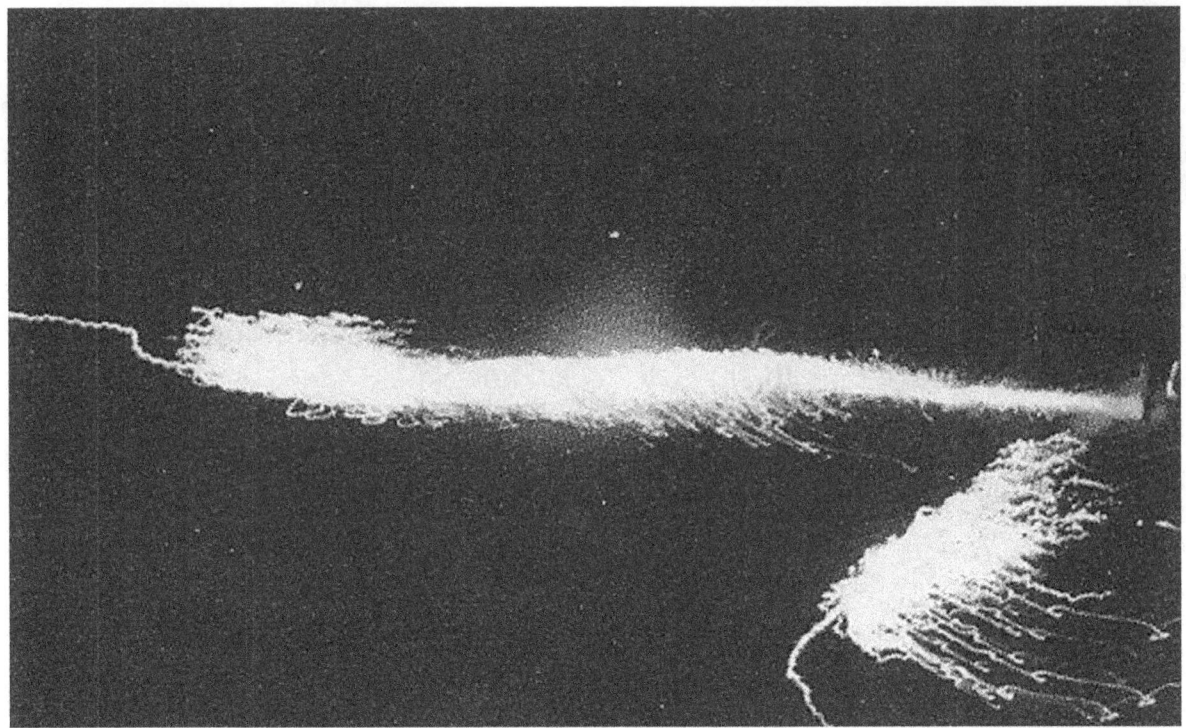

Above: Says Ellen about this shot: "We saw clear-cut triangle metallic craft about 200 feet in perimeter. This view is looking upwards at the belly. All emissions were unseen visually. Film is sensitive to short-wave radiation. There is a bluish burst in the center of the horizontal discharge. The blue is a textbook characteristic of ultra-violet radiation. The horizontal discharge contains an alternating current. This current also surrounds part of the body of the triangle."

Below: A shooting rod appears over the Jewish cemetery in Pine Bush.

origin but seemed to have grown jaded about the phenomenon through such frequent exposure to it. Meanwhile, Crystall wondered why the news media seemed to be ignoring what was happening, although she did recall numerous lyrical references to UFOs in the lyrics of rock groups like Jefferson Airplane and Crosby, Stills and Nash.

After a few weeks of routinely observing the craft, Crystall felt she wanted a closer look. She and a friend decided to go to a small hill about a mile from the apartment complex that provided an excellent view of the area. When Crystall announced that she also intended to photograph the ships, her neighbors vehemently told her it was "wrong" to do so, as though it would violate the sort of worshipful regard they felt toward the UFO occupants. Looking back, Crystall said she regretted taking those admonitions to heart at all.

Nevertheless, she took her camera to the aforementioned hill and the ships dutifully appeared after a few minutes.

"But instead of snapping off rolls of film like an experienced, professional photographer," she writes, "I merely took four pictures that first night and another three the next night, when we returned to the hill and the UFO behaved identically. During the two nights we were on the hill, the UFO circled us for hours. We could see other craft slightly farther away, also circling. On both nights, we felt the hill shake slightly. We left in the early hours of the morning. I did not feel afraid at any time, but we didn't return to the hill again."

THE FEARSOME PLAYMATE

On an August evening about four months after her arrival in Hollywood, Crystall was walking home from work around 9 p.m. when an extremely large, angular craft began to descend noiselessly toward her from above the rooftop of a small house. She froze in terror and awe. The interior of the craft was completely lit up and a being sitting in the front seat with its hand on a joy stick used to steer the vehicle was clearly visible. The being wore what looked like a rusty-brown metallic stretch knit jumpsuit with a hood. Its head was large and bulbous, but Crystall cannot recall any details about its face.

Crystall realized she could either stand firm, and accept any consequences, or run. She opted to run, another choice she would come to regret.

"How could I have thought I could run from the craft?" she writes.

UFO Repeaters! Seeing Is Believing - The Camera Doesn't Lie!

Above: "Squiggle"-type UFO photographed about a mile from the Jewish cemetery.

Below: Figures stand in a spray of lights. One is slightly out of range and appears to be somewhat taller than the others. "He seems to be wearing a dark jumpsuit with baggy legs which blow in the breeze," according to Ellen.

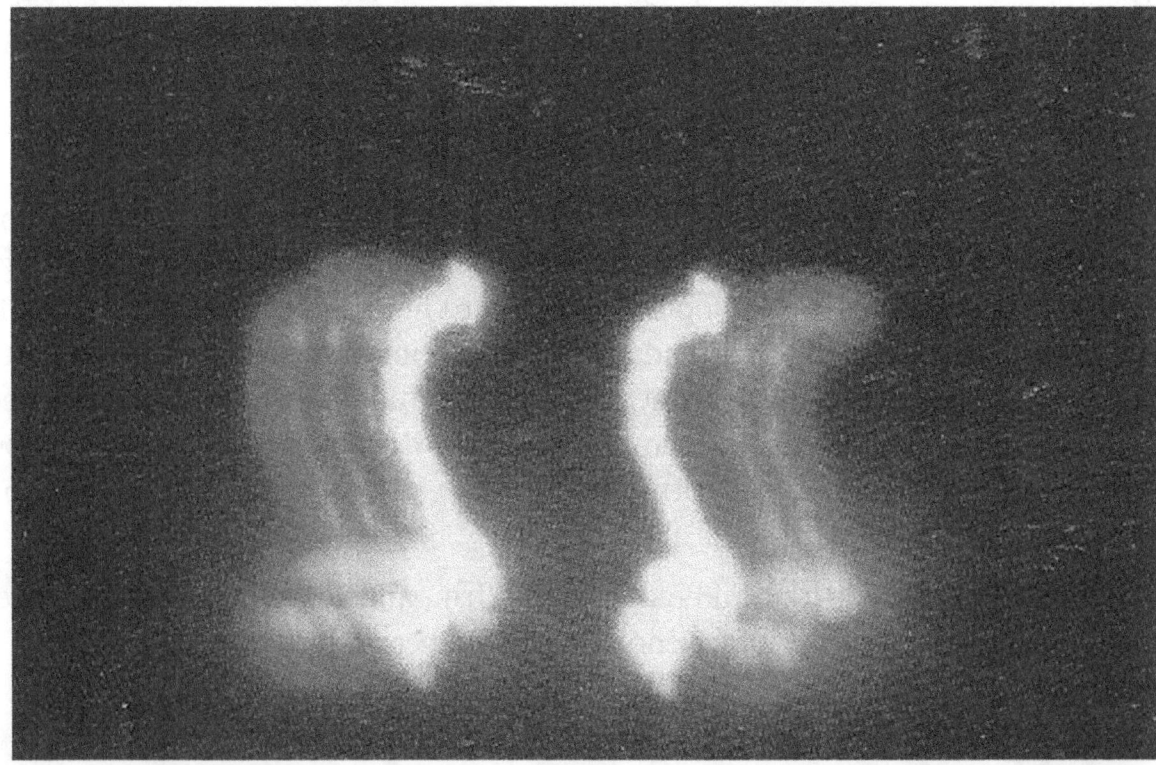

The UFO began to bob alongside her as she ran. It seemed to be playing an "amusing" game with her, though she did not see the humor in it. She returned to her apartment and, sobbing hysterically, began to pack her clothes. She flew back to New Jersey the next day and did not discuss her UFO encounters with anyone.

MAKING CONTACT IN PINE BUSH

In spite of the terror she had felt that night, Crystall continued to study the subject. After reading a column in "OMNI," written by Harry Lebelson, the friend Timothy Beckley mentioned in his introduction to this chapter, she called Lebelson and told him about her California experiences and the photos she had taken. She suggested that there must be other places where UFOs were seen frequently. Lebelson told her about Pine Bush and a young couple he knew there who claimed to see ships all the time. The couple's story sounded similar to her own, and Lebelson agreed to get in touch with them and set up a visit to the area.

"Thus began my most intensive, revealing – and continuing – field study of UFOs through direct observation," Crystall writes. "And when I say 'field,' I mean precisely that. I was to find myself in various fields and farm pastures in pursuit of elusive, wily but seemingly playful UFOs – and in search of answers to some very serious questions."

On Friday, July 18, 1980, Crystall and Lebelson drove to Pine Bush, a rural Orange County, New York, community nestled in hills and valleys some 60 miles upstate from Manhattan. As was typical of many small towns in the area, it had a few gas stations and restaurants, variety stores, a florist, etc. From the few paved roads, unpaved roads led into the scenic countryside.

The couple, Bruce and Wendy, were in their early twenties and lived in a secluded house off Hill Avenue on a short dirt road covered by an arcade of trees. Bruce and Wendy were quite upfront about the fact that they didn't want any publicity nor did they want anything to do with the UFOs. They had agreed, reluctantly and only as a favor to Lebelson, to simply take Crystall and Lebelson to the fields where the ships were landing.

Crystall says she expressed surprise that the ships had actually been landing in Pine Bush as opposed to merely hovering. When she told Bruce and Wendy about her Hollywood encounters, their standoffish attitude began to warm up. They explained that the ships had passed over their house several times, which quite simply terrified them. Other sky-watchers often barged in on

UFO Repeaters! Seeing Is Believing - The Camera Doesn't Lie!

Above: A UFO that resembles a flying "eel."

Below: With more than a little chutzpah, the objects dart out over the lonely highway near Pine Bush.

the weekend and practically took over the couple's home, only to see the ships disdainfully fly off in other directions.

At around 10 p.m., the foursome drove in Crystall's car to a field not quite a mile away. Almost immediately, they found themselves surrounded by about a dozen triangular craft with amber-yellow lights in the form of a "plus sign" on the front. Crystall says she came to call the lights "star lights" because she later learned they could be turned up to a blinding degree of illumination. When the intensity of the lights was raised to the full, the entire sky lit up. Crystall realized the ships were identical to the ones she had seen in California but now the exteriors of the craft were totally visible.

"I was ecstatic!" she writes. "My searching seemed over. I was reunited with 'my' ships after nine years. I hoped I could uncover the great secrets they held. I couldn't have been happier."

The ships were now filling the sky around the group and landing in the field. Some flew as close as 50 feet, but no occupants were visible. There was no sound.

At the time, Crystall was using a Zenite 35mm camera with an f2 lens loaded with a 36-shot roll of Kodacolor ASA 400 film. She began to shoot one picture after another while Lebelson, wielding a $1,500 Leica, did the same.

When they attempted to walk toward some of the landed ships, they were stopped by weeds grown five feet high. Wendy said that if they drove, the ships would follow, which turned out to be true. They decided to return to Bruce and Wendy's house to continue observing the ships. As they drove up the dirt road to the couple's home, a ship rose from a nearby field and came directly toward the car. Wendy started screaming and Bruce yelled out to keep on driving. At the last moment, the ship climbed slightly and skimmed over the car, missing it by inches. In spite of the frightening near-miss, Crystall returned to Pine Bush six times over the next few weeks and each time the ships "greeted" her in their ambiguous but seemingly playful fashion.

DEVELOPING THE FIRST ROLL OF FILM

Around this time, Crystall sent the first roll of film she'd shot in Pine Bush to a local Fotomat store. The photos showed bizarre bursts of multicolored lights, and "sprays" of shooting discharges and splashes of different hues were all over

UFO Repeaters! Seeing Is Believing - The Camera Doesn't Lie!

During her years of observing craft in the vicinity of Pine Bush, N.Y. Ellen has seen many types of craft. Some with rows of brightly lighted windows. Others with flashing strobes. And one with a large cross at the head of the ship.

This is how Ellen interpreted what she had photographed on numerous occasions.

the frames. Since the first three photos on the roll were of her home and family, there was no question that the film was hers and that it had been normally processed. But where were the triangular ships she and the others had so clearly seen? Lebelson's developed photos, meanwhile, were completely blank, in spite of his excellent camera and his skills as a photographer.

It would take two years before Crystall came to understand what had likely happened with the photos.

"Photography is a 'two-edged sword' for UFOlogists," she writes. "Everyone keeps hoping for a 'definitive' photo – the clear-cut 'real' picture of a craft in the sky. I understand and share those hopes, but I have to say, after my years of UFO photography and research, I've come up with some startling information."

Crystall goes on to explain that when she took the initial Pine Bush photos in 1980, she knew what she had seen – large triangular ships. But the developed photos had revealed only the aforementioned sprays and discharges of colored light. Although the lights seemed to begin where the outlines of the craft should have been, why were the craft themselves not visible?

She met a photographer who suggested she enlarge the color negatives in black and white, which she did in her own darkroom. Much to her disbelief, she was now able to discern not just the ship but also two figures standing beside it. She made an acetate tracing of the photo, saying "The details screamed out at me." In the second photo, there were five aliens visible, and the structure of the craft was clearly seen as well. Some of the remaining black and white enlargements had portions of the ships but no further aliens were visible.

WHAT THE PHOTOS REALLY REVEALED

A decision about who to talk to about the photos had to be made. Crystall had no desire to be sensational or cash in on her discovery. Her interest was purely in investigating the mystery. In spite of her fear of incurring more derision from people than she already had, she began to show the photos to experts in physics, commercial photography, scientific photography and the media. It was when she consulted scientists involved in radiation physics that she reached what she felt was a reasonable understanding.

"I learned some fascinating facts about phenomena above and below the human threshold of vision," she writes. "The human eye can see in the visible

UFO Repeaters! Seeing Is Believing - The Camera Doesn't Lie!

Above: You are about to enter the "Twilight Zone" of UFOlogy.

Below: Craft gets ready to touch down in Pine Bush. Seeing is believing - the camera doesn't lie!

portion of the electromagnetic radiation spectrum, which spans roughly 400 to 700 nanometers. This is the range of visible light. Shortwave radiation is defined as radiation from about 1 to 400 nanometers. The shorter wavelengths in this range are ultraviolet, x-rays and gamma rays. Longer wavelengths – those above 700 nanometers – consist of infrared, microwaves, television and radio waves. The Kodak Company's technical pamphlets on the many fields of scientific photography, and the technical specifications of the film, proved to be the critical factors in determining what was apparently occurring in the photographs."

All film sold over the counter, Crystall discovered, is sensitive to shortwave radiation. She deduced that the sprays or bursts of light in the photos must be due to shortwave radiation between what she and the others had seen and what the film is sensitive to. The ships had been discharging shortwave radiation her naked eyes could not see but that the camera and the film had. Physics textbooks state that any object surrounded by ultraviolet light will, when photographed, be blurred on the film. In addition to the blurring effect, ultraviolet light shows up as bluish bursts in photographs. Such bluish globule-type patterns are present in every one of the original prints from Pine Bush.

Crystall and Lebelson began to systematically go through the many UFO books that featured photos of the craft and discovered many like Crystall's that showed x-ray emissions and ultraviolet radiation. They realized that if anyone had done their homework and simply compared the many photographs against the technical specifications of their film, the person could have easily realized what was going on.

"I am sure there is specialized equipment," Crystall writes, "which would enable me to take clear photographs of the craft in their full, physical form. Two government employees whom I've talked with said special lenses had been constructed for government photographers to get clear moving film footage of the ships, as well as still photos. The film, I'm told, was spectacular. But I never had the financial resources necessary to obtain proper equipment, and I still don't."

A CLASSIC UFO REPEATER

What Crystall is saying is vitally important in the context of this book because it so clearly explains why so many UFO photos are often disappointing flashes of light. Even other UFO Repeaters who seem chosen by the aliens to regularly take such photos are sometimes subject to these same limitations, and

Crystall has done the field a service by helping to catalog some of the details of the radiation spectrum problem for the non-physicists in the UFO community.

She also writes that she once felt overcome with waves of love and compassion coming from the UFO occupants, which likely implies their establishing and/or demonstrating a bond of affection, in spite of her having described the aliens as "creatures" resembling grasshoppers when she spoke to Tim Beckley.

Under regressive hypnosis in 1979, she recalled nothing that constituted any major new revelations, though some details of her Hollywood adventures were freshened in her memory that later became more apparent when she journeyed to Pine Bush the following year. She doubted that she was an abductee, though she admitted she had remembered a very early childhood contact experience while under hypnosis. She did acknowledge that she was "a contactee with an extraordinary number of contacts."

But the point is that Ellen Crystall embodies the most important qualities of a UFO Repeater: she has had a lifelong relationship with the aliens, whether entirely consciously recalled or not, and she has been on the scene of UFO sightings that recurred on a sometimes nightly basis, with the ships leisurely, even "playfully," circling overhead for extended periods of time while her camera snapped away. With or without conclusive photographic evidence, Ellen Crystall has undeniably been caught up in the UFO phenomenon in a way few others can claim to equal.

SOURCES

"Silent Invasion: The Shocking Discoveries of a UFO Researcher"
By Ellen Crystall

"Touchdown in Pine Bush," by Ellen Crystal,
first published in "UFO Universe Magazine"

UFO Repeaters! Seeing Is Believing - The Camera Doesn't Lie!

CRYSTALL-CORNET UFO PHOTOS

IN some locations – often referred to as "window areas" or "UFO portals" – there can be several UFO Repeaters actively taking photographs. We can thus ask these questions: Is the person holding the camera attracting the phenomenon? Or is there something "funny" – maybe I should say "fuzzy" – about a specific location that attracts these objects and their strange occupants and brings them all into focus? Perhaps you need the person and the location working in tandem to get the best results. Give you or me a camera and it's possible we will come up with nothing – Zip! Nada!

All you can do is grab your camera and click away at the sky and at areas where you have a hunch "something" might be lurking on or near the ground. You can only hope that your results compare to that of Ellen Crystall and Bruce Cornet.

BRUCE CORNET – SECOND STRING REPEATER

I don't really know that much about Bruce Cornet. I have seen him several times on TV talking about his UFO sightings in and around Pine Bush. He knew Ellen Crystall. They had worked together on several occasions, taking pictures with their trusty cameras. Bruce does have a scientific background. He is not a flake. I found this brief bio on the "Coast To Coast AM" website at the time Bruce appeared as a guest on the show.

UFO Repeaters! Seeing Is Believing - The Camera Doesn't Lie!

With a little bit of research I discovered that Bruce is also a "fan" of Bigfoot and has taken at least one photograph of what could be "our boy." Below we see a photo taken by Dr. Cornet along with Sharon Eby on 8/8/2004, at 3:50 P.M., on the eastern side of the Franklin Mountains in El Paso, Texas, facing west with the El Paso power plant pond directly behind and to the east.

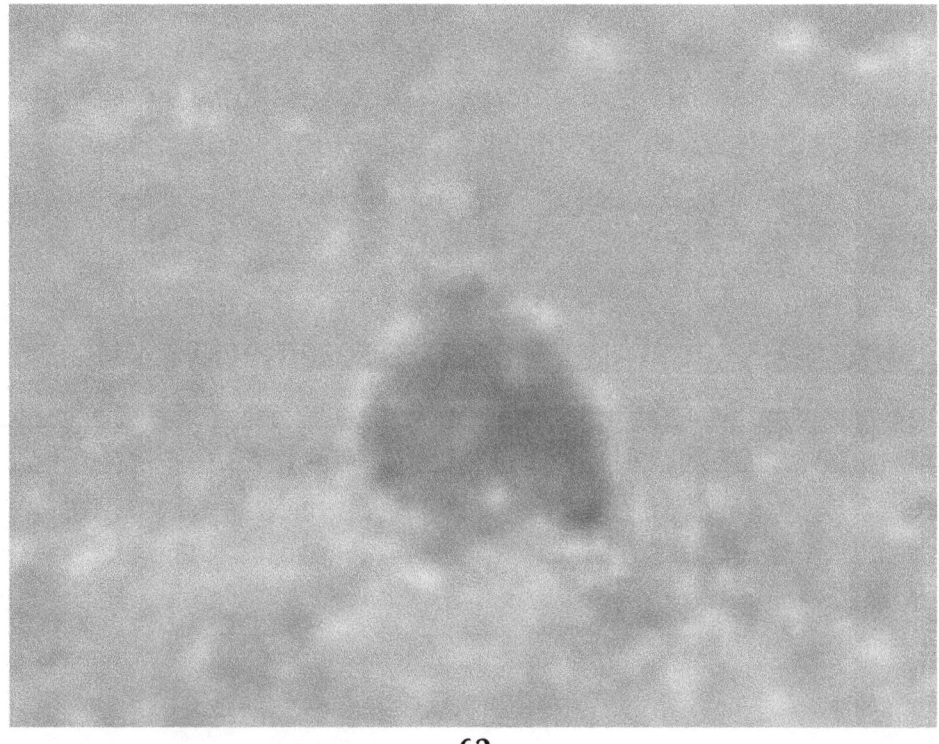

"Bruce Cornet has fourteen years of experience in the oil industry as a senior geologist, prospect geologist and palynologist. He has four years of academic research in geology as a palynologist, paleobotanist and well-site geologist. Currently, Dr. Cornet is Professor of Geology and Botany at the Raritan Valley Community College in Somerville, New Jersey. He is the author or co-author of 21 refereed scientific papers and two books, all on paleontological and/or geological subjects."

[Just in case you don't know, a "palynologist" studies living or fossil plant spores and pollen. Paleontology is the branch of geology devoted to fossils in general.]

– Tim Beckley

This photo was taken together by Bruce and Ellen in April 1993. It took nine seconds for the UFO to appear.

ELIZABETH KLARER OF SOUTH AFRICA

ELIZABETH Klarer was a most interesting early contactee. She had a friendly bond with the Space Brothers similar to that of famed fellow contactee George Adamski and was among the first women to claim a sexual relationship with an extraterrestrial. Klarer also took some remarkable photos of UFOs, some of which are included in this book.

Klarer was born in 1910 in Mooi River, Natal, which was at the time a province of South Africa. She studied meteorology and music in England and learned to fly light aircraft. She returned to South Africa and took her place as a well-respected member of high society there. Her husband was a major in the South African Air Force and she herself worked for Air Force Intelligence.

After reading George Adamski's books, "Flying Saucers Have Landed" (1953) and "Inside the Space Ships" (1955), Klarer recalled that she had been receiving occasional telepathic messages from a friendly space alien named Akon since her childhood. While her sudden return of memory has been mocked as "all-too-convenient," it is nevertheless true that contactees and abductees often experience such recall after their memories have been "reactivated" by some triggering mechanism, such as reading Adamski's books in Klarer's case.

As her story unfolded, Klarer said her initial sighting had taken place in 1917 and that she had had a second in 1937. After her recollections were refreshed, she began to venture out to take photos of the ships. Most famous

UFO Repeaters! Seeing Is Believing - The Camera Doesn't Lie!

Elizabeth Klarer, who worked for South African Air Force Intelligence, created international controversy when she wrote in her book, "*Beyond the Light Barrier*," that she became pregnant after her encounter with a tall, white-haired extraterrestrial.

among her photos are a series she took on July 17, 1955 or 1956 (the sources provide conflicting information).

The photos were taken in the presence of two witnesses to whom she wanted to show the site of her first contact. They accompanied her as she drove through the Zulu-Land to the foothills of the imposing Drakensberg Mountains. When she noticed a flash of light between some large thunderstorm clouds, she immediately stopped the car and exited the vehicle with her two companions. She brandished the Brownie Box Camera she had brought with her and a moment later she could see a metallic disc slowly approaching in the dark, clouded sky.

The disc was familiar to her, something she easily recognized from previous encounters. Klarer shot seven photos, reflexively and without thinking, and then the disc shot away. All at once, a thunderstorm started and a shower of hail covered the field. One can observe in the last two photos that the cloud formations do not change remarkably, which is proof that they were shot within seconds of each other. The disc seems to follow a clean curve, ruling out the possibility of a Frisbee or hubcap thrown in the air. She would later confirm the authenticity of the photos in a notarized affidavit and stood behind the story until her death in 1994 at age 83.

In 1954, a saucer flew over her farm in Natal, coming close enough that she could see one of its occupants. In April of 1956, a saucer scout ship landed and she was taken aboard. Some accounts say that on this occasion she had been able to call the ship down or "summon" it to her. In any case, it was then that she met Akon, a fair-haired and handsome Space Person, whom she recalled having known previously. This is reminiscent of the abduction literature that came decades later in which the abductee often feels the aliens are "familiar," as if they've known their abductors throughout their lives but are only remembering this fact at that moment.

Klarer was carried up to the mother ship in Earth orbit and was eventually taken to Akon's home planet, Meton, said to be orbiting in the nearby multiple-star system we call Alpha Centauri. Klarer became pregnant after intercourse with Akon and gave birth to a son named Ayling. Another version of the story says she was shown pictures of Meton while onboard the mother ship, fed a vegetarian meal and then given an introduction to the planet's culture.

Some accounts say that her son by Akon, Ayling, was unable to return to Earth with Klarer and stayed behind on Meton to be raised and educated there.

UFO Repeaters! Seeing Is Believing - The Camera Doesn't Lie!

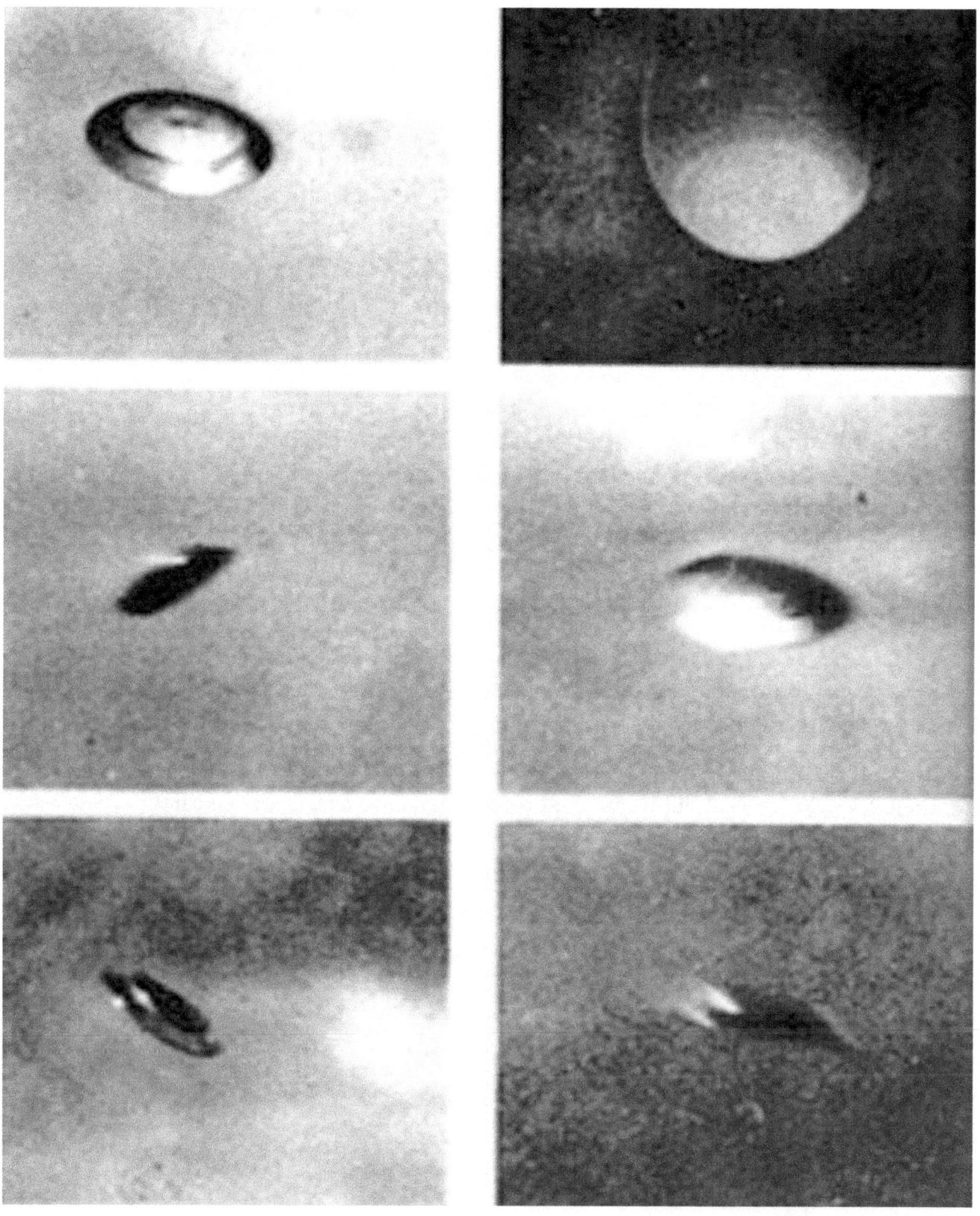

Close-ups of Akon's spaceship photographed by Elizabeth Klarer.

The entire process – the trip, lovemaking, pregnancy, delivery, and return voyage – is said to have required less than four months.

When George Adamski was on a world lecture tour in the late 1950s, he made a point of visiting South Africa and looking up Klarer for a chat on their various experiences with the friendly, wise Space Brothers. By that time there were more women among Adamski's followers claiming to have experienced "space-motherhood."

Klarer told her Akon/pregnancy story at UFO gatherings in South Africa as well as reporting on subsequent additional contacts. She was warmly and enthusiastically received at home, but her story was not believed by most North American and European UFO researchers, who found her tale of abduction and childbirth simply too farfetched to take seriously. It wasn't until the 1980s and 1990s that such stories became rather commonplace, and the existence of an extraterrestrial genetics program that produced human/alien hybrid babies was firmly established as perhaps the primary alien motive for abducting humans in the first place.

"Beyond the Light Barrier," Klarer's book about her extraterrestrial adventures, was published in 1980 and is said to have been written more in the style of a romantic novel rather than as a more straightforward autobiography. It also received an initially skeptical response.

But some of Klarer's photos are here, and readers are encouraged to form their own opinions about them. Just remember, the camera doesn't lie!

SOURCE

"Elizabeth Klarer Contacts," from the website at:

http://thenightsky.org/klarer.html

UFO Repeaters! Seeing Is Believing - The Camera Doesn't Lie!

1956-Rosetta/Natal, South Africa. July 17. Two photographs from South Africa were taken by alleged contactee Elizabeth Klarer. She claimed that she was impregnated by a tall, white-haired alien who piloted a UFO in one of her many contacts. Almost unbelievably, MUFON representative Cynthia Hind who was Africa's most respected Ufologist, found several eye witnesses to her contact cases.

1956-Rosetta, KwaZulu Natal, South Africa, by Elizabeth Klarer

WHEN UFOS GO BREEZING THROUGH

By Sean Casteel

THE photos of what could be alien spacecraft taken by Florida building contractor Ed Walters continue to be controversial. Photo analysis experts, both pro and con, have examined the photos in minute detail, often using computer enhancement techniques and a darkroom method called "light blasting" that brings the sometimes hazy images into sharper focus. If the photos are real, they rank as some of the most dramatically clear UFO photos ever captured on film.

Ed is also undeniably a UFO Repeater. His first photos were taken on November 11, 1987, and the pattern continued for several months, well into the spring of 1988. The small Florida town of Gulf Breeze, with a population of around 6,000 at the time, would never be quite the same.

In a book called "***The Gulf Breeze Sightings***," first published in 1990 and coauthored with his wife Frances, Ed told the story of how it all began. It was dinnertime and Frances needed to do some last-minute grocery shopping. Ed sat alone in his home office. He glanced out the window and was surprised to see a slight movement of light just across the street, partially obscured by a 30-foot pine tree in his front yard. He leaned over his desk to get a better look and saw that the light was something unusual and not simply a helicopter or plane from the nearby Naval Air Station.

"I still couldn't see clearly enough through the pine boughs to satisfy my curiosity," Ed writes. "I went to the front door and opened it. Whatever it was I had seen was still behind the tree. But I could tell now that this glowing, bluish-

UFO Repeaters! Seeing Is Believing - The Camera Doesn't Lie!

In 1988, Ed Walters took a photo of a UFO that seems to be drawing water up into itself. This is one of several "daytime" UFO photos taken by Walters that skeptics have all but ignored.

gray craft was like none I had ever seen before. This was right out of a Spielberg movie that had somehow escaped from the film studio. It was impossible, but there it was, glowing and gliding along like a cloud. There was a quiet in the air. As I stared at the craft, the hairs on my arms bristled. This was no movie prop gone astray."

Ed writes that his first thought was to call the police, but then he realized no one would believe him without proof. He rushed back into his office and grabbed the old Polaroid camera he frequently used on his job sites. He stepped out onto his small porch area and took his first photo as the craft came from behind a small tree.

A mind-numbing sense of shock and awe overcame Ed as he struggled with his camera. He simply could not process what he was seeing. He continued to stare at the enormous but silent spacecraft hovering in front of him.

"Bang!" he writes. "Something hit me. All over my body. I tried to lift my arms to point the camera. I couldn't move them. They were blue. I was blue. Everything was blue. I was in a blue light beam. The beam had hit me like compression. It was pressing me firmly, just enough to stop me from moving. I screamed, with my mouth frozen half open, but the sound was hollow. Dead, like a vacuum."

At that point, Ed believed he was dying. Then his feet lifted off the ground, and he heard a voice in his head saying "We will not harm you." Ed screamed again, and the mysterious voice said, "Calm down." Ed began to rise slowly from the pavement, unable to force his mind to see that he was only dreaming. The experience was really happening.

Inexplicably, he began to see visions of various dogs, with the images flashing by like pictures in a book, all accompanied by a strange humming sound. He sensed that he was suspended about four feet off the ground. He was abruptly dropped back to the pavement and fell forward on to his knees. The blue light was gone.

Ed felt confused and wondered if he had simply gone crazy and suffered some kind of hallucination. Then he saw the Polaroid photos scattered on the ground where he had let them fall as he took them. As he began to pick the photos up, his wife returned from her grocery shopping. The couple went into the kitchen to discuss what had happened. Frances poured Ed a glass of iced tea as he peeled the backing off his Polaroid photos.

UFO Repeaters! Seeing Is Believing - The Camera Doesn't Lie!

Above: Gulf Breeze UFO photo taken by Ed Walters showing object shooting out a "beam of light."

Below: Ed snapped this famous photo of a UFO just above the roadway.

"There it was, on the film," he writes. "It hadn't been my imagination or some sort of hallucination. What I had seen was real. It wasn't a comforting thought."

GOING TO THE MEDIA

The couple's first thought was to keep the whole experience, including the photos, to themselves for fear of ridicule, especially the kind that could hurt Ed's standing in the business community. But what if the UFO constituted a danger to their community? Didn't they have some obligation to warn their friends and neighbors? What if that had been their own daughter, or some other child, outside?

The decision was made to take the photos and an explanatory letter to "The Gulf Breeze Sentinel," the local newspaper. But Ed would say he was delivering the material as a favor to a "Mr. X," who preferred to remain anonymous. When the paper's editor, Duane Cook, saw the photos were taken with a Polaroid camera, he told Ed that made them less likely to have been tampered with.

Ed waited while the editor and the newspaper's photographer examined the photos. Cook's photographer made what are called "halftone blowups," which made the ship in some of the darker photos much easier to see. When asked who Mr. X was, Ed refused to budge and blow his cover. He knew some of the people in the newspaper office and was already concerned that they might talk about his presence there being unusual.

Two days later, the photos and letter were front page news. "The Gulf Breeze Sentinel" had published two of the five photos Ed had given them plus the entire "Mr. X" letter. The newspaper had added only a brief editorial comment asking anyone who also saw the incident or had any information about it to contact the "Sentinel."

Ed's letter had concluded: "Let me reassure you that this is not a hoax. I saw what I saw, took pictures of it, and have given these pictures to you. I wish I could come forward, but I cannot; for while I have nothing to gain, I have everything to lose. Thank you for your time and understanding."

Ed carried a copy of the newspaper with him from job site to job site, asking workers there if they had seen the newspaper report. One of his workers, on seeing the photos, said the craft must surely be the work of the devil and a sign

UFO Repeaters! Seeing Is Believing - The Camera Doesn't Lie!

Above: Strange craft photographed by Walters as it hovers over the city of Gulf Breeze, Florida.

Below: Gulf Breeze UFO photo taken by Ed Walters showing object emerging from behind a tree.

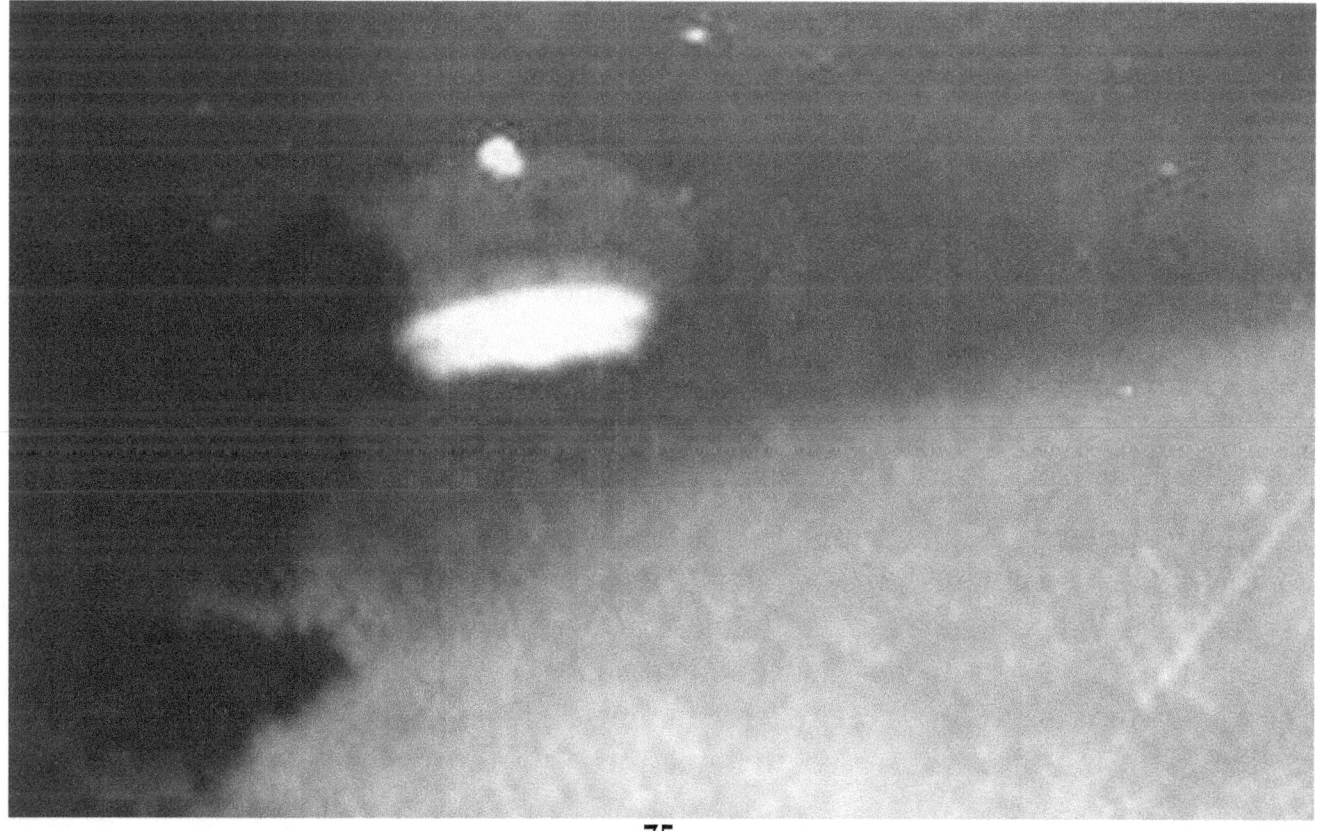

that the world was ending. The community was now abuzz with talk about flying saucers, much to Ed's satisfaction. He enjoyed the feeling that – whatever the consensus of opinion in Gulf Breeze, Florida, turned out to be – he had seen the UFO and knew the truth.

THE UFO RETURNS

On November 20, just a little more than a week after the first encounter, Ed was home and began to hear the same hum in his head along with the "UFO voice," which was speaking to him or someone else in a completely unknown language. He picked up his camera and stepped outside. He saw a speck of light high in the sky that was falling toward him at an incredible speed.

Ed spoke challengingly to the voice, saying he knew something was there. The voice then spoke, in English, "Be calm. Step forward." Ed raised his camera toward the falling UFO and the voice said, "Don't do that." Another voice said, in Spanish, "Los photos son prohibido." Ed was told that, even with photos, he would be unable to "expose" what was happening and that the aliens were there only to conduct a few tests. Ed replied, "If I want to be examined, I'll let you know." He then snapped photo number six as the falling craft stopped its descent and hung frozen in place just beyond the power pole at the front of his yard.

The alien voice declared their intention to bring Ed aboard, and Ed asked what right they had to suck people into the ships against their will. The eerie reply came: "We have the right."

As the discussion continued, Ed snapped photos seven, eight and nine. Finally, the UFO voice said, "We will come for you," and the ship shot upward into the sky and disappeared. This second encounter left Ed shaken and afraid, more so than the first, and he began to consider the idea of carrying a gun with him at all times.

Meanwhile, shortly after Ed's initial photos had appeared in "The Gulf Breeze Sentinel," the newspaper was inundated with stories from area witnesses who had seen something similar. Ed was elated to realize he was not alone. As the publicity continued, the Mutual UFO Network (MUFON) became aware of what was happening and began a full investigation, which ultimately concluded that the sightings were genuine and not a hoax. The organization's then-director, Walter Andrus, declared, "The overwhelming evidence is in. Gulf Breeze is indeed one of the most incredible cases in modern UFO history."

UFO Repeaters! Seeing Is Believing - The Camera Doesn't Lie!

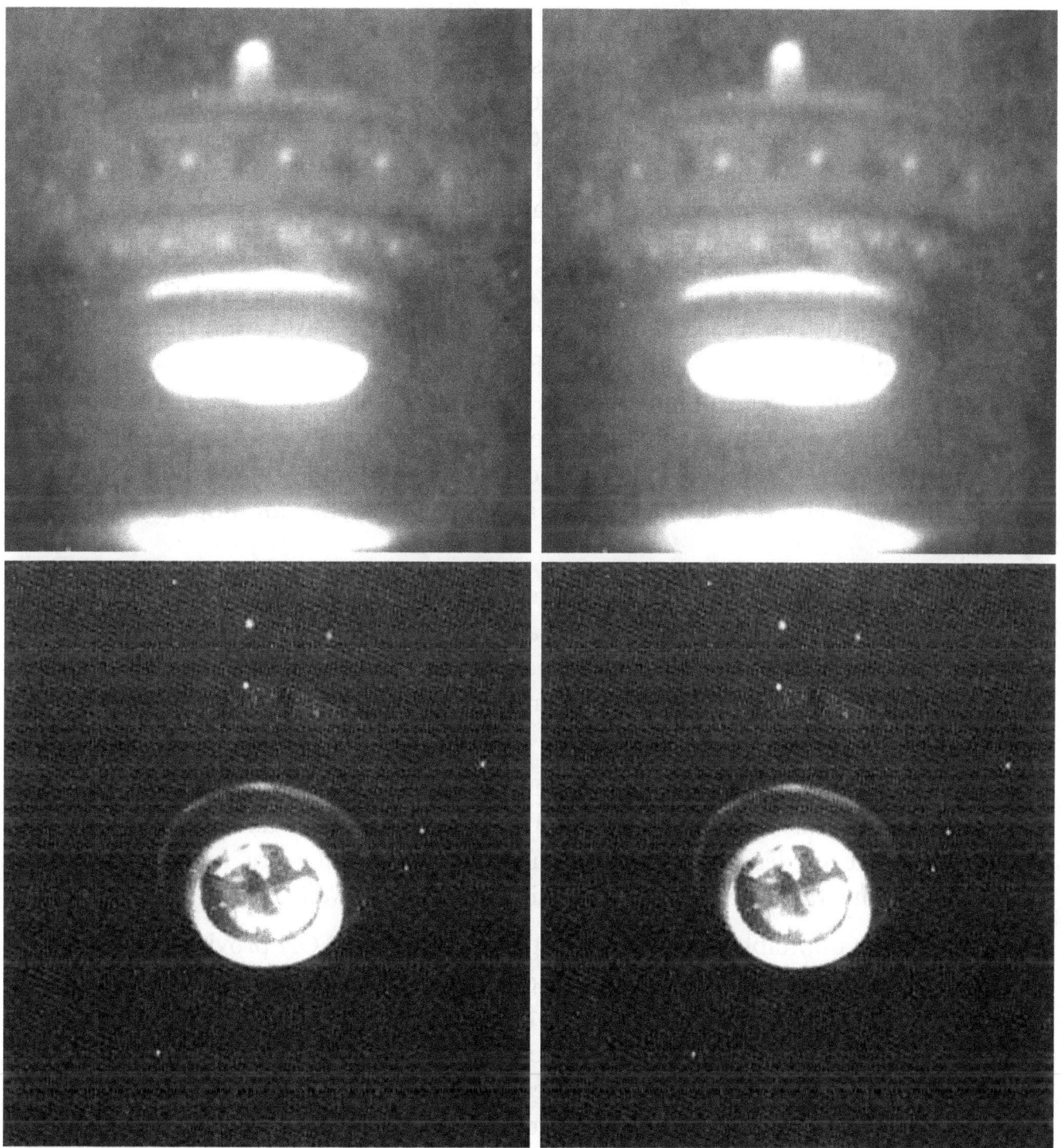

MUFON supplied Walters with a Nimslo 3D camera with 4 lenses that exposed four frames simultaneously when the shutter was released. Each lens captured the same image from a slightly different angle. The camera was sealed with wax to prevent tampering with the film. Shortly thereafter, Walters returned the unopened camera to MUFON, who found new UFO photos on the film.

As his anonymity began to slip away, Ed was still considered to be an honest and credible person. Nevertheless, as the sheer number of UFO photos he was producing grew, his believability began to come under fire. When Ed added claims of alien abduction to the mix, abduction researcher Budd Hopkins entered the picture at the request of Florida MUFON investigator Donald Ware. Around this same time, Ed underwent two separate polygraph tests and was assessed as telling the truth on both occasions.

Hopkins wrote an introduction to Ed and Frances' book, "The Gulf Breeze Sightings," in which he explained some of the reasons why he felt the case was genuine and not a hoax. For one thing, Ed and Frances did not make the standard contactee claims that Hopkins held in such contempt. Unlike George Adamski and Billy Meier, both of whom presented to the world unusually clear and detailed photos of UFOs taken at fairly close range, Ed and Frances did not try to "sell" the world on the kindness of the aliens or proselytize for a Space Brothers religion.

Adamski and Meier had presented themselves as "gurus" or "seers" with vital information to impart to one and all, and, in doing so, had profited greatly. But when Hopkins visited Ed and Frances at their home, he was struck by, even envied, their middle-class prosperity and thus concluded that they weren't in it for the money.

There were also familiar telltale signs of contact, like Ed's moments of recalled telepathic conversation with the aliens during an abduction event. A perfect circle of dead grass and peculiarly altered soil were found near the Walters' home that provided some physical evidence as well.

As the inevitable debunking campaign began, MUFON provided Ed with a special "tamper proof" camera, which Ed felt put him under too much pressure to produce further photos. Dr. Bruce Maccabee, an optical physicist who had worked for the government for many years, suggested Ed try using a "stereo" camera setup, meaning to mount two cameras parallel to each other to improve the odds of catching better quality photos that would prove the distances and sizes of the craft and silence the naysayers. With some hesitation, Ed took Maccabee's advice and used the stereo camera for some of his later photos.

Maccabee's analysis of Ed's photos led the Ph.D. physicist to believe the photos were genuine. Given Maccabee's credentials in the field of optics, that is nothing to sneer at. But the debunkers were not finished yet.

In an attempt to escape the pressures of unwanted fame and "celebrity," Ed had moved his family to a new home. On June 10, 1990, "The Pensacola News Journal" ran a story announcing that a UFO model had been found in the attic of the family's former residence. The following week the same newspaper reported that a Gulf Breeze teenager, later identified as Tommy Smith, had helped Ed hoax the photos.

On June 19, the MUFON state director for Florida announced that the organization was reopening its investigation into the Walters case to address these allegations. Their investigation concluded that the model was not constructed before September 1989, at least eight and a half months AFTER Ed and family had moved out of the home. Furthermore, close examination of the model and Ed's photographs did not show any exact match of markings, height/width ratios, etc. The investigator stated his belief that the model was built and planted by persons unknown hoping to discredit Ed.

TIM BECKLEY LOOKS BACK AT ED

Publisher and writer Tim Beckley has his own opinions on Ed's credibility. Beckley harkened back to Ed's appearance at the 27th National UFO Conference, held in Miami in May 1990. The conference was organized and sponsored by Beckley and fellow UFO journalist Jim Moseley.

"They had come out in droves," Beckley recalled. "But actually not so much the public as the press, who lined the beach with their mobile satellites, hoping that Ed would draw down a UFO or two, or maybe an entire fleet. The word had long since gotten out that 'UFO Ed' was known to attract swarms of brightly lit saucers complete with windows and laser-like beams of light that could hit you running if they wanted to.

"I can't believe that Ed Walters was a phony," Beckley continued. "I don't for one second think that he stuck a model into the walls of his attic so that someone would find it later and he would have the last laugh. He just wasn't that sort of guy. And besides, others did see the UFOs in close proximity to where Ed lived. He caused quite a hubbub for a number of years."

Unfortunately, Beckley said, Ed did not bring down any UFOs over the beach at the conference.

"Though there was a moment," Beckley said, "when the clouds started to part after an overcast and rainy day and the moon started to show itself. Everyone got their hopes up – but no such luck. The object that looked as big as the moon was – well – the moon!"

JIM MOSELEY WAS ALSO NOT A DOUBTER

The late Jim Moseley, for many years one of Beckley's primary "partners in crime," had similar feelings about Ed.

"I have met all kinds of people during my years in the UFO field," Moseley said. "While I admit that recording and analyzing technical information is probably not my forte, I believe I know how to evaluate someone's personality. Mr. Ed struck me as a perfectly normal husband and father. He has two children. He has also been honored on many occasions for his work in the fight against juvenile delinquency. In every way, he is a pillar of the community."

What Moseley believed to be Ed's last UFO encounter took place in the early morning hours of May 1, 1988. Ed said he had been abducted as he sat at a picnic table near the beach. He recalled feeling he had been assaulted physically or psychically and then deposited some 20 feet from the picnic table. He realized he was now bruised all over. In a panic, he collected his gear and sped off in his truck.

Ed said that he had experienced similar "missing time" effects four times before the beach incident. He decided to try hypnotic regression to recover the lost memories. The hypnosis uncovered a fairly typical story of aliens in tights brandishing rods the size of a flashlight that seemed to have some sort of power contained within them. Ed had consciously recalled touching a table on the ship at one point and getting some kind of foul-smelling, sticky substance on his fingers.

When he awoke the next morning, he could still smell the stench coming from his fingernails. He scraped some of the substance off, put it in a jar and refrigerated it. The substance, which continued to stink, was turned over to a MUFON investigator for analysis. It was never proven to be of non-earthly origin.

THE BUBBA UFO SIGHTINGS

One of the main reasons why the Ed Walters Gulf Breeze photos continue to have such credibility is that he was not alone in seeing and photographing the many appearances of the flying saucers. Throughout the early 1990s there was a series of sightings of strangely behaving lights and rings of light that traveled through the skies of Gulf Breeze. The observers nicknamed the phenomenon "Bubba UFOs."

As reported in a website called "My Baby Bubba in Gulf Breeze: "Although anomalous red lights have been occasionally reported throughout the world as UFOs in years past, they have usually been one-time events involving one or a few witnesses who had no means of recording the event. Hence these occasional sightings scattered throughout UFO history cannot compare to the unprecedented series of sightings between November 1990 and July 1992 in Gulf Breeze. During that time, the 'Gulf Breeze Research Team' logged about 170 sightings, most of which involved multiple witnesses and included still photography with telephoto lenses and/or recording by video cameras.

"In several cases," the website continues, "a light was observed simultaneously by two separated groups of people, thereby allowing for triangulation. There is no doubt that these sightings did involve some objects moving through the sky because there were 'too many' witnesses, videotapes and photographs to allow these sightings to be explained away as mere fabrications by a few people with some skill in photography, videography, etc."

The name "Bubba" is a Southern colloquialism roughly equivalent to "Good Ol' Boy," generally meaning a poorly-educated, white southerner. It is obvious this particular group of downhome Florida sky watchers had a sense of humor as they went about the serious work of photographing UFOs.

Some of the Gulf Breeze Research Team's photos are included here.

SOURCE

"Ed Walters, UFO Contactee," from the website at:
http://www.abovetopsecret.com/forum/thread1027093/pg1

UFO Repeaters! Seeing Is Believing - The Camera Doesn't Lie!

"The Gulf Breeze, Florida, UFOs," from the website at:
http://www.ufocasebook.com/gulfbreeze.html

"Bubba Comes To Gulf Breeze," from the website at:
http://brumac.8k.com/GulfBreeze/Bubba/GBBUBBA.html

"The Gulf Breeze Sightings," by Ed and Frances Walters, Avon Books, 1991.

Photos By Mike Hawkins. These are photos taken by independent witnesses most of whom do not accept Ed's photos as being legitimate.

82

UFO Repeaters! Seeing Is Believing - The Camera Doesn't Lie!

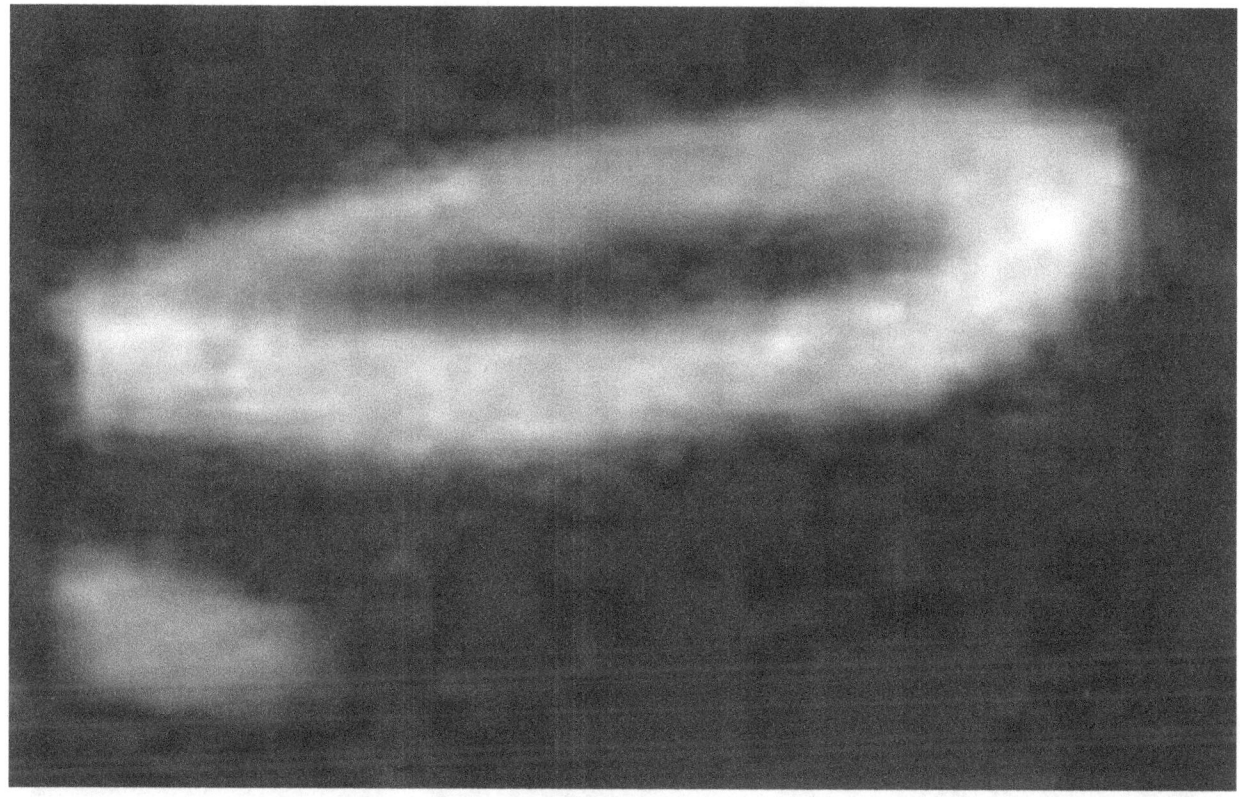

G. Bland Pugh, who was state director of Florida's Mutual UFO Network, took the above photo on January 10, 1992 at Gulf Breeze. The bottom photo was taken by Pugh while in the front yard of Ed Walter's home.

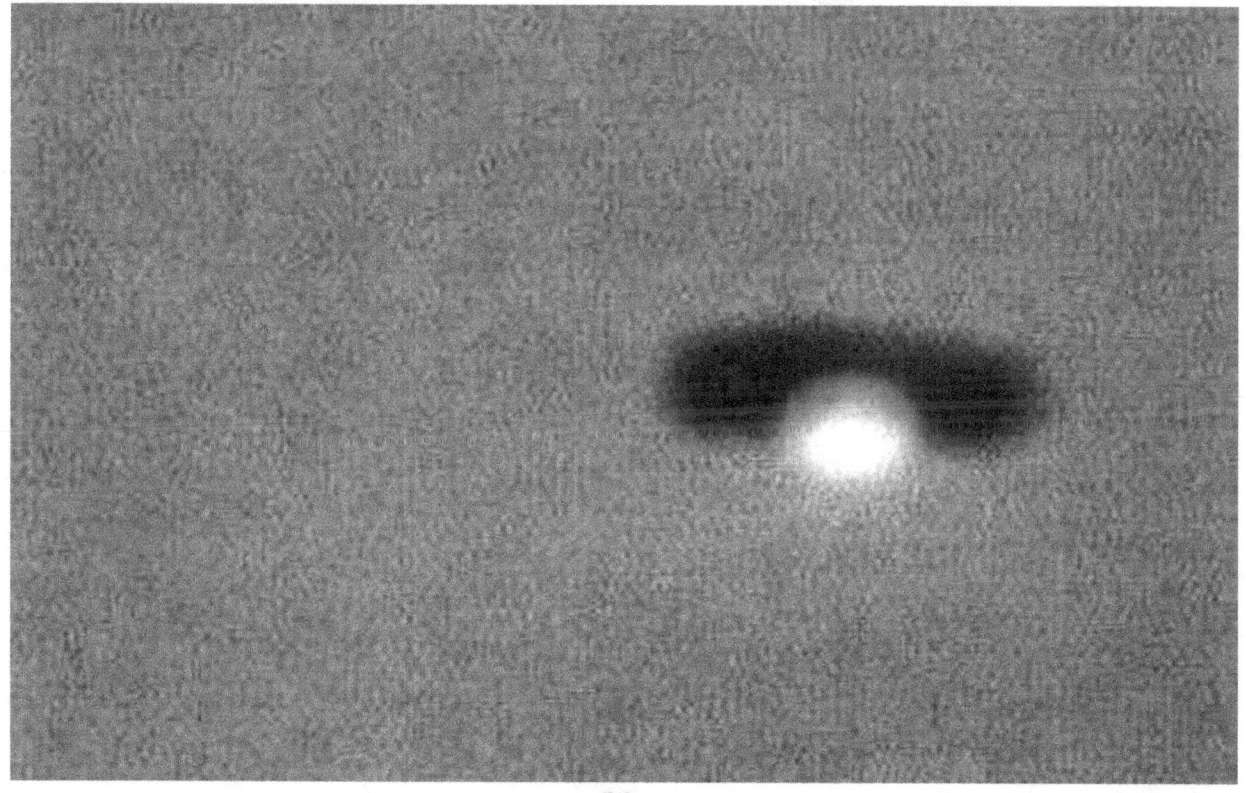

UFO Repeaters! Seeing Is Believing - The Camera Doesn't Lie!

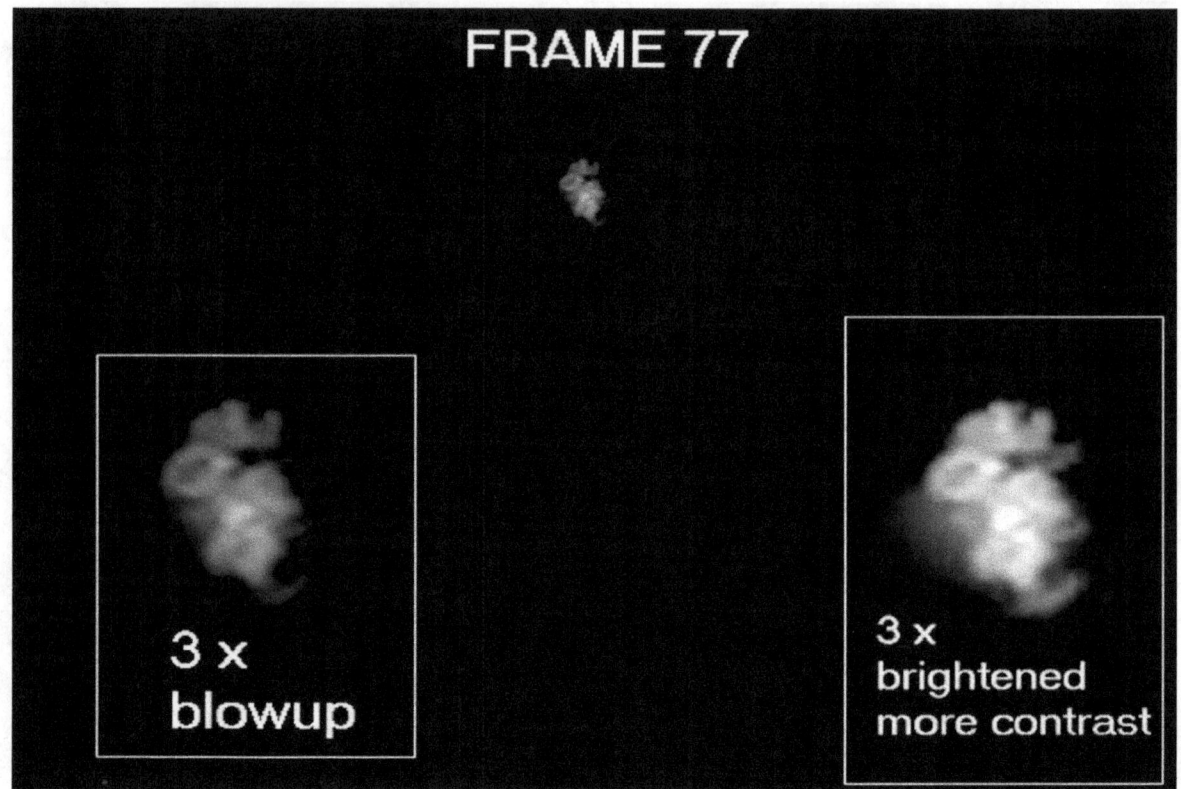

"Bubba" UFO photographed over Gulf Breeze, Florida

THE FASCINATING ELECTRIC UNIVERSE OF THE LATE HOWARD MENGER

By Timothy Green Beckley – "Mr. UFO"

I have to admit that I am sort of predisposed to believing at least part of Howard Menger's tales of meeting beautiful, highly advanced beings from other planets behind his home in what was once the sleepy farming community of High Bridge, New Jersey.

Truth is, I wouldn't be hitting the keys of this computer so persistently if it wasn't for Howard and his admittedly far out and sometimes outlandish stories of contact and communications with tantalizing Venusian gals and broad-shouldered Martian men.

It could all be a fantasy – albeit a beautiful one – but, as a kid listening to the crackling of the AM transistor radio under the covers late at night, it gave me something to believe in, to grab my attention, to propel me forward into a space/time continuum that seemed to promise great things for a planet that was itself just heading into the depth of space and looking to conquer the pathway to the moon and beyond.

I first heard Howard Menger on the Long John Nebel midnight-till-dawn "Party Line" show broadcast over the airwaves of WOR, a clear channel in those days that could be heard in over 20 states. It was in the mid-1960s, and I hadn't even reached my teens, but I was hooked on flying saucers and tales of angelic-like aliens walking and living amongst us. In front of a panel that was very often harshly skeptical, the mild mannered Howard Menger – who looked like a soap

UFO Repeaters! Seeing Is Believing - The Camera Doesn't Lie!

Howard and Connie Menger

opera star, his face perfectly chiseled – would spin yarns that would make the most susceptible listener scratch their head in puzzlement and awe. . . and maybe a bit of disbelief.

Though the majority of his contacts with "space people" took place far from the lamppost lights of the city, Howard was by no means a country boy. Howard's folks came from Brooklyn, where he was born on February 17, 1922, and it was only at the age of ten that Howard's mother and father decided a quieter, rural lifestyle was far more suitable for growing children, thus moving to the spacious, rustic property that was to become their homestead for years to come.

Well, quiet might not be the most appropriate word when you consider that Howard and his brother loved to romp in the pastures and over the hills, just like any young tykes would love to do. The only difference? On several occasions, the youths maintained, they were cornered by weird objects resembling Buck Rodgers-like spacecraft that came out of the tree line, prompting them to run like the dickens. Strange as this was, matters got even weirder when, Howard claimed, a ten-foot diameter disc landed pretty darn close to them. Meanwhile, a larger object hovered overhead, as if to gauge their reaction to what was happening in front of their bewildered eyes. It was an amazing science fiction-like episode that might otherwise have been forgotten except that it was the beginning of a half century of amazing experiences for the little boy named Howard, who would grow up to be among the most famous contactees in America, perhaps second only to George Adamski. Howard was in many ways a bigger puzzle to all those who attempted to unravel the mysteries that seemed to surround him and his controversial claims of contact with extraterrestrials and shadowy figures who always seemed to be just on the fringes of the action, perhaps directing his moves and egging him on to be a bit more fanciful and provocative in his claims so as to gauge public reaction to the idea that aliens are walking the Earth right here amongst us.

But let us not get ahead of ourselves, as there is much to tell and a great deal to ponder.

THE GIRL ON THE ROCKS

Little by little, Howard, being more "sensitive" than his brother, started to venture out into the pastures and meadowlands on his own. He noticed that he easily made friends with the smallest of beasts, such as squirrels and rabbits. He

UFO Repeaters! Seeing Is Believing - The Camera Doesn't Lie!

Howard Menger says that, as a boy, he spoke with a beautiful space woman who sat on a rock behind his parents' home. His life would never be the same.

enjoyed the sounds and the smells of nature and found himself drawn to a specific spot near a slow-running stream that ebbed and flowed in back of his home. As he tells it, the sun was shining brightly on that day in 1932 – a day that was to change Howard Menger's life forever and shape the belief patterns of many who were to be drawn in the years ahead to his uniquely divergent sense of reality.

"There, sitting on a rock by the brook," Menger poetically reminisced in his memoirs **The High Bridge Incident**, "was the most exquisite woman my young eyes had ever beheld! The warm sunlight caught the highlights of her long golden hair as it cascaded around her face and shoulders. The curves of her lovely body were delicately contoured . . . revealed through the translucent material of clothing which reminded me of the habit that skiers wear." To say that the young Menger was more "unworldly wise" than his age would seem to allow is no minor point to bring up when relating his life's most impacting moments.

Though Howard might have had every reason to be at least momentarily blown away by the appearance of this woman, who seemed to have just dropped in from nowhere, he reveals that he was not in the least frightened, "but was overcome by an overwhelming sense of wonderment" which nevertheless made him freeze in his tracks.

Howard continues by explaining that the lady on the rock "turned her head in my direction. Even though very young, the feeling I received was unmistakable. It was a tremendous surge of warmth, love and physical attraction, which emanated from her to me. Suddenly, all my anxiety was gone, and I approached her as one would an old friend or loved one. She seemed to radiate and glow as she sat on the rock, and I wondered if it were due to the unusual quality of the material she wore, which had a shimmering, shiny texture not unlike but far surpassing the sheen of nylon. The clothing had no buttons, fasteners or seams I could discern. She wore no makeup, which would have been unnecessary to the fragile transparency of her camellia-like skin with pinkish undertones. Her eyes, opalescent discs of gold, turned their smiling affection on me with a tranquil luminescence."

"Howard." The woman spoke the little boy's name and he trembled with joy. "I have come a long way," she said and then paused, smiling, "to see you and to talk with you." As long as he lived, Howard said, he could never forget those first words exactly as she spoke them; but "then my thoughts swirled in a maelstrom of emotion and slowly coalescing understanding as she continued to

UFO Repeaters! Seeing Is Believing - The Camera Doesn't Lie!

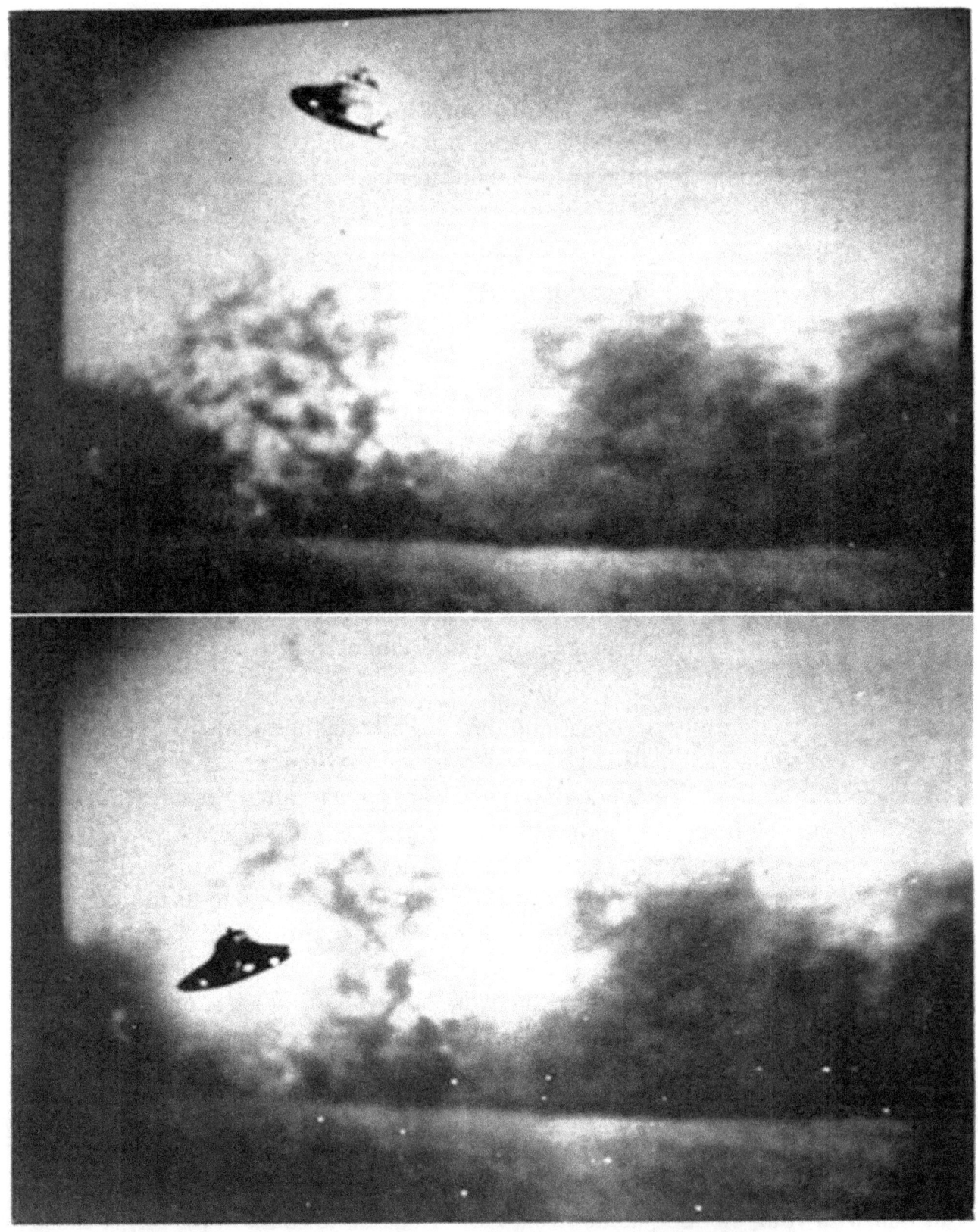

Two scenes from motion picture filmed by author at Field Location No. 1. These two pictures, shot from a movie screen in close sequence, show a space ship coming down and landing.

talk. Nobody had ever spoken to me as she did. She talked with me as if I were much older. She said she knew where I had come from and what my purpose would be here on Earth. She and her people had observed me for a long time and in ways I would not quickly understand. When she spoke of her 'people,' I still could not understand they were from another planet; as I listened in awe, my eyes delighted in feasting on the beauty of this lovely creature. Every movement of her body, as she stood up and walked toward me and reached out her hands to me, was a symphony of rhythm, grace and beauty. I seemed to be encompassed by the very glow, almost visible, that emanated from her presence. Somehow the entire area surrounding us appeared to take on a greater kind of radiance. I have often tried to describe it as like seeing a Technicolor movie in three dimensions and being a part of the action in the film.

"Again she pronounced my name and reassured me she knew who I was, 'from a long, long time.' And then some words that have taken on even more joy and meaning as I have grown older: 'We are contacting our own.' She told me that even though I did not understand many of the things she told me, later in life I would. Her words would be impressed on my mind – I suppose she said "subconscious" – but it was difficult, as she said again, to make me understand. I remember that she compared the idea to that of a phonograph, which would be played back to me time and again. "It is no fault of yours, Howard, that you cannot understand everything. Do not worry." And she laughed musically. She continued to speak to me as if I were an adult. Time has dimmed many of her exact phrasings, but the 'phonograph' has played back the ideas, each 'replay' taking on more and more meaning. Some of the actual words were beyond me, for they were words that meant nothing to a ten-year-old: 'frequency...vibration . . . evolvement."

Howard maintained that the lady on the rock seemed to know every thought that he had in his head. But, as she spoke, a look of sadness came over her face. Howard says he grew at that point not to envy her as she spoke of grave changes, destruction and torment to move as a dark cloud over the country and the world. "As you grow older, you will learn of your purpose," the alluring lady in the translucent, tight-fitting garb intoned dramatically. "And you will grow to help other people learn of their purpose as well."

I mean, come on now! How can you go away without being incredibly touched by this account as given by an adolescent who should be reading the

Hardy Boys finding himself mixed up with some Gypsy Rose Lee from outer space?

The lady told Menger that she would see him again but that it might not be for a long while. Trying to keep the spark in his heart alive, Howard said he returned to the same spot time and time again, hoping to rekindle their friendship, but the lady did not reappear. As the months and years rolled by, Howard confessed, the spot near the brook seemed to have lost its power to attract the boy who was now growing rapidly into manhood.

But Howard was soon to learn the incredible – that he would never truly be alone the rest of his life, for the world "out there" was rapidly closing in on him, and the lady on the rock was only the first of many strange episodes in his life involving phenomenological lifeforms.

HE'S IN THE ARMY NOW

Being a patriotic American, when his country called, Howard was happy to serve. But, while never one to be non-personable, Menger found that he had little in common with his fellow GIs. While they wasted no time in wanting to shoot the breeze, play craps and drink whatever alcohol was handy, Howard was drawn to more esoteric activities. While on leave, for example, he says he was content with window shopping, taking long walks and doing a bit of people watching. It was the latter that led to some interesting adventures in interplanetary communications.

While south of the border, Howard was trying to catch a taxi when he noticed there was already someone in the cab he had hailed. The gentleman in the backseat had blonde, shoulder length hair and was all too happy to open the door for him. Howard backed off, thinking the situation a bit peculiar. And it became even more so when Menger realized the passenger was attempting to speak to him but his lips were not moving. No! Better not get into that taxi, Howard. You have no way of knowing for sure where it might take you.

Later, it was confirmed to him that the man in the Mexican livery was "one of them." It was not unusual, his unearthly contact explained, for them to hang out in Mexico, as they had been doing so since the time of the great Aztec empire. There they taught those brave young men "some of the secrets that had to do with the use of sound and light necessary to produce power and run machinery." This individual explained to Howard that they had been selected for a series of ongoing contacts and that, while superior in many ways, these beings were not infallible and had deep emotions just like earthlings. And while they revealed in true prophetic terms that Howard's life might be in danger while in the military, they said it would never be necessary for him to have to kill another living individual. This part of their otherworldly prediction seemed momentarily inaccurate when Howard was attacked by a burly Japanese soldier who came at him with a razor sharp bayonet, cutting a hole in his tent in the middle of the night. Quick on the draw, Menger started blasting away. The Japanese soldier was injured by a blast of fire from Menger's service weapon, but the enemy was not mortally wounded nor were his two other companions.

It seemed that everywhere he went, Menger was bumping into "them." It was widely thought that aliens from space would have to be monstrous in appearance. But these people were not. If anything, they were a bit more delicate then we are. Were opposed to war. Didn't consume meat and believed in the sanctity of each individual and professed a love for the Creator. Surely, they looked human enough, but there was just something odd about their appearance – something a bit "off" perhaps – that convinced him these visitors meant what they said when they claimed to be from other neighboring planets. They intimated that they had selected Howard to become a "contactee" because he had some of the same benevolent qualities about him that they had.

THE BEAT GOES ON

Returning back to the same area of New Jersey after the war, Howard's contacts increased, and so did the sightings of their craft. He met them in his home as well as outdoors in several remote rendezvous spots where he had been told to go. One was a "landing field" in Pennsylvania where he would see their craft touch down several times. On a number of occasions, he carried a camera with him to record some of their aerial activities. He even managed to get several still photographs of the beings approaching him against the lit up hull of their craft, creating eerie shadows and figures which some have tried to say were "painted in" because, after all, Howard was a sign painter and could create all sorts of effects against the right backdrops. This was, however, years before the creation of the "blue screen" effect and I don't think Howard was quite sophisticated enough to create such special effects. Still photographs are easy to fake, 8mm and 16mm footage quite a bit harder back before Photo Shop and the age of computer enhancement. Plus there was the fact that Menger was not alone in reporting extraterrestrial craft and their occupants around the town of High Bridge, New Jersey.

In fact, people were coming from far and wide to meet Howard. Some of them went away impressed and feeling he was the real McCoy, while others felt he was definitely trying to pull the wool over the eyes of a public fascinated with space travel and UFOs. Not only that, but there were others – some of whom did not even know Howard – who professed to have met the space people and undergone incredible experiences of their own right near where Howard lived, some while walking about in the now famous apple orchard behind the Menger's home.

In 1958, Howard married Connie, who still lives in Vero Beach, Florida, where they had gone to retire. But the couple ended up "holding court" again, as well as starting up their sign painting business once more, this time with the assistance of their grown children.

But we are getting a bit ahead of our story – and a fascinating one it will continue to be. Yet to come was a supposed trip to the moon, the invention of a disc-shaped craft that could fly without rocket fuel, a career as a radio and TV guest acting on behalf of the Space Brotherhood, the promotion of a highly successful outdoor UFO conference, and authoring a controversial book entitled FROM OUTER SPACE TO YOU, which created so much of a stir that Menger found himself backtracking away from telling about his experiences with extraterrestrials. There were hints now that something perhaps a bit more sinister and strange had taken ahold of him, and he had become an unwilling – or perhaps all-too-willing – pawn of the military industrial complex.

Had Menger fallen into the hands of the silence group? There is much more to be said as we become even more deeply wound up in telling our story.

ENTER TALK SHOW HOST LONG JOHN NEBEL

Long John had a voice and a personality and a way of doing things that was unique. He started out as a sidewalk pitchman, became an auctioneer and finally turned up on Broadway in the studios of WOR from midnight till dawn on his **"Party Line Show"** with some of the most incredible guests the world has ever known. He might have been the first all night talk show host in America and certainly was the first to use the phones to pose questions to his guests live over the air. At first, it was a one-sided conversation where the caller would ask the guest a question, but only Long John could hear it. Long John would then repeat it over the air to his guest and his assorted panel of "experts," who all took diverse views on whatever the topic of the evening was going to be.

Later on, the beeper system was developed, and two-sided conversations went LIVE in all 30 states where Long John was heard . . . and we're talking about hundreds of thousands of listeners in a time when everyone normally went to bed long before midnight. Hell, **"The Tonight Show"** wasn't even on the air yet and CBS's **"The Late Show"** – which broadcast a full-length movie every night – went off around 1 a.m. the latest. It was dead air and dead silence, and good night till around 6 a.m., when the airwaves started to hum again. But then came Long John and his Friends from Outer Space. America's sleeping habits would be changed forever – just ask Art Bell and George Noorey, whose careers would not have been so easy if it wasn't for a man who stood six feet-seven inches tall.

And the tales that he aired on a regular basis were as tall as the man who broadcast them . . . perhaps even a bit taller, as we shall see.

Long John never said he believed any of the stories told him and his audience. "I don't buy that," he relished saying, but that doesn't mean he couldn't use a particular guest to boost his ratings. He must have had some inkling that, after midnight, there is a little bit of paranoia in all of us and he profitably tapped into those feelings. Nebel was the first radio show host to be given a salary of a hundred thousand dollars annually, the equivalent of what Mickey Mantle was making over at Yankee Stadium just a short subway ride away.

LONG JOHN'S GUESTS, THE USUAL SUSPECTS

There was George Adamski, who said he had met Orthon, a long-haired space visitor from Venus, in the desert near Sun City, California.

The Mystic Barber, who wore an antenna on his head to protect himself from the bad vibes of the bad space people and who everyone thought was a complete whack job. And he was, but a nice man just the same who had a reputation for giving the best haircuts in his Brooklyn neighborhood.

Stuart Robb, who talked about the prophecies of Nostradamus before anyone else did, could pick up the voices of the dead on his reel to reel tape recorder, and had proof that Shakespeare did not write any of those plays, couldn't read or write, but offered a safety net for Francis Bacon, who really penned these incredible works.

There was Gray Barker, who told about Albert K. Bender being silenced by the Men-In-Black and who later published, in hardback, Menger's **"FROM OUTER SPACE TO YOU,"** only to have Menger blow off the opportunity to promote the book and instead decide to change his story in midstream.

Jim Moseley, publisher of **"SAUCER NEWS,"** which later morphed into the satirical **"SAUCER SMEAR,"** before the days when he became the acknowledged "Court Jester" of UFOlogy.

And even the mighty visionaries, like science fiction's Arthur C. Clark and the Great One himself, Jackie Gleason, who stopped by the Times Square studio of WOR from time to time to discuss UFOs and to voice his opinion that contactees were charlatans. He once agreed to go for a ride onboard a flying saucer, but I guess the Space Brothers passed him by because he never made it to the far side of the moon like the man who became Long John Nebel's biggest drawing card claimed he did.

Howard Menger was, for all intents and purposes, the East Coast version of George Adamski, except that Menger's accounts seemed a tad more believable, there was at least some scant independent evidence that something pretty unearthly was happening on Menger's property in the Garden State, and, finally, his ability to communicate a good story was heads above any of the other contactees, who mostly resided on the West Coast, thus giving Menger an uncluttered field to operate in.

And operate he did. Howard's contacts seemed to take on a life of their own. On weekends, dozens of cars headed for the open road in order to pull into one of Menger's fields and speak with him personally about what had been going on when the sun went down and the heavens came alive with shooting stars and the flickering lights of the flying saucers.

And the stories did get wild – they seemed to have no boundaries. But the public ate them up and Howard Menger became, in his own right, a star with his 15 minutes of fame long before that amount of time was allocated to anyone and everyone by the highly-hyped artist Andy Warhol.

UFO Repeaters! Seeing Is Believing - The Camera Doesn't Lie!

Above: Howard in front of a prototype of a "free energy" flying saucer that he had invested in and which he said could take us to the moon.

Below: Howard and Connie stand next to the illuminated form of a space person.

AN INTERVIEW WITH CONTACTEE HOWARD MENGER

Long John's questions came fast and furious. Nebel would often try to trip up his guests, but Howard either outfoxed one of the greatest fox hunters of all time because he was smooth and polished or because he totally believed in what he was saying. You can decide (or just maybe you can't) by reading the following interview that Howard did around this time period.

Q. What is a flying saucer?

A. An interplanetary space craft.

Q. Where do these come from?

A. From other planets in this system, such as Mars, Venus, Saturn; also from planets outside this solar system.*

* There are also space craft, though of inferior design, which are built by people of this planet. These people are in communication and in service with people from other planets. They are people who possess a high spiritual understanding and have reached an awareness of natural law; therefore they have been entrusted with information enabling them to construct such a craft.

Q. Who has seen them?

A. Thousands of people all over the world.

Q. What do they look like?

A. Saucer-shaped (as the name implies), disc shaped, bell-shaped and so on. They may often appear to take on different shapes and colors due to the magnetic fields surrounding them.

Q. Where do we see them?

A. In flight, in the sky all over the world. They land only in secluded areas where they may contact people without attracting attention.

Q. How fast do they fly?

A. In the Earth's atmosphere, they travel in excess of 20,000 miles per hour; outside the Earth's atmosphere, they can exceed the speed of light.

Q. Has anyone seen them land?

A. Yes, many people have seen them land – such as myself, and countless others who have not told of their experiences.

Q. Do they have people in them?

A. Yes, physical beings like ourselves operate the craft.

Q. Do the people get out?

A. Yes, when they need to make contact or gather information.

Q. What do the people look like?

A. They are humans and look just like we do, excepting their manner of dress. They have solid physical bodies.

Q. How many people are aboard a flying saucer?

A. I have never seen more than six in one craft; however, they can travel in units of 3-6-9, or 4-8-12, depending on the planet from which they originate, or the polarized balance of the people in connection with the mechanics of the craft traveling through space.

Q. Do the people say anything or communicate in any way?

A. They communicate telepathically and orally with whomever they may contact.

Q. What do they say?

A. They say they come in love and compassion for us, their brothers, to help us to help ourselves to reach a higher understanding of life and its meaning.

Q. What language do they speak?

A. They have their own language, unintelligible to us because of the higher frequency and different harmonics in the tonal scale; however, they can speak any language on Earth after a short period of study aided by electronic instruments.

Q. Do they indicate where they have come from?

A. Yes, usually. The ones who have contacted me have come from Mars, Saturn, Venus and probably Jupiter.

Q. Do they seem peacefully disposed towards us?

A. They say no man can leave his planet with the purpose of conquering or controlling another world. They are not hostile. They come in love and service to the Infinite Father.

Q. Did anyone ever see a craft take off?

A. Yes, hundreds of people have seen them take off and have ridden in them.

Q. Do the craft make any noise?

A. None audible to our physical ears.

Q. Are there any pictures of craft taking off?

A. Yes. I have color movie films of craft taking off and landing, people getting out and stepping into the craft. I have Polaroid shots of the same, which will be shown in the future.

Q. Is the viewer of a craft affected in any way – emotionally, physically or mentally?

A. What happens is that we ourselves may unwittingly cause our own fear or panic. Some cases have been reported where an individual got too close to the craft while the power was still on.

Q. If there are such craft in our skies, why are they not a more common sight, such as our regular aircraft?

A. First, they are not our regular aircraft; second, they are considered alien to our skies; thirdly, it has to be a slow process in reaching the people because of the hostile nature of this planet.

Q. Why don't they make proper visits through channels of government, or mass meetings and landings?

A. Mass landings, great displays, and the like would only cause confusion. The military would be involved immediately; the governments of the world would be in turmoil, each seeking its own advantage. There would be hysteria and, possibly, panic. And so, in the interest of humanity, the space people approach us cautiously. Incidentally, space visitors do not have identification papers and passports. If we now investigate and counter-investigate every suspected alien who might be suspected of being a foreign agent, what would we do if confronted with people who are entirely new, strange and alien to our planet? There would be endless investigations and controversy, and the work and message the space people have come to deliver would be snowed under by red tape. I doubt whether they have the time or inclination to play this silly Earth game of intrigue and counter-espionage. So they come directly to the people, by contacting their own; and the people will learn of them over a period of time – gradually, without fear, panic, or censorship. Every great movement has always started with the people, and that is where the story belongs: with the people.

Q. If they can speak our language, why don't they come among us and announce themselves, as we would do if we went to another planet?

A. They have tried, but people would not believe them – mainly because they look and act like us and are not monsters with six or eight arms.

Q. How long have they been coming into our atmosphere?

A. For thousands and thousands of years.

Q. Why don't they tell us about the wonderful experience of space flight?

A. They have, through certain people, and these certain people are willing to listen and believe whether or not they see; and also some of the information divulged must be kept secret.

Q. What is the place of the space people in the cosmos – do they come from different dimensions?

A. They are spiritual beings, like ourselves, using physical forms adapted to their own planets. There is time around their planets within their atmosphere just as on Earth; but there is no time in space.

Q. Is this their first or early beginning of flight into space?

A. No, they have been traveling in space for thousands of years.

Q. How do they regard us?

A. As brothers. They love us.

Q. Why do they come here – what is their purpose?

A. To try to awaken within us a yearning for higher understanding so we can help ourselves in preventing any further destruction of our planet, which could conceivably have a bad effect in our solar system. It is about time we grew up as a humanity.

Q. What planets are they coming from?

A. From Mars, Venus, Saturn, Jupiter, and some planets outside our own solar system.

Q. Are any craft coming from beyond our solar system?

A. Yes. And some mother ships have come from distant galaxies.

Q. What are the main different types of craft?

A. Discs are remotely-controlled objects sent out from the masterships, to record thoughts, emotions, feelings and other conditions of the people in the area; also to detect hostility before landing. Some of these recordings are used for future contacts with the individuals concerned. These discs range in size from eight inches to more than eight feet in diameter. Bell-shaped Saturnian craft are about 509 feet or so in diameter, 18 to 20 feet high; metallic, grey, somewhat flatter in appearance than a Venusian scout ship. A Mother Ship or Carrier is elliptical, cigar-shaped or egg-shaped. They have been reported up to 3,500 feet in length; however, there is no limit to their size. Green Fire Balls are a means used by space people to protect us from the effects of the atomic and hydrogen explosions in our atmosphere.

Q. What are other planets like? For example, Venus or Mars?

A. Venus is a planet slightly smaller than our Earth. It is in the stage that the Earth was in many thousands of years ago; young and healthy, with beautiful foliage, streams, forests, large bodies of water, mountains, and hills. As a matter of fact, there are some places in California today that resemble Venus. It is beautiful and verdant and a veritable paradise. There are also places in South America similar to places I have seen on Venus. They plan to keep their planet young, beautiful and healthy. Their atmosphere is very similar to ours, but the sun cannot penetrate it with destructive rays.

Q. Do they have governments, cities, country places, farms, gardens, factories, schools, etc.?

A. They do not have authorities or government officials of any kind. They live in peace and harmony and everyone knows what his or her particular talent is so that they work at that particular job – and they love their work.

FACTORIES: There are buildings where work is done, or where the craft are built; but the buildings are beautiful places and not like our factories at all. They receive no coin in exchange for work. Instead, they exchange talents, and everything is shared to the extent of their talents and desires and no one wants for anything. We work because we have to work. They work in service of their Infinite Father.

FARMS: They grow fruit and vegetables and flowers. They do not raise meat-producing animals since they do not eat meat. Animals roam free and complete their cycle of life naturally. They are not over-bred and over-produced for food.

SCHOOLS: There are schools of wisdom that children or adults can attend. Most knowledge is inherent in the children, since they are born with the knowledge of the past. Their education is their past learning, which they apply in their present life to gain wisdom for future use.

CITIES: They live in small communities, built in the forests and close to natural surroundings. They do not denude the land of all trees and shrubs and then build boxes. Their communities are kept small and usually contain no more than a few thousand people. They are spread out and decentralized.

Q. If well-known people have been contacted, why don't they tell about their contacts?

A. Government officials in particular refuse to tell because it would upset our economy. The knowledge they have gained depicts an entirely different way of life. It is living under God's law rather than man's law. Most mechanical energy sources would become obsolete.

Q. Have all countries been contacted?

A. People in every country of this world have been contacted.

Q. Why do they contact only certain people?

A. Certain people are born with an awareness of truths within themselves, or they are reborn from another planet, in which case their own are contacting them and awakening within them that one small spark of truth so that they become the flame of truth. These people must have the courage of their own convictions and the ability to take it, for they will suffer ridicule and attacks.

Q. If they are coming here to help us, why are they concealing their identity?

A. They are not particularly trying to conceal their identity, and to those they have contacted they have revealed themselves.

Q. Are space people living here on the Earth among us?

A. Yes, thousands of people from other planets are living among us. Some are rebirths, some have come directly from their home planets in spacecraft. They may live next door to you. One of them may be your co-worker, the person who serves you in a store or a restaurant. They have one identifying trait: love of fellowman.

Q. Why don't they tell us how to build a craft?

A. Because it is like giving a child a firecracker, an automobile or gun. We cannot live with ourselves, let alone trying to live with people of other planets. We would use this power to conquer. On other planets there are no wars – they would like to keep it that way.

Q. If, as some reports indicate, some of our airline pilots are seeing flying saucers and are said to be suffering from hallucinations or seeing weather balloons, why are they not fired since the safety of our flights depend upon the pilots?

A. Because authorities know the pilots are NOT suffering from hallucinations. They know the pilots are telling the truth, and saucers are being seen by too many airmen to adequately squelch the story.

Q. What is the average life span on other planets?

A. Eight hundred years.

Q. Have the space people brought us any picture or films of their home planets?

A. Yes. In the future, pictures taken on other planets will be shown here. These will include scenes of the planet, people, animals, etc.

Q. What kind of clothing do the space people wear?

A. On Venus and some planets, the women wear knee-length, billowing, tunic-like gowns of pastel colors, sometimes held by a jeweled belt. The women do not wear girdles, bandeaux, or any tight undergarments. The clothes are comfortable, airy, loose and beautiful, enhancing the contours of the female form. The men wear ski-type trousers, translucent and soft, something like nylon. The clothing both for men and women adjusts to the bodily heat so that it can keep them cool or warm as the temperature varies. A sandal-type foot gear is worn by both men and women.

Q. Do they have families, children? What is their social setup?

A. Two beings, when perfectly mated, stay together as long as their desire and mutual progress continue, sometimes for many of our lifetimes. They have children, and the children are loved by all. However the children mature at a very early age. Their social setup is communal. They share the goods of life with one another. Yet, if it is their desire, they can have isolation and privacy at any time they wish.

Q. At what age do children reach maturity on other planets, such as Venus?

A. They mature in three to five years. A child on Venus shortly after birth is already equal to an Earth child of seven.

Q. Do they nurse their children?

A. Yes, the children are breast-fed in a few months, then are weaned on natural foods, such as fruit and vegetable pulp. They are not given animal milk.

Q. Do the children go to school?

A. They have communal-type schools or places where they are briefed on their own spiritual development. Most of their knowledge is within themselves and in such schools it is encouraged to develop.

Q. Do people work?

A. There is no work as we know it. They have advanced mechanics and apparatus that do the work quickly and efficiently. All services are voluntary and rendered with love. All products are shared. They do have buildings where people go to perform services, where the various conveniences of life are made.

Q. What is their religion? Do they believe in God? Do they believe in Jesus?

A. Their religion, or more properly, way of life, is serving their Infinite Father, and attaining more knowledge so they can serve their Creator to a higher degree. Jesus was one of them in the highest degree of development.

Q. What are their homes like?

A. On Venus, the buildings are dome-shaped and semi-translucent to permit light and color to enter. Some of the buildings resemble our own modern organic architecture.

Q. Can we go to the other plants and be accepted and live as they do?

A. Generally, no. We might, due to the differences in development and vibration, atmospheric pressures, etc., suffer a nervous breakdown. Some people from Earth, however, have gone physically to other planets aboard a craft and stayed there (not wishing to return); others have returned after a learning period or visit, to help their Earth brothers. Those who do return usually remain silent as to their experiences lest they be confined to a mental institution or suffer ridicule.

Q. Can a disc-type craft return to Venus without having to depend upon a mother ship to transport it back?

A. Yes, the craft has the ability to return to Venus on its own power without transport by a mother ship.

Q. What is the purpose of the mother ship or carrier?

A. The space carrier is used outside this system for extended trips into outer space. It transports cargo and equipment, along with many people.

Q. Can space people take goods or plants from here back to their own planets?

A. Yes. Many craft are sent here for specific botanical studies and take many of our plants back with them for study and transplanting.

Q. Can we transplant plants from their planets to Earth?

A. Yes. Plants can adapt themselves to the conditions of varying frequencies in time.

Q. Have some of our terrestrial plants been brought here from other planets?

A. Yes. Some of our plants have been brought here from space.

Q. Are the planets known by names different from the ones we call them?

A. Yes. In some cases. In other cases, planets are designated by symbols. Our Earth, for example, has a specific symbol.

Q. Do people from other planets have hair on their bodies as we do?

A. They are not as hairy. In some cases, however, when a person from Venus comes here, he will, after a short while, grow hair much faster than the ordinary Earth person. When they return to their own planets, they lose the hairy condition.

Q. Does the frequency of a planet affect the mental development of its people?

A. Yes.

Q. Are men and women equal in social level on other planets?

A. Yes. In fact, from a physical standpoint, it is more pleasurable to be a woman on other planets. Childbirth, for instance, is a thrilling and pleasurable event, not associated with pain or discomfort.

Q. What is the difference between a reborn and a reincarnated being?

A. A REBORN (or rebirth) is a being who has volunteered to come to this planet from a higher planet or dimension on a mission to teach his or her brothers and sisters and assist them in helping themselves gain more insight and understanding of the Universal laws of the Creator.

Q. Is it difficult for a reborn to understand the reasoning of Earth people? Is their reasoning or understanding different?

A. The reborn are usually masters or near-masters; therefore, it is not difficult for them to understand the Earth reasoning or its people; however, it is, at times, difficult to live among them.

Q. What is the difference between a master and a near-master?

A. A MASTER can do anything, but does not. A NEAR-MASTER (such as an adept) can do almost everything, and does. There is that small percentage of the ego still operating that prefers to demonstrate through the individual ego, rather than operate God's law through many forms and people. A MASTER appears confused, but is not, among those who are confused, just to be one of them. A NEAR-MASTER appears calm and in control before the confused, and prefers to remain aloof from humanity. A MASTER can leave (mentally and etherically) a group of people engaged in conversation at any time he wishes, without the people being aware of his spiritual absence, or partial absence, since a master can be several places at one time. A NEAR-MASTER can leave, mentally or physically, and appear before those people then, as a master. A MASTER directs indirectly the laws of God through the confused people around him, because when they act on what they term as their own thoughts, these actions are recorded in their own subconscious and they then learn through their own mental processing what the master has known for centuries. A NEAR-MASTER directs throughout what HE knows as God's laws and the beings in the physical illusion do what they think HE knows is right and do not learn as much. There are four real master in the world today. One is in the United States, one is in India, one is in Australia, and one is in South America.

Q. Are the master celibates?

A. No. God is married to the Infinite Universe. All masters are married. It takes a master to get married and perform physically that which is taken for granted that a master would not do. Sometimes it is a matter of choice. The sexual expression is one of the highest expressions of God, in that it takes in the sense of touch. When we speak of sex, we interpret it to mean physical union expressed through love and understanding – not sex as expressed for and by itself. Sex expressed purely on the physical plane for itself and its beings, perfectly combined in all areas, that is, in the spiritual, mental, emotional, and physical, should be joined as one. Wedded incompatibility is the true adultery.

Q. What is a flashback?

A. A mental picture of an experience, or a feeling of remembering a place or lifetime on this planet or another planet. Only the brains and mental makeup of reborns can tune in to flashbacks. Certain granules in their brain cells, which are present by previous development, will respond to flashbacks.

Q. Why don't we remember past lives?

A. The memory of past lives is trained out of us from childhood onward. Children's fantasies, imagination and play are sometimes really flashbacks and/or regressive memory.

Q. How are the visitors trying to raise the mass consciousness of the people?

A. By various methods such as: a. Dissemination of saucer research data. b. Stories of contact with their own. c. Their signs in the sky. d. Mechanically by means of mental capsulation, and machines. Mental capsulation can be projected by sound, color, vibration. A high-frequency sound can be a mental capsulation; a song or a selection of music can be a mental capsulation. Music in the form of a mental capsulation helps push certain buttons in the mind and releases something which is there. However, because of the way we eat, think, and act on this third-dimensional planet, this knowingness is held dormant, sometimes through several lifetimes. Nevertheless, God's laws shall prevail, and those who are due this release toward an awareness will have it when the time in the cycle of expression of this planet is ripe. The machines which send out super-sonic high frequency sounds use a man's body as a terminal in conjunction with the mental capsulation. There are three terminal bodies in each state. The machines operate on a silent carrier wave.

Q. What is the Will of the Father and how can it be developed?

A. The will of the Infinite Father is to EXPRESS, in ALL dimensions, the love of the Infinite Father in ALL FORMS, COLORS, SOUNDS, TASTES, and EXPRESSIONS.

Q. Will there ever be an interchange of people, ideas and cultures between the planets in our solar system so that there will be a brotherhood throughout our solar system?

A. This is inevitable. You can delay God's plan, but never stop it. Interplanetary brotherhood for Earth's people is dependent upon the degree of decline of hostility and the degree of increase towards tolerance, love and good will toward our fellow men. The near-masters do not know of the masters, but the masters know of the near-masters, and of the reborn, who do not know of themselves as near-masters and/or reborn. This realization of one's near-mastership usually comes somewhere between the ages of thirty and forty.

THINGS START TO GET REALLY BIZARRE

Around the time Howard began to reach his stride, he suddenly grew silent. Noted UFO/New Age publisher Gray Barker had just issued **"FROM OUTER SPACE TO YOU"** in a deluxe hardback edition which featured an illustration on the cover that Menger had painted himself of the girl on the rock. Barker needed to recoup quite a bit of dough and, like all publishers, figured that the author would be more than happy to promote the work in all media, especially on the Long John Show where he could possibly sell several thousand copies. Nebel's Party Line had just gotten onto WOR-TV in New York and Menger was invited on to hype the book.

He did show up, but his story had changed from that of fact to a possible work of science fiction. His space friends might have been imaginary. Perhaps he had been duped by secret agents – Russians? – into believing what was basically a lot of hog wash. Barker was ready to pull his hair out. Long John would probably have liked to put a hit out on him.

UFO Repeaters! Seeing Is Believing - The Camera Doesn't Lie!

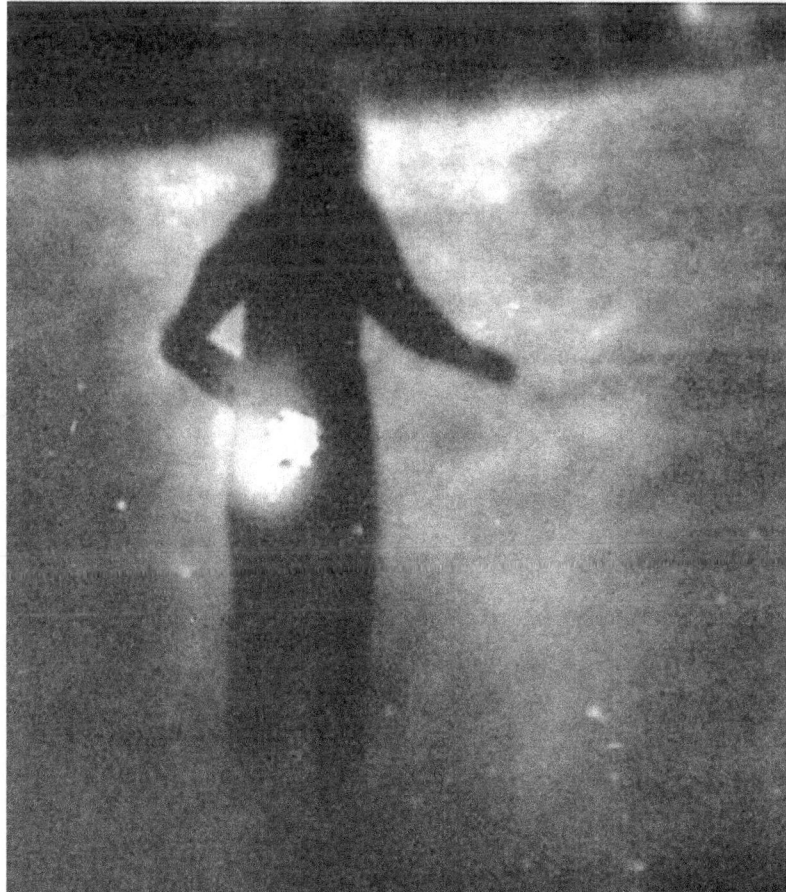

Above: Menger took this photo of a landed "Adamski-type" craft with one of the occupants silhouetted against the brightly glowing spaceship.

Left: Photograph of a "Venusian woman" who, equipped with a diving-suit, left the spacecraft and approached Menger, then used a luminous device that she carried and disappeared.

Others saw Howard's space people from a safe distance. Often they hung out in a glade not too far away from the house.

Rumor had it that Menger had been visited by the Men-In-Black and they had warned him for the safety of his family that he should tone this all way down. This does not seem out of the realm of possibility because, as we mentioned earlier, shadowy types were often seen in the vicinity of Menger while he told his stories. Some folks thought they might be space people themselves – others figured far worse.

At the time, I was publishing a monthly newsletter called **"THE SEARCHLIGHT."** Being the journalist that I am, I tried to get Menger to comment on these stories. I wanted to know why he had copped out on Barker, Long John and those who wanted to believe his experiences were real and not fabrications. After all, how could such a seemingly sincere person be such a liar?

Menger did not talk to me for several years but he did send me some material which he hoped would shed some light on what was happening and why he was not "hanging out" in the limelight for the time being. In addition to Menger's remarks, I tried to feel out those in the field who I thought might have some insights into this troubling situation.

The following are the notes that I collected – some of which I published – at the time.

Notes on the High Bridge Incident—A Turn of the Screw

Menger wrote in his book, ***"From Outer Space To You"*** (Saucerian Press, 1958), that he had met people from outer space on his farm in High Bridge, New Jersey. Later, while appearing on the Long John Nebel TV show, he backed away from many of the controversial statements presented in his book. As our readers know, even though we attack the subject of contact claims with a completely open mind, it doesn't take much to know that many of the stories told by the contactees over the years leave a lot to be desired in the way of solid evidence. We now seem to have some additional information which might shed some light on the Menger claim in particular and on "contact" cases in general.

The following are extracts drawn from an eight-page letter sent by Menger on September 18, 1965, to a Colonel Jordan, United States Army (Ret.), who was then the City Clerk of Sebastian, Florida. At the time this letter was written, Menger was attempting to hold a three-day space convention with the help of the City Council. But because of "negative publicity" received from such then-active groups as NICAP and CSI, the council refused to pledge their full support.

Because of the length of this letter, we will not reproduce it here in full, but will give the bulk of the relevant parts of its text.

Menger Explains His Positions On Contact Claims

"I wrote a book, *"From Outer Space To You,"* (Fact/Fiction) based on an actual experience, which I accidentally stumbled upon in an isolated field to the rear of my property in High Bridge, NJ. These photographs (I took) I sent to a department in the Pentagon. It wasn't long afterward that I was contacted and asked if I would cooperate in an experiment based on what I had inadvertently seen and project into this experience an expanded futuristic view of 'things to come' with their help and information. (I suppose they must have figured the only way to obtain my silence and cooperation was to put me on the 'team.') In other words, the 'High Bridge Incident.'

"'The High Bridge Incident' was used as a gauge to indicate the people's reaction to alien contact. You will think this not so strange when you consider that our astronauts today are being thoroughly conditioned and trained to meet any and every strange condition or situation they may face upon landing on an alien world! The psychology of human reaction to the strange and unknown, the utter desolation of hostile terrain, the complete isolation in the black void of space, and the awesome feeling of looking back at a dimly glowing globe called Earth, so distant, small . . . these are the feelings our astronauts must feel, conquer, control and cope with. Space Medicine is dealing with unknown factors and human reactions to them, and if our scientists sometimes obtain their much-needed information in bizarre ways, it is because they have only one known quantity with which to work, namely the human factor. Bearing this in mind, let us suppose they superimpose a hypothetical condition, based on truth, like a spacecraft landing in an obscure country town, and some alien creatures disembarking, giving messages of good will to a local yokel acting as 'contactee.' This would be one way of getting an index of human reaction . . . .

"I agreed to cooperate in the above experiment, and when the press picked up the story of flying saucers over High Bridge (and they were there and the people did see them – don't ask me how or why) they really had a ball. They worked it up into a real sensation. However, all the publicity did not help me, my work, or my family, as I had little or no privacy left. But this was all part of it. I had to meet and talk to people. At first, I was a little shy and more or less tongue-tied, but after many lectures I gained in confidence and with the material and suggestions handed to me, I was able to carry on.

"Yes, I was handed a specimen that was claimed to be a potato from the Moon Base. It's the finest piece of dehydration you have ever seen on Earth to date. There is no dehydration plant that can safely dehydrate a whole specimen. I never said I married a Venusian. My wife never said that she came here in a spaceship from Venus. She was born in Elizabeth, N.J. In my own UFO investigations, I have come across many accounts of aliens claiming to be from Venus and being described as fair-complexioned with long blonde hair. In my own futuristic account of space, I mentioned a blonde Venusian woman, as does George Adamski in his book . . . I have remarked rather whimsically that my wife, who is small, fair and blonde, is a 'Venusian type' . . . The press really went to town on that and made money turning out copy.

"After the 'High Bridge Incident' had been widely publicized and the experiment was considered finished, I completely withdrew from all activities in saucer research. I refused to give lectures or show movies or speak to anyone about it. I had completed my mission. I wanted peace . . . .

"Whatever bizarre circumstances occasioned my entrance into the UFO field, it was with proper motivations and the desire to help that so involved me . . . ."

Perhaps you will say that this account, given above by Menger, will add more confusion to the saucer picture than it subtracts. And, in all probability, you are correct. Were all the various contactees put on the "team," as Menger says he was? Or did they have actual experiences? Perhaps, as Dr. Davidson has suggested many times, they were hoaxed, unknowingly, by the CIA or some other government agencies, into believing that they were talking with friendly space people and then relaying the space people's "message" of good will and brotherly love to the general public. Perhaps Menger was smart enough to find out what was going on. But, just the same, how does one go about explaining the strange objects seen over High Bridge?

Saucers were seen. We've talked to some of Menger's close associates, who say they saw UFOs landing near Menger's home. One person even goes so far as to claim some sort of mental contact with the "visitors." Or perhaps, as our own Staff Advisor, Harry Hoffman, suggests, this is merely an attempt by Menger to somehow connect the past with the present. Perhaps things, as Menger indicates, got too hot for him and, being unable to get one second of privacy, he decided that he had better change his story. These are all questions which remain to this date unanswered. Menger's book (now out of print) has just been translated into French by Dr. J. P. Crouzet and has been published under the title of "*My Friends, the Men from Space*" in Paris by Dervy Livres Publishing Company. Presently, Menger is working on a new book which he says "will drop a few bombs in certain places." But this may not be released for some time.

WHAT I BELIEVE

By Gray Barker, Publisher of "*From Outer Space To You*"

After ten years or more of saucering, I'm afraid I'm a rather jaded individual when it comes to getting excited, but, very frankly, this statement from Menger interests me greatly. Although no doubt there is much fiction in many of the contactee accounts, I have always thought in my mind that SOMETHING actually happened to many of these "extremist" saucerers. I cannot say in all certainty that Menger is telling everything when he talks about the Pentagon bit, but it certainly does ring a bell somewhere in the corner of my mind.

After Menger's book was published, you will recall that it was a source of some disappointment to me that, on a Long John Nebel TV appearance, Menger really backed down by saying that he wasn't sure about some of the contacts.

Although I knew this wouldn't help book sales, strangely enough here was the point where I began to take Menger more seriously than before. Especially after he had told me in a phone conversation that he was still contacting people but that he wasn't quite sure whether they were from other planets or not!

You will also recall Dr. Leon Davidson and his many articles for "Saucer News" and "Flying Saucer Review." Although "Dr. D." had some pretty far out stuff, he did come up with an interesting accusation – that the CIA had set up some of Adamski's contacts. He also accused my publisher of having been subsidized by some government agency. Well, like Ray Palmer, I had a "fact" here: I knew that I wasn't working with any government setup and doubted very much that the publisher of **"They Knew Too Much About Flying Saucers"** was. But Dr. Davidson did leave some suspicions in my mind.

In regard to Menger, I do know that nobody subsidized me in any way in publishing his book (except the thousands of people who ordered the book in advance of printing). Although I had contact with the FBI early in the Bender mystery days, and several disquieting contacts during the (Adamski-related) Straith Letter matter (also from the State Department), I have never had any contacts with the Air Force on saucers nor with any government agency which offered any sort of encouragement or subsidy.

And I still think that if you take Menger's experience, add either encouragement of a government agency, or some other party besides himself, you will come up with a clearer picture of what may actually have happened. The same may well be true of Adamski.

Take Albert K Bender's book, **"Flying Saucers And The Three Men,"** also. It could be an invention to cover-up, as sort of a red herring, something that may have happened involving government intervention.

As a publisher of various saucer books, however, I have tried to retain a completely open mind, as you have done, and much of what I have expressed above is at best only speculation.

A Dire Warning To "Watch My Step"

Charles Marcoux, who has been a student of UFO matters and a follower of the Inner Earth and, more pointedly, the Shaver Mystery, since the very beginning, has some rather interesting comments regarding Menger that would tend to add some credibility to Menger's claim that he was an agent for the Pentagon. These observations are in a seven-page report written on April 28, 1957, at the time Menger was lecturing in Michigan. Since the report is most lengthy, we will once again quote only its most important sections.

"At this lecture, Menger played a tape recording of a saucer sound as it 'hovers and vibrates' before landing. The sound was sort of a high-pitched whine which reminded me of the Atlantic communication system. It was also very similar to a hydroelectric generator. After this, the tape seemed to change to a high pitched Morse code effect . . .

"Menger in his lecture claimed that there were no monsters coming here in spaceships and any such things as Deros and subsurface races were hoaxes. I thus proceeded to question Menger further about this since I am very familiar with the Shaver Mystery and know there is a lot to it. He told me that if there were such things the space people would have informed him about them . . . .

"After I put the pressure on Menger, he sort of shrugged his shoulders and asked me if I didn't think it better to be in contact with the higher forces than such low ones and proceeded to warn me to 'watch my step'....

"But perhaps the most unusual thing was the two men who traveled constantly with Menger wherever he went. After I left the meeting, one of the men (I believe his first name was Dave) asked me point blank, 'Don't you think that it would be better if you followed the higher contacts, rather than those lower ones, as Menger said?' To this I replied that I could have knocked loopholes in everything that Menger had stated but that it wouldn't be wise to do so on Menger's field of battle. To this the fellow agreed....

"These two men watched Menger like a hawk about to pounce on its unsuspecting prey. They were silent and did not noise about too much but instead remained in the background and let Menger hold the attention of the group. I knew that the money taken in from his lectures in the area did not cover the expense of the three persons and also keep up the cost of operating a five thousand dollar automobile....

"A few weeks later, I was threatened by three men who attempted to force their way into my home. I cannot say for certain whether there was any connection between the two events but, following the Menger lecture, I also received a number of very strange notes and letters through the mail....

"There is more that I could tell you, but think it not advisable at this time."

Comments By "Saucer News" Editor James Moseley

"I think you will agree that it certainly does take courage for a contactee, or anyone else, to change his story. Although I tend to disbelieve all saucer contact stories, we must admit that Menger is apparently sincere.

"I am almost ready to believe that the government DID put him up to his pseudo-contact stories, for reasons best known to themselves. Why should he, in effect, admit he was lying, when he could just as well stick to his old story or remain completely silent as he has done for a couple of years now? In other words, I really think he may have something.

"Longtime readers of **"SAUCER NEWS"** will recall that Dr. Leon Davidson has propounded the idea that UFOs are a hoax perpetrated by the

Central Intelligence Agency. The letter from Menger to Col. Jordan sounds like he is expressing a view very similar to Dr. Davidson's.

"I do hope he writes another book, as it sounds like it might contain some very interesting material . . . ."

Dr. Leon Davidson Comments

"My earlier opinions on this matter still apply, without adding or subtracting a word, as is indicated in my '**Open Letter to Saucer Researchers**,' published in the March 1962 issue of '**Flying Saucers**,' Ray Palmer's magazine . . . .

"My view of the CIA involvement also remains exactly as I expressed in my article '**Why I Believe Adamski**,' as published in the British '**Flying Saucer Review**,' Jan-Feb 1960. The CIA contact man in the Menger case was, I believe, the 'electrical engineer' from Califon, N.J., whose identity is known to Richard Harpster, a reporter on a New Jersey paper.

"The recent activities of flying saucers may be linked to other and newer secret agencies than the CIA, such as the DIA (Defense Intelligence Agency). As long as government money may be spent without public accountability, for reasons of 'military secrecy,' we can expect continued 'psychological warfare' as represented in the Menger case and its aftermath."

Although Menger's letter has brought to light a new possibility for many of the contact stories, this is not the first time that it has been suggested that the people contacted were in reality from this planet. In a **"New York Daily News"** column, written by Ben Gross on April 4, 1957, noted naturalist and author Ivan T. Sanderson suggests that agents from other nations may be behind some saucer contacts!

Ivan is quoted as saying: "Some of those who tell such stories can't be dismissed as liars, psychotics or conscious charlatans. Menger, for instance, appears to be utterly sincere.

"All of these stories have certain similarities: the alleged spacemen appear only at night; their craft land in out of the way places; and they warn their contacts never to approach them while carrying any weapons, even flashlights.

"Furthermore, these space visitors preach a doctrine of brotherly love and are reported to harp constantly on the suggestion that we abandon our experimentation with atom and hydrogen bombs. Also, they are said to be giving secret instructions of some kind to their earth-people contacts.

"But most suspicious of all is this: Persons who say they have had contacts insist that occasionally they recognize 'people from other planets' working in our factories and riding along our highways in cars. How do they identify these individuals as being from outer space?

"Well, they tell you that this is a secret. But some have gone so far as to say there are hidden means of identification, including code words, involved."

Sanderson goes on to say he is beyond the point of dismissing all such stories as fiction since "There is now quite a considerable mass of such reports. Some of these alleged contacts have been witnessed by as many as six persons at a time, in one case even a Princeton University physicist . . ."

To bring this story up to date, Ivan wrote us on February 4, 1966:

"Ben Gross and Long John were at that time deeply intrigued by and concerned with the drive behind the new rash of contactees, from a purely news point of view. Put it this way: there were either UFOs or there were not; assuming there were, where did the contactees fit in? And, if all they said was make-believe, why did they do it? In view of certain things that were definitely recorded, it was manifest that there must have been some very good reason for this drive because, if for nothing else, the amount of money these people were able to spend . . . .

"As for Menger's claim that he was used or virtually employed by the government, I am afraid that I can have no comment. It amazes me that it should have been so claimed and I frankly don't believe it. If true, it would seem to me that Menger is behaving in a most improper manner in so disclosing without official permission and he should therefore produce such permission.

"'Howie' Menger, whom I met at least fifteen years ago near here when he contracted to paint the road signs for my zoo, is, as everybody knows, a most likable chap, and I feel pretty confident in saying that he certainly never intended to harm anybody. Whether he was deluded, misguided or, frankly, blackmailed, I don't know and nobody will ever know most probably; but, published stories (press clippings) show that he caused a tremendous disturbance for a couple of years, and there are those photographs. Both may have been pure 'games,' but as more experienced newsmen than I (like Ben Gross) pointed out: just how much money will you spend on games, and where in the heck do you get it? . . . ."

Dr. Berthold E. Schwarz, the Kindly, Credulous Psychiatrist

Over the years, a few of the more liberal-minded investigators of the phenomenon decided to give Menger's accounts a second look. Timothy Good, the very popular British UFO writer, spent crucial time checking out Menger's claims, found additional witnesses and was not afraid to include these accounts in his books. But, more than most others, one of Menger's prime supporters was the late Dr. Berthold E. Schwarz, who received his M.D. from the New York University of Medicine and was a Diplomat of the American Board of Psychiatry and Neurology, a Fellow of the American Psychiatric Association and also of the Academy of Medicine of New Jersey.

When Menger passed on February 25, 2009, Dr. Schwarz gave a very touching eulogy at Howard's funeral service, making mention of those who not only respected Howard's claims but actually might have participated in some sort of contact or sighting themselves, sometimes in the presence or vicinity of Howard or while they were out and about on their own.

In the heavily footnoted **"UFO Dynamics"** (Rainbow Books, ISBN: 0935834648), Schwarz recounts several incidents in which Menger apparently was somehow linked to the events in question.

In one case he recollects the time a couple were on their way to hear Menger speak when suddenly their radio apparently was "possessed" – or "taken over" might be a better way to phrase it – by a voice which stated: "It's been reported that the British have communicated with a saucer in England and have made arrangements with the occupants." It was a bulletin broadcast over WOR radio in New York. When the husband and wife arrived at their destination "the people there were also listening to that particular radio show, (yet) they hadn't heard what we did! I could hardly believe what I had heard. I never had an experience like that before or since. A hoax would have been highly unlikely."

In addition, Dr. Schwarz recounts how he interviewed a physicist from Princeton University who said he had seen "a noiseless disc three feet in diameter" in a rural New Jersey ravine near the home of Howard Menger. "The disc changed in color for approximately 15 to 20 minutes and was observed at a distance of 6 to 8 feet. The physicist was unable to offer a plausible explanation."

Another witness was present who added more details when he said, "A little light came out of the disc and circled around."

The most remarkable of the cases discussed by Dr. Schwarz centers around the time one of Menger's sons, then aged 12, was dying of brain cancer. The family had gathered around, having given up on doctors, and were down to using advice from the space brothers.

Let us quote directly from Dr. Schwarz's text, which contains the statement of one individual who was present on this rather remarkable night: "We were sitting in the kitchen and the boy was in the other room with the nurse, who was on twenty-four hour duty. The sick boy then called urgently. His mother rushed into the room and we followed. The nurse took his pulse; it was very slow. The boy had a convulsion and a light started to show up above his bed. It began as a light blue and was about eight inches from the wall but not casting any light on the wall. It was like a bar of light. It pulsated and grew whiter and then it faded. The whole manifestation lasted about one and a half minutes.

"The nurse left to call the doctor . . . When the boy relaxed, the light was white. By the time the doctor came there was no light and the boy was all right. When I saw the light I turned my head sideways to make sure it was not an optical illusion which would travel with me, but it was still there . . .

"The night of the column of light, I saw four men in luminous uniforms. They were about three hundred feet away on a hilltop in the pasture. They stood in front of a dark grove of trees behind a fence. It was a moonlit night. They were on the edge of the rise and walking and flowing. If they were stooges, it would have been a very strange hoax. The sick boy's mother was with us; the other children were too small to fake this. The contactee was in the house, as was everyone else whom we had met when we first came . . ."

During his illness, the son had other remarkable experiences which are recounted in *"UFO Dynamics,"* which I believe is one of the best books ever written on the high strangeness element apparent in many UFO cases. And it may be the only positive UFO book ever written by a psychiatrist with impeccable credentials.

UFO Repeaters! Seeing Is Believing - The Camera Doesn't Lie!

Spaceships coming down for a visual inspection. Or are they about ready to land in Howard's famous apple orchard?

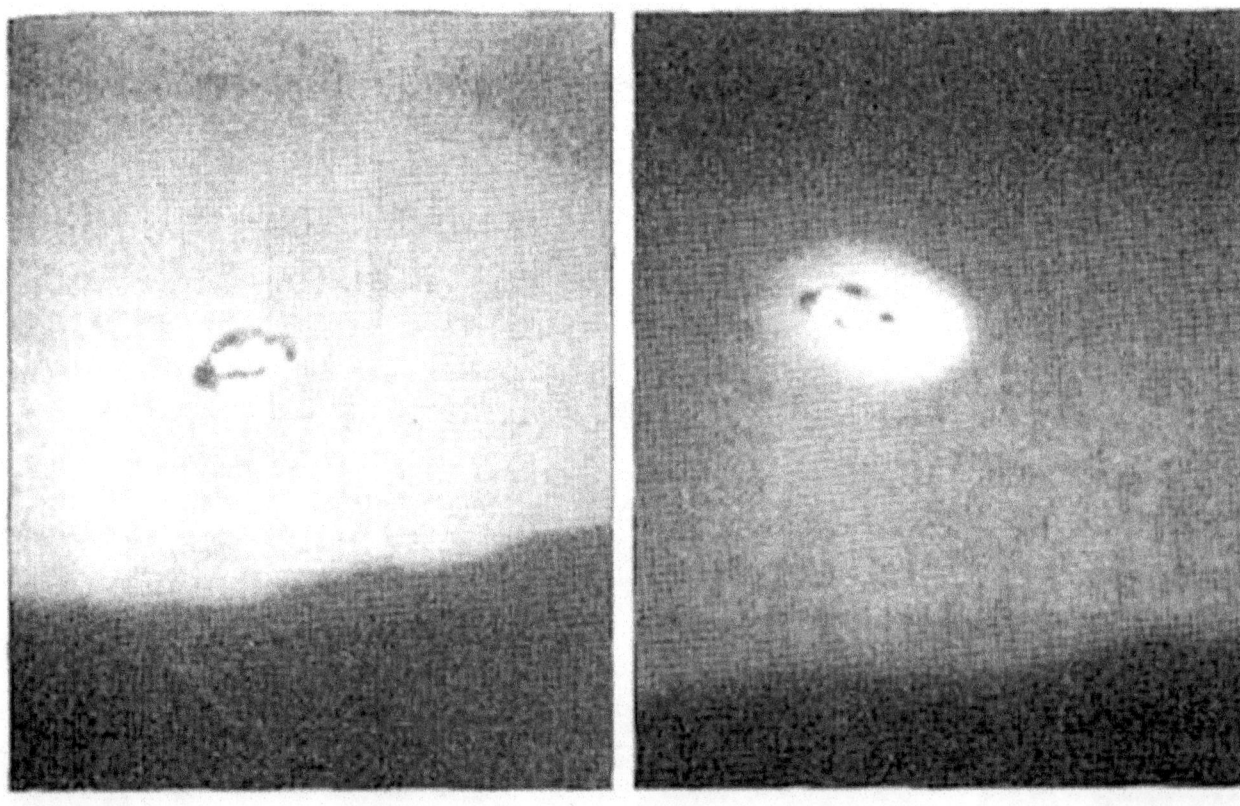

MY CONCLUSION IS THAT THERE IS NO CONCLUSION

I have tried to cover as much of the Howard Menger story as I possibly can. I have tried to present all the highlights as best as I remember them. And I am not blind to the fact that there are some inconsistencies in Howard's recollections. He had made different statements on various occasions, even in his own **"High Bridge Incident"** book (privately published and co-authored by Connie Menger).

On one page we are told, for example: "Years ago, on a television program, when I first voiced my opinion that the people I met and talked with from the craft might not be extraterrestrial, it was thought that I had recanted. However, they (the aliens) said they had just come from the planet we call Venus (or Mars). It is my opinion that these space travelers may have bypassed or visited other planets (as we are planning to do) but were not native to those planets any more than our astronauts are native to the moon."

Shortly after, we are hit with the following statement: "The authors believe that the underlying pattern of the UFO phenomenon is controlled by a central network from which contrived information, such as sightings, holograms, photographs, specimens and documented accounts are fed to the public. This central network consists of various top secret agencies in our government working with specialized personnel of the Army, Navy and Air Force in secret locations. But why is the public uninformed? The authors believe they know why but cannot prove it. Their main purpose is to let people know their side of the story, the story behind the story, and then let the reader decide the answer."

Menger even takes into account the notion that they could be other than extraterrestrial in the sense that we think of ET . . . that they could be life forms, time travelers or perhaps beings crossing time and space from some other dimension.

Connie Menger sums it all up quite beautifully when she states: "Despite the testimonies, witness accounts, photographs, movies and even specimens of dehydrated food samples, scientists will not and cannot accept any of the foregoing as proof of extraterrestrial visits. They would like to see and examine a landed craft, see and talk with the visitors, see and visit the planet of origin, inspect some alien artifact and obtain scientific information about their culture.

"The proof as required for scientific analysis was never really offered. The contactees, witnesses, abductees and others did their best to present the facts as they perceived them. They never had access to artifacts, books, language, culture, bodies or hardware. They did get a story, photos and a whole lot of philosophy. But perhaps that's the way the visitors and government wanted it. The whole point, we believe, was to introduce the possibility of alien culture from other worlds through consciousness. Have you ever used flash cards to teach a small child numbers, letters or images? Maybe, someone is flashing images to us, a childlike humanity, in the hope that we will learn."

And so it is – and so it was.

And, in conclusion, all we can do is repeat the words of Dr. Schwarz given at the end of the day – a day perhaps when Howard Menger passed over to a place full of peace and kindness, where some of the most vital questions of the cosmos could finally be put to rest at least for one of the most interesting individuals of our time.

WE MISS YOU, HOWARD MENGER. WE WILL NOT FORGET YOU, HOWARD. MEMORIES AND YOUR SPIRIT LIVE ON. FOR YOU AND THE PAST, THE PRESENT AND THE FUTURE, THERE IS ALWAYS CONTACT!

JOSEPH FERRIERE – A SMOKING CIGAR AND A TOP-SHAPED SHIP

By Timothy Green Beckley

JOE had to be one of my first correspondents in the UFO field. He lived up in Rhode Island and I was down in New Jersey. I was publishing *"The Interplanetary News Service Report,"* a mimeographed newsletter that grew to have the fairly large circulation of around fifteen hundred. Actually, that made us just about as "big" as APRO, which was a highly-touted research organization out of Tucson. Despite repeated membership drives, they couldn't seem to gather much thunder, although they did have a real office and some really dedicated volunteers, including librarian Allen Benz, who I see from time to time when I am in the Southwest.

Joseph Ferriere, on the other hand, was putting out a digest-sized zine called *"The Controversial Phenomena Newsletter."* His co-publisher was a fellow named Armond Laprade, and together they must have printed, collated, stapled and mailed their publication much the same as I did. Their magazine wasn't just about UFOs but all things strange and unusual. I remember a particular article about a Brooklyn woman who was hanging out the family laundry when she disappeared – straight up! – and was never seen again.

But Joe was a "multitasker" way before the term was invented. He definitely was a man of many callings, which included being a talk show host, a publisher, a collector of old records, and, for our purposes, a top notch UFO Repeater, ala have camera will travel!

UFO Repeaters! Seeing Is Believing - The Camera Doesn't Lie!

Joe Ferriere displays negative strips showing evidence of his close encounter.

UFO Repeaters! Seeing Is Believing - The Camera Doesn't Lie!

After his passing, the local paper in Woonsock, Rhode Island, *"The Call,"* published the following obit, which we have abbreviated, centering on his professional career(s):

* * * * *

Joseph L. Ferriere, Jr.

August 6, 2012

WOONSOCKET- Joseph L. Ferriere, Jr., 73, of Beacon Ave., Woonsocket, died Saturday at Massachusetts General Hospital in Boston. Born in Woonsocket, he was a son of the late Joseph L. and Helen (Marchand) Ferriere. He was a lifelong resident of Woonsocket and a graduate of Mount St. Charles, Class of 1957.

Joe was employed for many years at the Fairmount Dye House. Joe was widely known in the city as the proprietor of Joe's Moldy Oldies on Rathbun Street. Joe also had a career spanning over 40 years on local radio and was a longtime personality on WOON.

A man of a great many interests, Joe was an avid collector of books, magazines, records and all types of memorabilia. He had an extensive knowledge of trivia and could easily recall any and all details.

Joe was passionate about baseball and in his younger years played as a pitcher, almost making it to the big leagues. He was also involved in amateur boxing and trained and fought with Al Costa. Joe was a talented musician and a member of the Deltones, a local band well-known during the 50s and 60s.

Joe produced and edited his own magazine dealing with his special expertise on UFOs and extraterrestrial matters, his parting words known to many listeners – "Watch the Skies."

* * * * *

Somewhere along the line, I hooked up with Joe to do his radio show. Now understand, this was no Coast to Coast AM. As far as I know Joe seldom mentioned the UFO topic, although he was personally engrossed in it. I guess you can say he was one of the many "Silent Contactees," as John Keel liked to refer to

UFO Repeaters! Seeing Is Believing - The Camera Doesn't Lie!

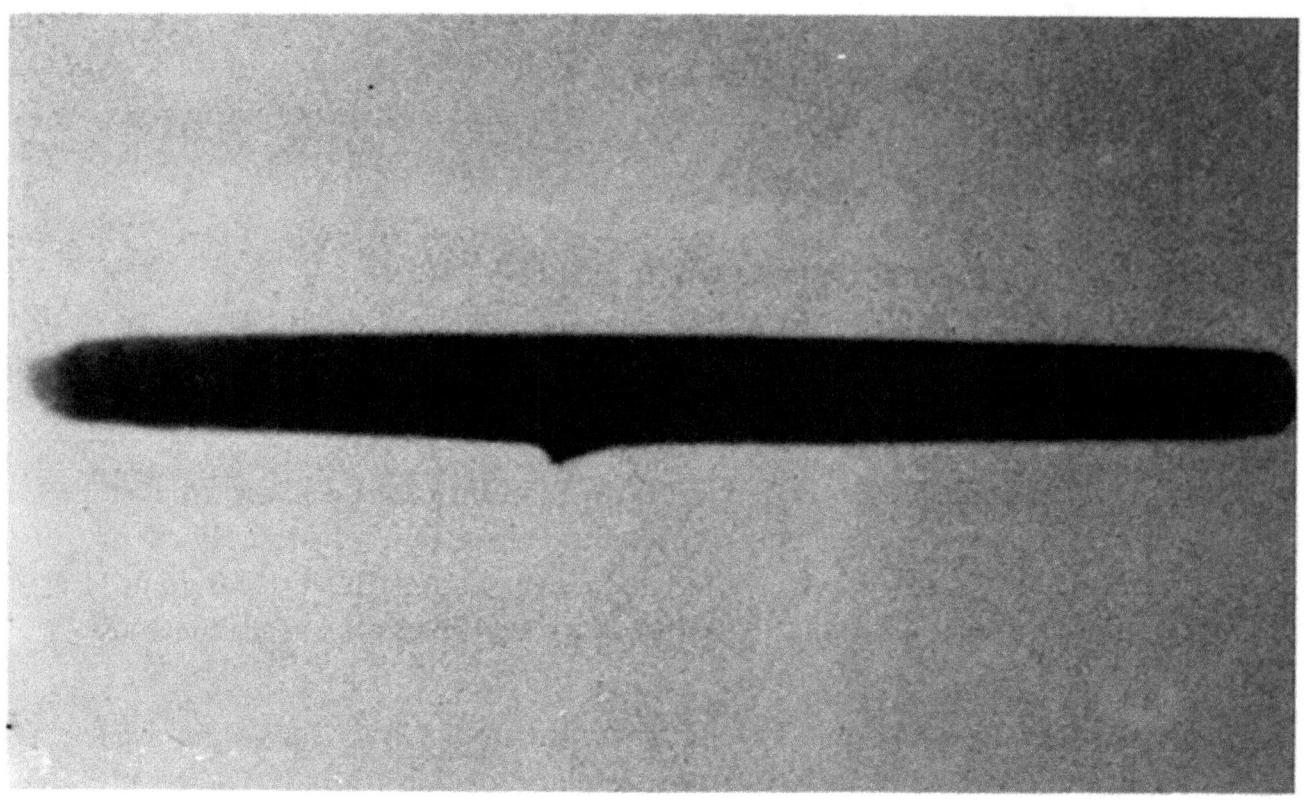

Above: No cigar, but the real thing! A UFO taken over Cumberland, Rhode Island.

Below: The object begins to tilt in the sky.

UFO Repeaters! Seeing Is Believing - The Camera Doesn't Lie!

those experiencing encounters but not interested in attracting attention and instead keeping a low profile. I believe Joe hosted the drive time program, "Woonsocket Open Line," in the evening between 4 and 7. This is normally a station's peak hours, with listeners tuned in while they try to beat the traffic to get home in time for dinner. On a local station like WOON, it's not unusual to fill the time with traffic, sports and birthday "shout outs," and, of course, lots of commercials. It's the period when a station makes money.

But I guess the day I was on Joe had fallen from grace. We talked shop over the open microphones for a good part of New England to hear. I was so young at the time I was still wet behind the ears, UFO-wise at least. There is an old copy of *"Midnight," the* supermarket tabloid now known as *"The Globe,"* which features a photo of Joe and me in the studio. I had a crewcut, black horn-rimmed glasses and a bit of acne. A frightening photo, but I would still publish it if I could locate it in one of the 50 file drawers here. I am hypersensitive to dust and there is nothing like old newspapers to bring out the worst allergies.

But we're not here to talk about my health but to discuss Joe's UFO experiences, which are numerous, even though he managed to keep them under the radar for the most part.

I wish I had a collection of the magazine *"Probe"* that Joe published over the course of several years. Fairly polished looking for a UFO fanzine, it was backed by my longtime friend and roommate for a while, the late Harold Salkin, and it contained descriptions of Joe's encounters as well as dozens and dozens of photos that he was able to capture of UFOs, mostly cigar and hat-shaped vehicles. Indeed, they put Adamski's pictures to shame, and, as far as I am concerned, Joe was a much more honorable individual. I don't think anyone ever caught him in a lie.

Thus, for our information, we must seek out another friend who just happens to broadcast from the same studio in Woonsocket. Paul Eno co-hosts the Monday night program *"Behind the Paranormal"* along with his son Ben, who has just graduated from college. The program has been beaming out over the airwaves for over seven years. Many believe *"Behind the Paranormal"* to be the most intelligent paranormal show out there, and the fact that I have been on the show numerous times serves to prove that point. Paul began his long career as a paranormal investigator in 1970, at the age of 17. He is a graduate of two seminaries, holds a degree in philosophy and is an award-winning New England journalist. Paul is also the author of seven books, including five on paranormal

UFO Repeaters! Seeing Is Believing - The Camera Doesn't Lie!

Above: UFO postcard based on a photo taken in Rhode Island at around the same time.

Below: What unearthly group is responsible for these objects hovering over our heads?

subjects. He is a fellow of the American Society for Psychical Research and a veteran of the U.S. Coast Guard. In addition, Paul has had hair-raising adventures with famous hauntings and has unique theories about the paranormal and its implications for our understanding of God, the world and ourselves.

I point all this out to show that *"Behind the Paranormal"* is not a fluff, lightweight, pop culture podcast but a real radio program, with hundreds of shows archived at http://www.behindtheparanormal.com/ to support my contention. After trying to get Joe on the air for ages it seems, Joe finally broke down and agreed to do *a* show emono emono, no holds barred. *[Those who want to listen to the broadcast can find it on the website under the year 2009, Program #21, Blackstone Valley Mysteries.]*

During the broadcast, the listener is privy to lots of information that would otherwise have been lost to time.

For example, Joe admits that his UFO experiences have been episodic but ongoing since he was a toddler. "I am approximately four years old. This memory is so clear, even though most people cannot remember that far back. It's precise, but it's short. It's just a brief glimpse. I was sitting in the backyard and I am playing in a sand box with my little pail and my little shovel when all of a sudden I am aware of the presence of a huge silver color – I want to call it a rocket ship. It looked like something out of a Buck Rodgers or Flash Gordon movie. It had no wings. It was enormous and very, very low to the ground. That was unnerving. I was a little bit afraid of it but then I noticed there were a lot of windows on this thing and that there were people in the windows smiling and waving and apparently having a great ole time. I had never seen anything that low. I called to my grandmother to come out and see it but by that time it was gone." Joe says he has no recollection of anything else at this age, but that this memory stuck with him throughout his life.

For Joe's second brush with the aerial unknown, we have to move ahead perhaps three years. "I am in school now, and it is recess time and we are outside when some UFOs overfly the schoolyard. Even the teachers are pointing to the UFOs as they fly over." Talk about multiple witnesses. Readers might be surprised to know how many sightings take place over schools – especially elementary schools. There is one case where a girl of about eleven or twelve was in the play yard and a UFO flew over. She proceeded to grow like five inches in the next few months. UFOs do influence the growth of plants and animal life, so why not humans? But this is not our target subject for now.

UFO Repeaters! Seeing Is Believing - The Camera Doesn't Lie!

Photos taken by Harold Trudel, also of Woonsocket. Trudel and Ferriere's photos often get confused as they were taken during the same time period, near the same locations and both gentlemen knew each other.

With the objects still in his mind, Joe says he ran home to tell his grandfather what he had seen. Joe says his grandfather had certain abilities, like being able to heal people, and his grandfather said that there was life on other planets and someday Joe would get to meet them.

Talk about a premonition.

The next incident Joe can remember took place when he was in the fifth grade. "Frequently, I would walk home from school. There was a short cut I would take that cut across the ball field that would take me pretty much right to my backyard. Once, I saw this disc maneuvering around the smokestack of a manufacturing plant. So I stopped and I sat down and I am watching it and it is effortlessly moving around this smokestack and that's the last thing I remember. I don't remember it leaving. I don't remember getting up and leaving."

Joe says he doesn't want to give the impression that these had to be extraterrestrial in origin. "I don't know what they were. But these three occurrences did take place in a short period of time."

Then, in 1962, Joe says he was working at the dye factory. It was a cold day, and someone offered to go get coffee for everyone. "They come running back in and say there are flying saucers outside. There were four of us, and we went out and observed these silent UFOs in V-formation silently flying over the area. They are reflecting the sunlight but they also appear to be diaphanous, like you could see through them. Translucent. There was a solidity to them but there was also an apparent non-solidity to them. They were really weird."

Joe says that this sighting triggered something in him. "It made me compulsive about finding out more about UFOs. I was more open to space travel. Alien life. I began to hunt down people who knew about these things, like George Fawcett, a speaker on the subject at the YMCA, and researchers like Tim Beckley and Ray Palmer. There was this urge to communicate information on this topic."

As for his ability to take photographs of the celestial visitors, Joe says this first started when people began to call into a talk show he was hosting. "It was just before the 4th of July, 1967, and I went to the vicinity of a neighboring town, Cumberland, where people told me they were seeing this great shining silver bar hanging in the sky. I went three days in a row. I wasn't sure what I was looking for. I thought perhaps I might find some traces of something unusual on the ground."

UFO Repeaters! Seeing Is Believing - The Camera Doesn't Lie!

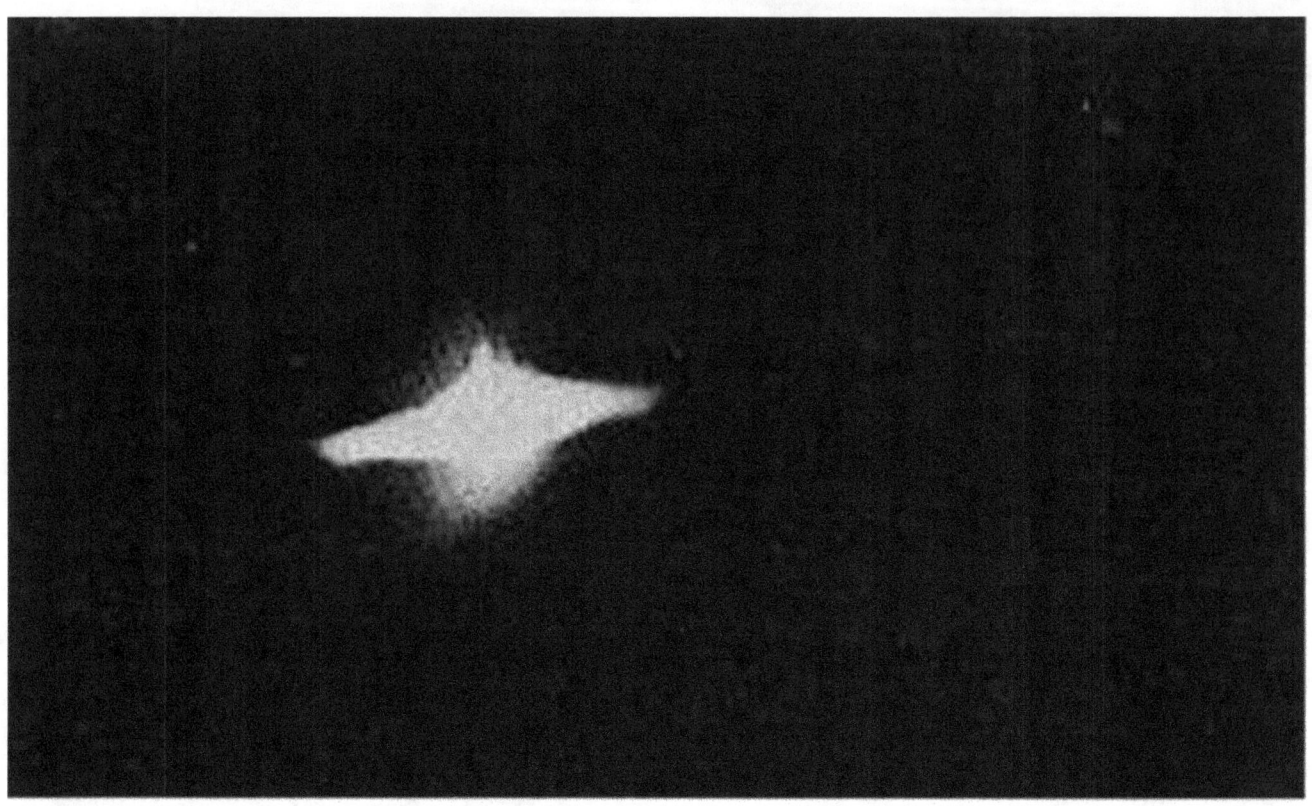

Above: A UFO at night over Woonsocket.

Below: Another view of the craft over Cumberland, Rhode Island.

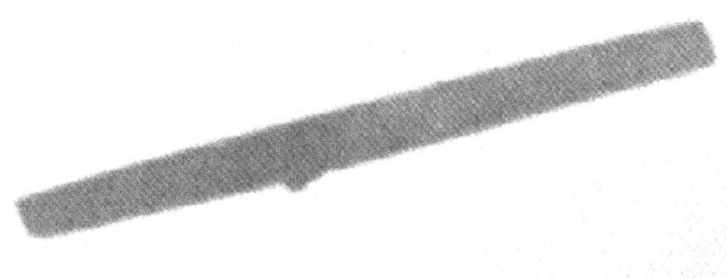

UFO Repeaters! Seeing Is Believing - The Camera Doesn't Lie!

Joe says he was walking along some high tension lines that ran besides a reservoir. "I was looking around for some sort of debris indicating that an object had landed. When I turned and looked over my shoulder to the left, there it was! It was just hanging there in space, parallel with the ground. I hadn't heard it approach but, when I turned, it was just there." To Joe's way of thinking it – this elongated, tube or cigar-shaped object – was "superb!" Almost immediately, he notes, "The UFO began to move very slowly. First it leaned to one side and then to the other. It looked like a boat rocked by the water." And as soon as he realized what he was watching, he took aim with the camera that he had bought with him mainly to photograph trace markings on the ground.

Then things got a bit weirder, if that were possible.

"After I took two shots, a door falls open on the bottom of the object, and suddenly something is expelled, spherical in shape, from within."

Joe says he was in a quandary as to which object he should follow.

"The smaller one started to move away very swiftly. I took two more pictures of the large object before it shot off straight up."

Joe was interviewed extensively on this incident by August C. Roberts, a professional photographer who had taken some unexplainable pictures of his own. "Joe states that in his first impression he estimated the size of the object – which was about a city block away – at over 200 feet in length. Later, when he had calmed down a bit, he judged the larger object to be between 100 and 150 feet long and the smaller one about 15 feet in diameter. The larger cigar-shaped object seemed to have four lights running along the side, but these Joe guessed were not portholes as they did not give the impression of glass or plastic but rather gave off a translucent glow from within the object."

With all his years of photo analysis, Roberts did not believe the photos to be hoaxed in any way, shape or form.

Joes says that at one point Dr. J. Allen Hynek, who had just left the staff of the Air Force's Project Blue Book, contacted him about obtaining the negatives. "I told him he could make a field trip to investigate the matter but I knew what happened in a lot of cases where negatives were sent to the Air Force for purposes of analysis – they simply vanished!"

No one can doubt that these are wonderful pictures of an unknown craft. And Joe has taken others in the Woonsocket area, including spherical blasts of light in the sky as well as a "top-shaped UFO," is the best I can describe it. He has also had his share of strange experiences that would seem to indicate even more that he was "hand-selected" to get out the word.

"Behind the Paranormal" host Paul Eno manages to extract from Joe a tale involving two very unusual people. Paul says, "It's a real whopper," and Joe has to agree.

"I'm in Hartford, Connecticut, and I'm hitching a ride back home. This is the early to mid-1950s. I'm a teenager now. I'm picked up by two people. One is a gentlemen with dark bushy hair; the woman was a beautiful blonde. They sat me in the back seat of the car. I am not alone in that there were all these little black boxes. And I am told, 'Whatever you do, don't touch the boxes.' That was clear to me. These people are very happy. Very outgoing. Very cheerful. And they are laughing and joking. I asked them where they were from and they asked me where I was going. They said that they could bring me pretty close to the area I was looking to be dropped off near. They said they were from very, very far away, and that I would not recognize where they were from. And that their job was to go around the country delivering these little black boxes to different people and helping to install them. And they're laughing while they are telling me this. I am impressed by these people – once in a while you meet someone who is different, who is out of the mainstream. These people are that different. They radiated an aura of warmth and friendliness and compassion. You felt safe in their presence."

Many years later, Joe says, he met August C. Roberts, who was a very well-known UFO photographer and had a fabulous collection of pictures taken all over the world. "So August came to Woonsocket to visit as we were working on a magazine, getting it ready for the printer, and he handed me a book called **"Stranger At The Pentagon"** by Dr. Frank Stranges. And so I am thumbing through the book and there are photos taken at a UFO conference in New Jersey. One of the gentlemen is supposed to be an alien who has lived inside the Pentagon and who had no fingerprints and whose clothing could not be torn or burned. And seated next to him are a small group of people – also thought to be extraterrestrials – including the same two people who had picked me up while hitchhiking."

"Twilight Zone" theme, please.

UFO Repeaters! Seeing Is Believing - The Camera Doesn't Lie!

There are so many questions we would like to ask Mr. Ferriere about his ongoing experiences, but, alas, he is no longer with us, nor is Augie Roberts, who carefully examined Joe's photographs and declared them "Authentic!"

I know there are many other photos that Joe took that I hope will surface eventually. In the meantime, here are the remarkable ones we have that definitely place him in the UFO Repeater category.

Not necessary to spook the neighbors.

Paul and Ben Eno.

Paul Eno is the author of such books as: "Footsteps in the Attic", "Faces at the Window", and "Rhode Island: A Genial History"

http://www.behindtheparanormal.com/

VIVA MEXICO!

By Timothy Green Beckley

THANKS to Mexico's top journalist turned professional UFOlogist, Jaime Maussan, we in the English-speaking world know all about the many unexplained bogies seen in the sky south of the border and further down in Central and South America. There have been some really dramatic sightings of both craft and humanoid creatures, and the truth is that this is not at all a new phenomenon. Our Spanish-speaking friends have been confronting an unparalleled bizarre entity or two for muchos de luna llena.

As early as the late 1940s, it wasn't unique for an unsuspecting individual to be confronted by something completely terrifying while walking alone along a dark and lonely path in areas where streetlights were nonexistent. To say that such confrontations would cause a heightened degree of frightfulness is simply putting it mildly. A journeyman's heart was certain to skip a mighty beat, and fear could easily encompass a person's soul without any difficulty. A vast majority of the initial encounters between ultra-terrestrials and hombres were not of an overtly friendly variety, causing emotional distress and sometimes even physical harm. A few of the reports, however, were of a decisively benevolent nature. As in the U.S. at the time, there were those coming forward with unbelievable tales of face-to-face contact with extraterrestrials who looked and acted remarkably human.

UFO Repeaters! Seeing Is Believing - The Camera Doesn't Lie!

Above: George Adamski is seated next to the first Mexican contactee, Salvador Villanueva, a taxi driver who in 1953 claimed to have visited with human-looking space beings.

Villanueva said that while trying to repair his car, he was joined by two men who told him that they were from another planet. Villanueva accompanied them to their craft which looked like two soup plates joined at the rim and a shallow dome with portholes

Left: The first contactee book ever to emerge from Mexico was authored by Salvador Villanueva.

Perhaps the most heralded contactee of this bygone era was taxi driver Salvador Villanueva, who, toward the end of August 1953, was trying to repair his broken down cab out in the country near Ciudad Valles. He was joined unexpectedly by two pleasant looking men, 4.5 feet tall, wearing one-piece gray corduroy garments covering even their feet, with wide shiny belts. They had, according to Alien-UFOs,com, metal collars and small black shiny boxes on the back of their necks. They carried football-type helmets under their arms. As it was raining, he invited them to shelter in the car, where a conversation with one of them was conducted all night.

The spokesperson eventually told him they were from another planet, which Villanueva scarcely believed. Despite being confused and bewildered, he accompanied them to their craft. He noticed that the mud puddles did not wet their feet and that their belts glowed whenever the mud was repelled. The UFO looked like two soup plates joined at the rim, with a shallow dome with portholes, and rested on three spheres. He was invited in, but refused. Glowing white, the vessel zigzagged upwards and then shot up vertically with only a faint whistling sound. Upon later examination, a 40-foot circle of broken down bushes was found at the spot.

Because of the novelty of the incident, Villanueva was propelled into the media's public spotlight and received more than his requisite 15 minutes of fame long before there was any such recognition factor to deal with. Salvador received so much attention that he was the driving force behind inviting pioneer contactee George Adamski to Mexico, where he enthralled a bullfight arena full of the curious who were just becoming aware of OVNIs (the Mexican acronym for "UFOs"). Villanueva wrote that country's first contactee book – maybe even the first Mexican book on OVNIs themselves – which would have been on the bestseller list in Mexico – if Mexico had one!

Within a few months another individual joined the ranks of Mexican contactees.

While driving the winding roads that separate Mexico City from Acapulco, Armando Zurbaran's only concern was arriving at the Pacific port city before sunrise in order to meet a business partner. At some point during the drive, he was overcome by an almost hypnotic state of lethargy, which caused him to pull over. Not far ahead on the road, he was able to see a number of men clad in overalls with wide belts gathered around a strange, brilliantly lit object. Before he realized it, and having no idea how it happened, he was walking toward the object, escorted by the longhaired men.

A slight buzzing sound filled his ears as he entered the saucer. Zurbaran was going down in history as a pioneering contactee, and this was his first question to the ship's captain: "Why have I been chosen for this honor?" "You are neither the first nor last earthman to be chosen for testing," his host replied. "Our task, slow though it may seem, is designed to persuade. We choose the likeliest, most malleable persons for contact, so that they might better transmit our messages." Zurbaran was then treated to a review of the smallest details of his life on a screen within the vehicle's wall and a tour of the ship's interior, guided by one of the fair, longhaired crewmen (reminiscent of Adamski's visitors), who answered each of the puzzled human's questions in detail. The space travelers, he learned, employed a gravity repulsion system to cover the distance between their home world and Earth, scanning the space ahead of them with a radar-like device to dispel any objects that may lie in their path. Unlike other contactee stories of the time, Zurbaran's visitors did not claim to originate from any planet in the Solar System nor did they mention their planet of origin by name. The craft, he realized, had taken off while he was unaware and was now in space.

ENTER HISPANIC RESEARCHER SCOTT CORRALES

Scott Corrales became interested in the UFO phenomenon as a result of the heavy UFO activity that occurred while he lived in both Mexico and Puerto Rico. He was also influenced by Mexican UFOlogists Pedro Ferriz and Salvador Freixedo, the latter being a former Jesuit priest who advocated a paranormal, interdimensional interpretation of the phenomenon. In 1990, Scott began translating the works of Freixedo into English, making the literature and research of experts and journalists available to English-reading audiences everywhere. This led to the creation of the *"SAMIZDAT"* journal in 1993 and to his collaboration with Mexico's CEFP group, Puerto Rico's PRRG, and the foremost researchers of Spain's so-called third generation of UFO researchers.

In 1998, the *SAMIZDAT* bulletin was replaced by *"Inexplicata: The Journal of Hispanic Ufology"* as the official publication of the nascent Institute of Hispanic Ufology. In addition, Scott has been a guest on numerous radio shows and his articles have been featured in several national publications. Scott has worked with the authors on numerous occasions and before going into limbo was a regular contributor to the now-defunct "*UFO Universe,*" edited by myself and one of the most popular newsstand UFO magazines ever published in the English language.

In this section, Scott helps us coordinate efforts to place the UFO Repeaters of Mexico and Central/South America into some consecutive order, though this is somewhat of a difficult task. There is a mountain of material to be examined along with the fact that the phenomenon is so all-encompassing, is spread out across thousands of miles, covers a variety of terrain and has been happening for more than half a century.

As Scott points out, "Reports of unusual objects in the sky were not unknown in the Spanish-speaking Americas. As has been written elsewhere, the first 'UFO flap' can be dated back to the Aztec era in Mexico, and South America and the Caribbean had filed away sightings of oddities as prodigios (prodigies or miracles) contained in sea captain's logs and the formal reports made by government ministers to higher-ups. Religious significance was attached to some of them, especially if the sighting coincided with a religious holiday. Early on, nocturnal lights had been considered a welcome phenomenon, as they reputedly marked the location of buried treasure, thus sending locals on digging sprees. In the 1970s, few UFO books could go by without mentioning the objects seen 'against the disk of the sun' by astronomer José Bonilla in Mexico a century earlier."

Scott also reports that Puerto Rico has from the start been a hotbed of UFO activity. "UFO activity over Puerto Rico was commonplace in 1952. Cases were being reported from one part of the island to another, mentioning specific locations that would become familiar 'hot spots' later in the century. The turbulent waters of the Mona Passage, separating Puerto Rico from the island of Hispaniola, were a particularly rich source of sightings. On May 13, 1952, at seven o'clock in the evening, prominent politician Miguel Angel Garcia was spending time with his family at their home in the city of Mayaguez. The house commanded a view of the city and its bay from a considerable elevation. Garcia, his wife, daughter and son-in-law interrupted their conversation to look at two orange disks – one larger than the other – flying high over the Mona Passage. The politician promptly went inside for his field glasses and returned to study the unusual objects. The larger of the disks had 'the apparent size of the sun,' according to Garcia, and was static, while the smaller one maneuvered around, switching positions with the other. Garcia's daughter, Fredita, managed to photograph the strange aerial ballet between the orange disks, but nothing appeared on the film due to shortcomings in the Verichrome film employed. Other residents of Mayaguez also saw the disks but believed them to be military devices undergoing flight tests out of Ramey AFB. In an age of technical wonders, it seemed like a perfectly reasonable possibility."

Nor could even Cuba be placed behind in the lineup of UFO activity: "The earliest UFO report from the largest island in the Caribbean comes not from terrestrial onlookers but from a pilot: On March 16, 1950, Captain Miguel Murciano of the Compañía de Aviación Cubana reported having timed the progress of an unknown object over Antilla airport on the island's eastern edge. The strange object, he said, was traveling at extraordinary speeds at an altitude in excess of five thousand feet 'covering eight degrees in sixteen minutes' – a measurement aided by a theodolite. According to Captain Murciano, he first saw the object at 10:15 A.M. during a routine flight from Santiago de Cuba to Antilla. All crewmembers and passengers saw the object due to the excellent visual conditions, agreeing that whatever it was, it wasn't an airplane.

"Dr. Sergio Cervera of the Comisión Investigadora de Fenómenos Aéreos (CIFA) compiled a list of significant UFO-related cases in Cuba going as far back as the 1930s. Dr. Cervera's notes for the year 1952 include a sighting by some fifty witnesses in the village of Candonga, Palma Soriano Municipality, in Oriente Province. A very bright light appeared over the community, remained suspended, and then began zigzagging, engaging in a 'cosmic ballet' that mesmerized onlookers for nearly an hour."

By no means could we be expected to cover here this massive an amount of time and geographical area. And, in any case, this is not the thrust of our current efforts. Being mainly concerned with UFO Repeaters, we zero in on two Mexican individuals who seem to be "camera happy" when it comes to photographing the unexplained. Once this has been accomplished, we will turn Scott Corrales loose so that he may follow up with some additional cases from South America which are as interesting as anything we have encountered so far, though they may lack the photographic proof we have so readily accumulated up to this point.

A SUCCESSFUL BUSINESSMAN COMES FORTH

Raul Dominguez is a successful businessman who owns a clothing store and lives in the Ocotlan region of Jalisco, Mexico. He had no previous interest in

UFO Repeaters! Seeing Is Believing - The Camera Doesn't Lie!

Raul Dominguez took some fantastic shots of a hat-shaped UFO that stumped the experts.

UFOs. However, over a period of several weeks, Raul's neighbors began to speak of unearthly phenomena in the sky above Mount Chiquihuitillo. He wasn't sure how much of this chatter was based on truth or was just idle gossip being circulated for the purposes of sensationalism.

For several days in a row in February 1993 – with camera in tow – Raul hid himself in the underbrush in the vicinity of the purported sightings, hoping to see something but not really expecting to. Finally, on April 24, Raul hit pay dirt when he spotted a hat-shaped object coming from out of the lake and headed in his direction as it flew low over the mountains. The object was quite huge and cast a menacing shadow down over the valley. The witness said the hat-shaped object seemed to have a force field that appeared to be sucking up air and almost pulled him into the sky with great suction. The hair on his dog was standing on end and Raul felt an uncomfortable sensation of dread.

Barely able to lift his camera, Raul did manage to take a series of very clear photos of the UFO which show the craft as being similar to that of a flying hat but with a metallic structure like a copper pot. Those who later examined the photos believed that the craft had lit up windows, but Raul did his best to explain that these "windows" were in reality some sort of signaling device. "I think the object was emitting signals because the light pattern changed from picture to picture. There was a definite code with a definite purpose," he opined. And who were the UFO occupants signaling? "Well, there were several small spheres resting on a nearby hilltop whose attention I think they were trying to get."

Raul says he heard a faint hum as the object passed directly overhead. At times, the bottom of the craft seemed to open and close like the aperture of a camera. The craft, the witness states, was so large that it hardly fit into the view finder.

The sightings in the vicinity of Mount Chiquihuitillo went on for a while, with Raul returning to the scene to try and get more photos of this perplexing puzzle that had everyone on pins and needles. Raul's photos were put under rigorous examination and no hoaxing has ever been discerned.

Raul has also had more recent sightings.

"The latest is what I photographed Sunday, November 5, 2006. It was an object that was far away and remained in the sky for 20 minutes. Not sure if it was a sphere or a kind of dish. To capture the images, I used a short telephoto 135 mm lens. I have also seen evidence of areas that remain static on the airway of

UFO Repeaters! Seeing Is Believing - The Camera Doesn't Lie!

Close ups of the Dominguez UFOs.

UFO Repeaters! Seeing Is Believing - The Camera Doesn't Lie!

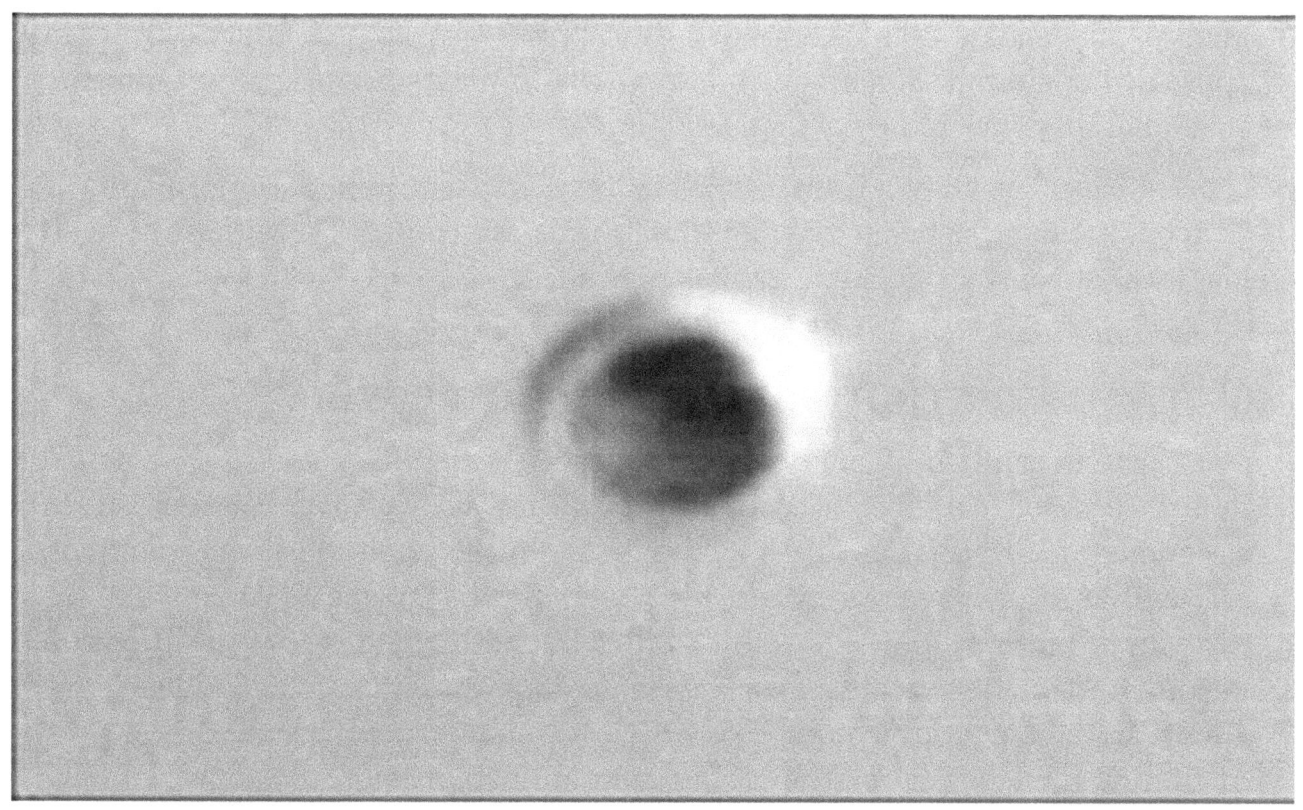

The UFO was photographed by Mr. Dominguez from a variety of angles.

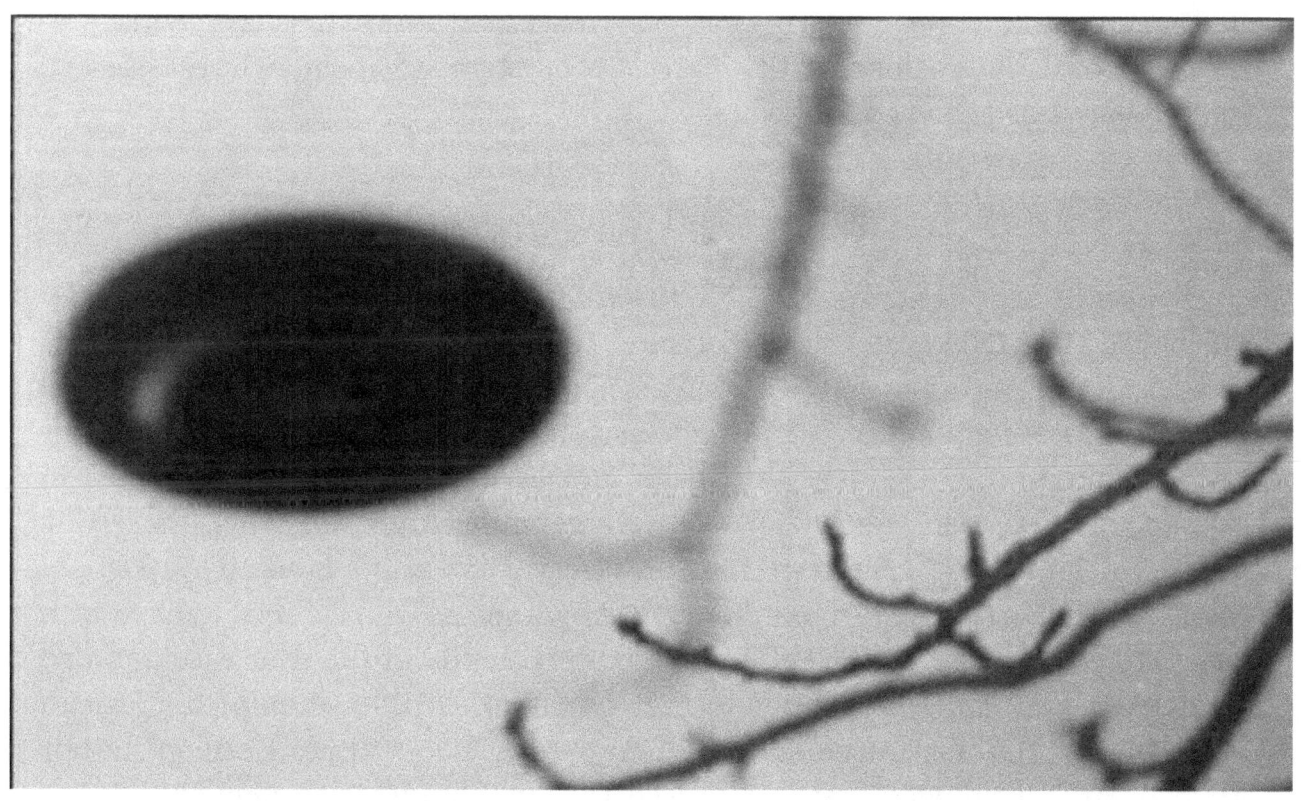

Mexico-Guadalajara and seen how the ships want to go unnoticed when approaching aircraft. Sometimes the UFO will lower its brightness or be made small, but they stay in the sky for a long time."

We do not know of any other sightings by Raul, but the information is sketchy. We hope someone reading these words can contact the witness to see if his "luck" at being a UFO Repeater has continued.

THE LIGHT-BEAM SHIPS OF CARLOS DIAZ

One morning in January 1981, Mexican photographer Carlos Diaz pulled into a deserted car port at Ajusco Park near Mexico City. He was on an assignment for a magazine and had arranged to meet a journalist who was yet to arrive. Diaz sat in his car, preparing his camera for the job ahead. Although it was early in the morning, the air was thick with a humidity that made even sitting still uncomfortable. Impatiently, Diaz began to look at his watch. Suddenly, his attention was caught by a strange yellow glow coming from the valley below him. At first he thought it was a forest fire, but, an instant later, the source of light revealed itself to be a large, orange, oval-shaped UFO, slowly hovering about 30 meters from his car. The craft got closer and eventually landed. This turned out to be Diaz's first in an ongoing series of experiences with ETs that have led him to travel to different regions of the Earth's ecosystem, to include forest, desert, jungle, shoreline and even Arctic areas.

INDISPUTABLE PROOF?

According to "*Phantoms and Monsters*" (a dot com web site), "Mexican TV journalist and UFOlogist Jaime Maussan, who has been at the center of UFO investigations in Mexico since the wave began in 1991, believes that Diaz's UFO photographs are among the most impressive he has seen. Maussan took Diaz's photographs to Jim Dilettoso, an image processing expert at Village Labs, in Tucson, Arizona, who concluded they were genuine. After satisfying himself he was not dealing with a hoaxer, Maussan visited Diaz at his home in Tepoztlan, Mexico. There, he spoke to a number of other witnesses who claimed to have seen exactly the same type of UFO. The apparent credibility of the Diaz case has also attracted UFO researchers from further afield, who have attempted to glean insights into the alien agenda from Diaz's contactee claims. German author Michael Hesemann, who first interviewed Diaz in June 1994, is convinced of the

UFO Repeaters! Seeing Is Believing - The Camera Doesn't Lie!

Carlos Diaz

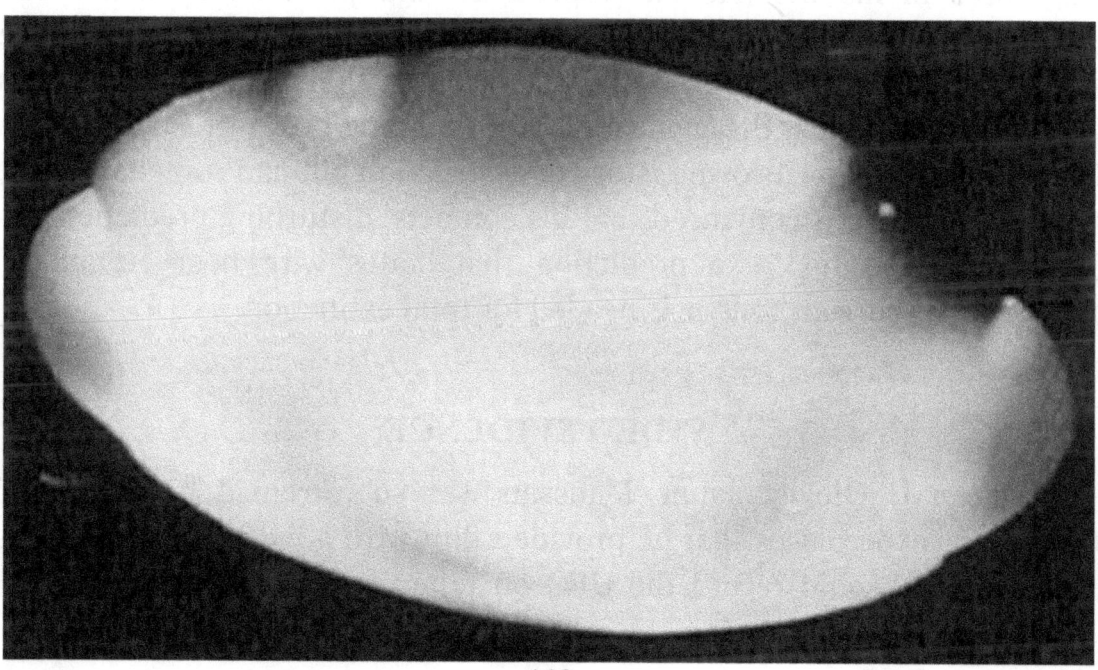

credibility of Diaz's story. 'Not only is he contacting these beings through encounters on the ships,' says Hesemann, 'but he claims to be meeting these beings socially, since he believes some of them are living among us.' However, Hesemann explains that, according to Diaz, the beings are reluctant to fully disclose their origins. 'Apparently,' says Hesemann, 'they did, however, explain that they have been visiting Earth for thousands of years and are particularly interested in our evolution which, compared to their own, has happened at a much faster rate. They are trying to learn why.'

"Another UFO researcher intrigued by Diaz's case," says the above-mentioned Internet portal, "is Professor of Psychiatry at Harvard Medical School, John Mack. Mack has a long history of dealing with abductees and contactees and believes that the Diaz case is among the most convincing he has come across. In his book, 'Passport to the Cosmos,' Dr. Mack states: 'Out of all the experiencers I have worked with, it is Carlos Diaz who seems to have developed the richest understanding of the interconnected web of nature. Diaz's experience of connecting with living creatures is so intense that he seems literally to become the thing he is describing.'

"Diaz's experience, Mack claims, constitutes an 'awakening,' a process which, he says, is common in abductees. Diaz told Mack that his contact with the ETs had instilled in him a need to preserve the environment and the ability to 'enjoy a beautiful planet.' Whether or not an extraterrestrial influence was involved, Diaz's new-found concern for the environment has certainly become a driving force in his life. He has repeatedly and passionately conveyed this environmental warning publicly, most notably at a UFO conference in Dusseldorf, Germany, in 1995. Diaz has revealed that he had been informed through his contacts that the civilization of the visiting extraterrestrials, like ours, had been threatened by its own history of destruction but had somehow managed to survive. He remains convinced that his contacts' disturbing prediction for our future is only too real – a prediction that states with near certainty that humanity, on its current course, is headed for total extinction."

VIDEO EVIDENCE

Mexican UFOlogist Jaime Maussan was so intrigued by Carlos Diaz's account of his experiences that he provided him with a video camera and asked Diaz to see if he could record the UFO on tape when it next appeared. A few

UFO Repeaters! Seeing Is Believing - The Camera Doesn't Lie!

A beam ship against the darkness of space makes for a spectacular sight.

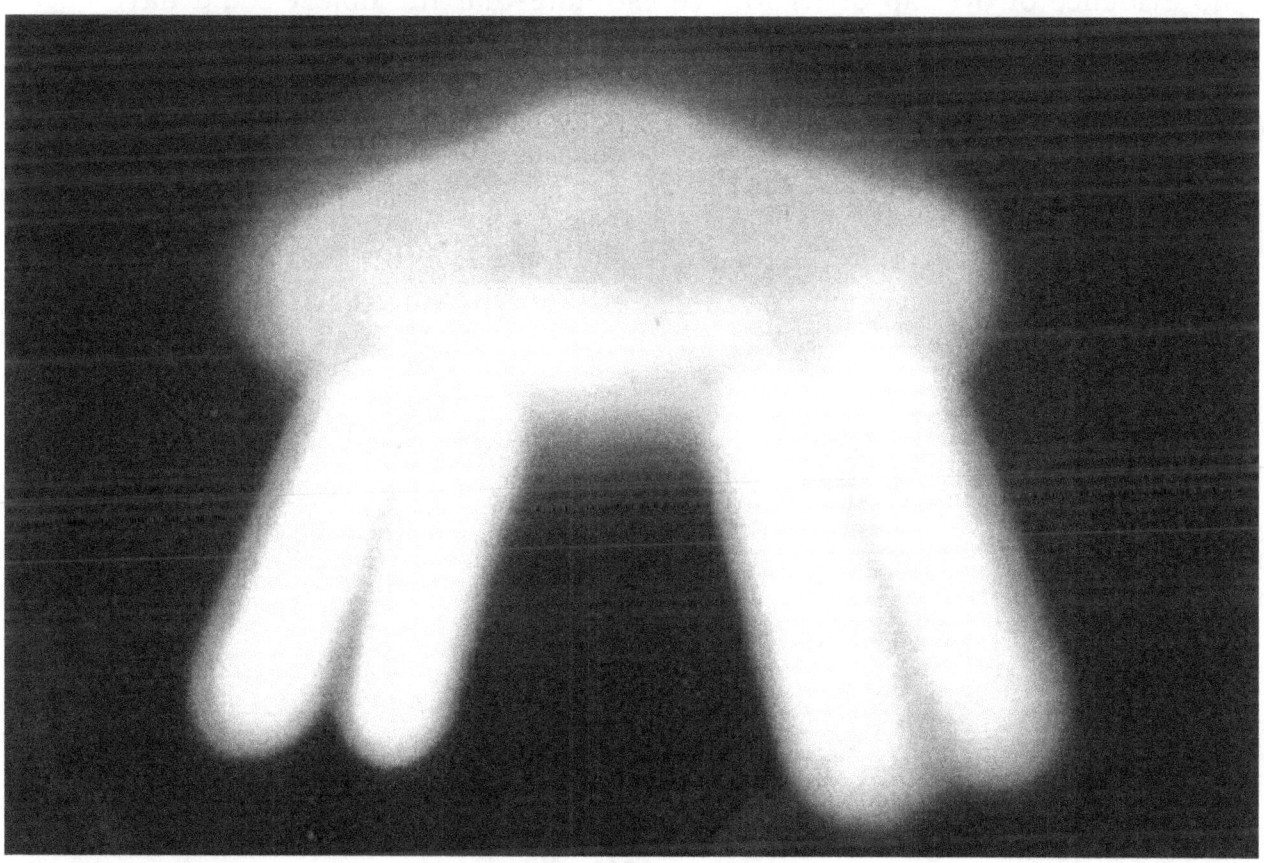

weeks later, Diaz awoke at 5 A.M. and grabbed his camera. He walked out and waited. Apparently, within minutes, the craft appeared and hovered over the house, where Diaz filmed it. When Maussan saw the remarkable footage, he asked Diaz if he could get even closer to the craft while filming. Two months later, Diaz was once again able to film the craft, which this time hovered directly above him without moving.

However, it is Diaz's third attempt to capture the craft on video that is the most spectacular. In this footage, Diaz, having mounted his camera on a tripod, walks to the bottom of a field waving a flash light. Responding to this, the craft suddenly materializes directly above Diaz's head and sends beams of light down towards him. Then the unidentified object remains motionless for 30 seconds before blinking out. It is universally recognized that this video contains some of the best UFO footage ever taken.

The original transparencies were given to Professor Victor Quesada of The Instituto Politecnico at the University of Mexico for verification. Quesada says: "We were shocked to see that the spectrum of the light of the photographs of the object is unlike anything we've ever seen, broke all parameters and does not fit with any data from our database. The light was extraordinarily intense. There is no evidence of overlap or fraud. We estimate that the object could have been between 30-50 meters in diameter. "

Interestingly, the photographs were also analyzed by Dr. Robert Nathan at NASA's Jet Propulsion Laboratory in California, and Nathan – a notorious UFO skeptic – failed to find evidence of fraud.

Diaz's videos can be found throughout the Internet and are a part of the UFOTV channel archived on YouTube. Certainly the videos are more than an idle viewing.

UFO Repeaters! Seeing Is Believing - The Camera Doesn't Lie!

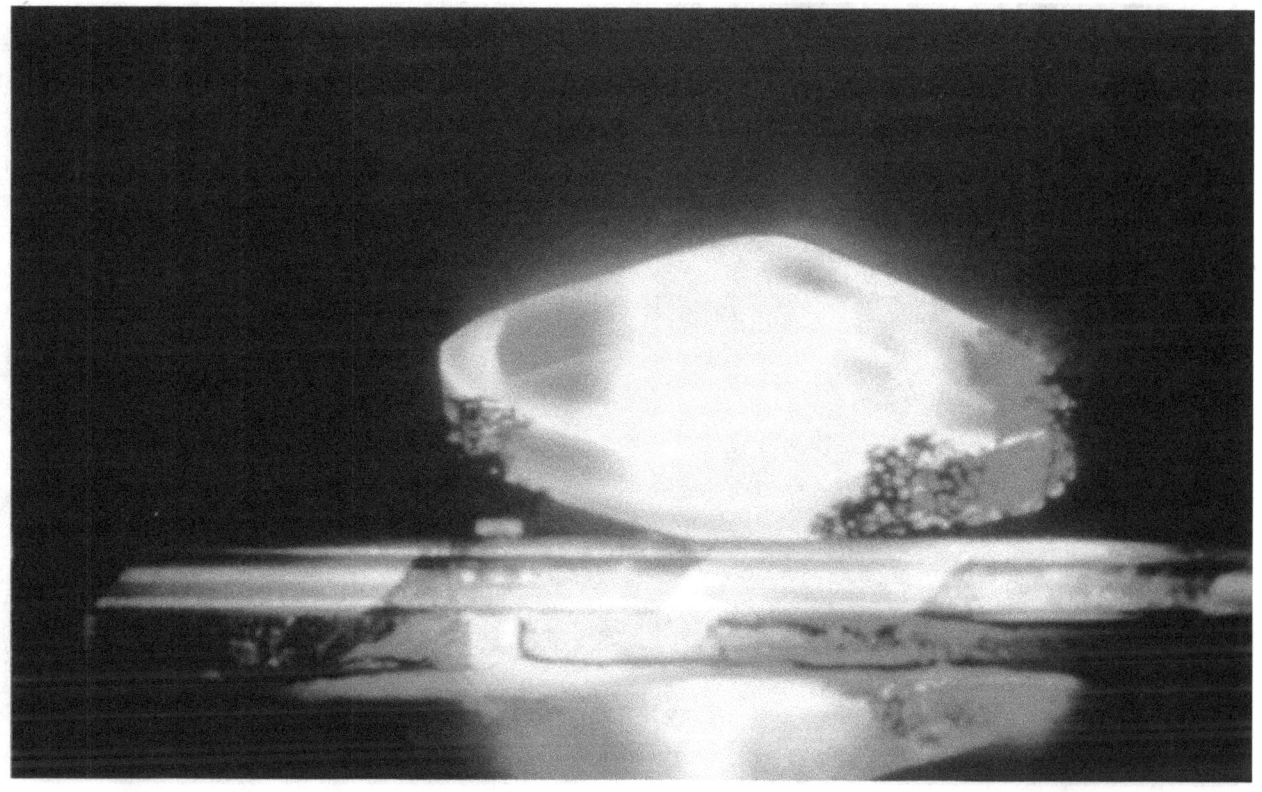

Above: A plasma ship appears to be sitting on the roof of a building.

Below: And out comes a beam of light.

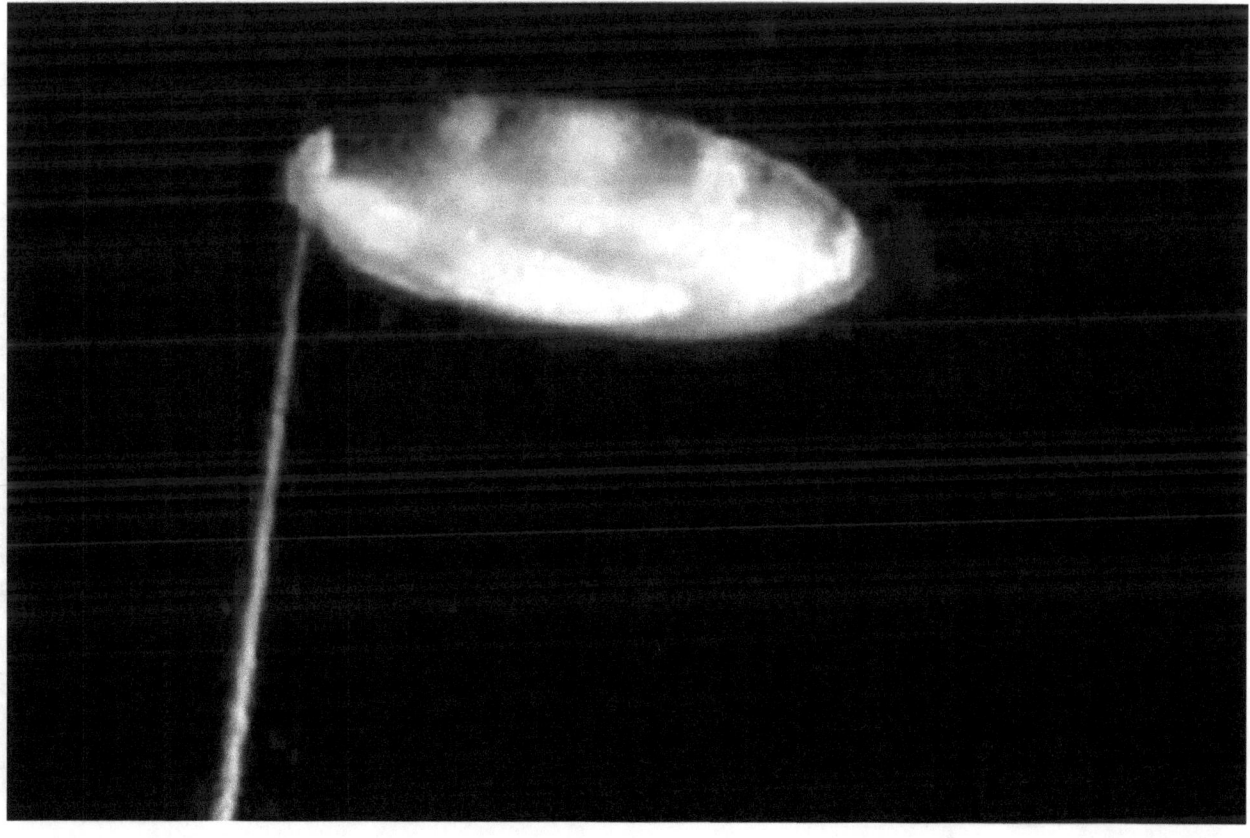

UFO Repeaters! Seeing Is Believing - The Camera Doesn't Lie!

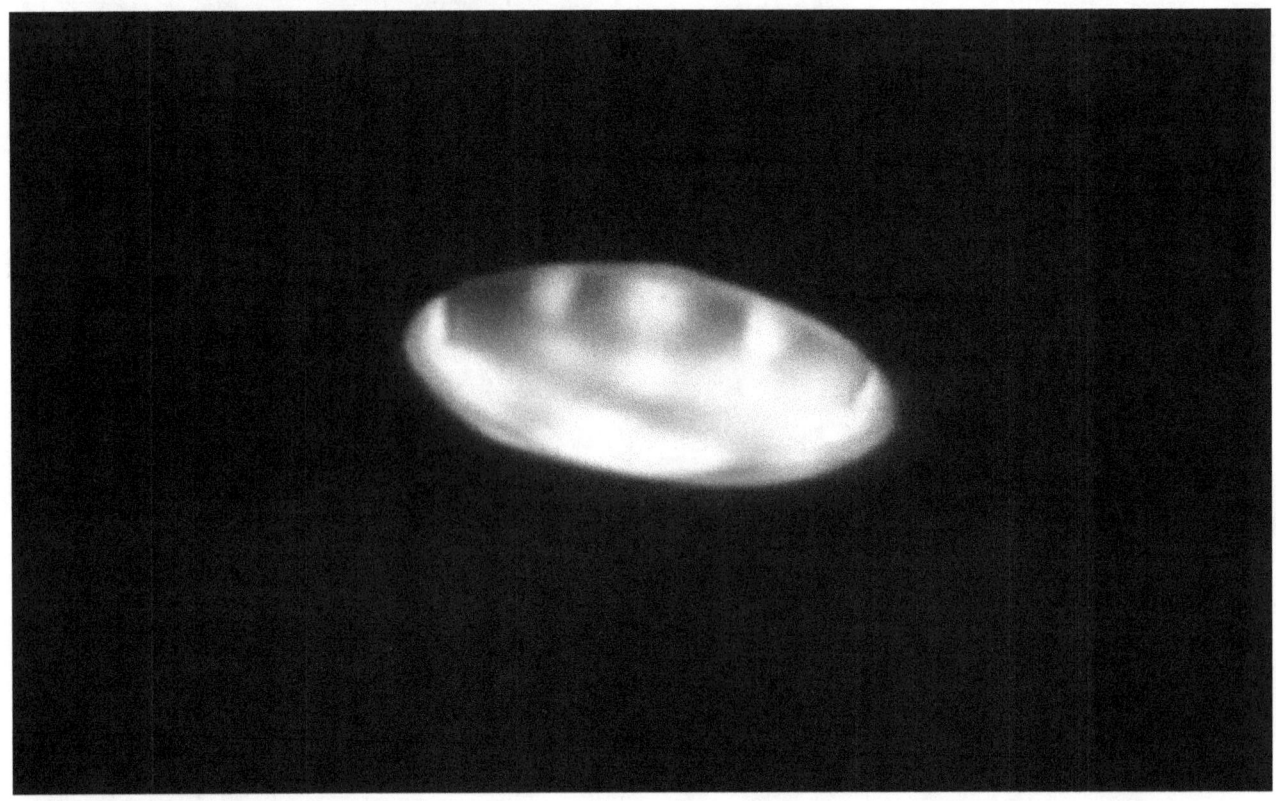

Above: One of Diaz's plasma ships of light hovering in the sky for all to see.

Below: The plasma ship with the branches of a nearby tree for perspective.

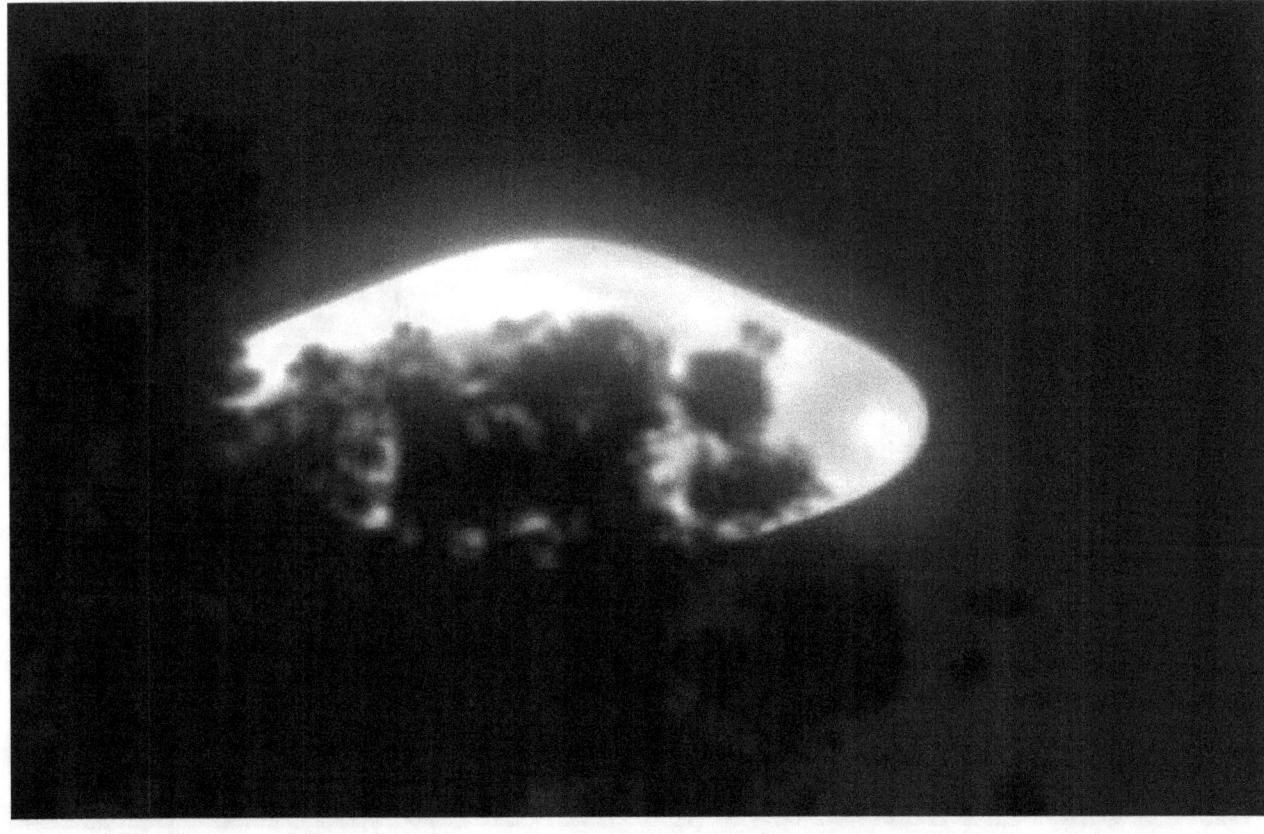

A SPANIARD IN THE WORKS – MULTIPLE BRUSHES WITH THE UNKNOWN

By Scott Corrales

THE "MICHELIN MEN" OF LERIDA

IN the spring of 1977, UFO Repeater Juan Soler had gone to a farm which his brother-in-law had just purchased at Binefar, in the Spanish Province of Huesca, hoping to lend him a hand with plumbing and sundry duties. Once the chores were complete, both men boarded their respective cars and drove away. Soler, however, had trouble with his ignition and made a wrong turn down a country road that led him to an open field. The road came to an abrupt end, marked by a large toolshed surrounded by farm implements. It was at that inopportune moment that the engine died.

Things were about to get markedly worse.

According to Soler, who was struggling with the ignition, he noticed a strange figure appear out of nowhere – an entity with a shocking physical appearance. This is how he described it to UFO researcher Ramon Nava-Osorio: "It had no neck and its big round head was directly joined to the body. Its head was enormous and ended in a green-colored crest that resembled a fin. This fin seemed to have something like a corkscrew halfway down. The body was covered in large scales, some three centimeters in diameter, green and darker than the rest of the skin. Stunned as I was, I then saw a second and third figure appear, all of them having similar characteristics. The third figure walked to the middle, and all three turned to look at me. They all came from the same place and walked like regular people. I was able to see their eyes, which looked like a horse's eyes – round, bulging, black and white – and they showed anger. There was considerable distance between the eyes; they had no noses and small mouths; carrying something in their hands that I couldn't see clearly.

"I felt invaded by a sense of terror," Soler continued. "It was a hellish nightmare. As I kept looking at them, I continued to turn the key over in the ignition until the engine started. I put the car in reverse without looking and got out of there the best I could. I normally tend to revisit places where I've had experiences, but I've never gone back there."

The last few words of Soler's testimony are important. Since his earliest experience with nonhuman entities, he has felt compelled to learn more about the phenomenon with an intensity that researcher Nava-Osorio compares to that of the Roy Neary character in Spielberg's "Close Encounters of the Third Kind." These experiences went back to his early childhood, but none was as vivid as his encounter in September 1966 on the banks of the Marganell River.

At that time, Juan Soler had taken his then-girlfriend on a picnic to a heavily wooded area frequented by families from the Manresa area. Around 2 P.M., Soler went off to a spring to bring back water, but something caught his eye: a metallic structure he took at first for a motorcycle sidecar, but, as he approached, he realized that the object was a long white cylinder standing some 60 centimeters over the ground and "looking like a small submarine," relatively speaking. Soler estimated its length at some five meters and its width at 120 centimeters, featuring portholes through which brown seats could be seen.

Nava-Osorio notes that Soler was at least ten meters distant from the object at this point. It was then that he saw two humanoid figures who must have descended from the sub-shaped structure shortly before the experiencer's arrival.

Soler described the occupants as follows: "They were two beings, dressed in white, wearing helmets similar to those worn by motorcyclists. They were dressed in segmented outfits whose rings made them look like the Michelin Man. [This is a reference to Bibendum, the logo of the Michelin tire company, whose image has been used as a descriptor in many CE-3 cases.] But their segments were much thinner than those of the advertising character. The vehicle and the occupants' clothing was the same color. I couldn't make out their faces clearly due to the fear I felt and the swiftness with which it all occurred. But they seemed Nordic, although I had the impression they'd gotten suntanned, given the look of their skin. Their suits ended where their helmets started – it had no support or collar. They walked ponderously, wearing short-leg boots and gloves. They looked at me in surprise."

This is where the "Marganell CE-3" – as we might call it – took a detour into high strangeness.

Gripped by fear, Juan Soler felt the urge to flee, which is understandable in such a situation, but rather than escaping back to the picnic and his waiting girlfriend, he ran TOWARD the humanoids, charging between both figures and brushing against one of them. Even more startling was the fact that the owner of the property containing the spring – described as an older man dressed in blue and wearing a cap – was standing there as if witnessing the proceedings.

"He shouted an order, and the two humanoids hurriedly boarded their craft. Once aboard, they managed to touch me with the sharp end of the vehicle. I also felt something in my head. I turned around a little and told them: 'Go ahead, go ahead. I'm not about to do anything to you.' When the vehicle had reached the height of my own head, I was gripped by excruciating pain. I felt as though my hair was on fire, and the pain spread down my arms to my legs. Fully turning around to look, I saw the portholes [on the vehicle] were closed. They both looked at me from their seats and took off uphill. The pain was similar to an electric shock, like something I'd experienced in the factory I worked for."

Nava-Osorio did not press the witness for a better explanation of events. The description regarding the vehicle "going uphill" is unsatisfactory, and no mention is made of Soler returning to his girlfriend's side.

"I showed up late for work on Monday morning," Soler added. "Rather than reporting at 5 A.M. I showed up at 9 A.M. In the afternoon I went to see the doctor, but he didn't put me on leave. He did on the following day, and I was on leave for fifteen days. I told the story to a number of people: friends, contemporaries and people at the factory, all of them serious, well-informed people, but no one believed me."

There was an added detail to the story. Soler's description of the entities as resembling Bibendum the Michelin Man was ironic in view of the fact that he worked at the Pirelli tire factory for many years, and his buddies began calling him "Gangarin" after the history-making Soviet astronaut.

Soler made efforts over the years to speak to the landowner who had fearlessly barked at the nonhumans, prompting their departure. On one occasion, he went to the man's home to discuss the bizarre experience, only to be slapped by the old man's fiery-tempered daughter. "The man died in later years, and I never had the pleasure of talking to him. In 1994, the daughter's husband agreed to speak to me, but he had nothing new to say. His father-in-law died nearly at age 90 at the farmhouse." An attempt to discuss the subject with the parish priest also earned Soler a slap in the face.

"A long time after the incident," Soler reminisced, "and while I was in the town of Peralta de la Sal, I got to speak to Jose Rami, the community's jack-of-all-trades. He described an incident very similar to my own. He was a kilometer outside the town of Peralta with some mules and their tackle when he saw a white vehicle with two pilots. He was so frightened that he covered his eyes for a while, allowing the mules to lead him into town."

The fact that Juan Soler would later drift into contactee circles would only cause serious researchers and journalists to overlook his experiences. Scientists are tired of telling us that the odds of finding human-looking intelligent beings somewhere in the universe are impossible, citing a number of evolutionary and genetic factors.

But one researcher, Edward Ashpole, allows a loophole that will be of interest to those interested in humanoid CE-3s and which many will find vindicating. "This line of thinking," writes Ashpole in his book "**The UFO Phenomena: A Scientific Look at the Evidence for Extraterrestrial Contacts**" (London: Headline Books, 1995), "leads us to the conclusion that creatures with some kind of primate form, though not like us, might emerge from flying saucers, should flying saucers have a physical reality with biological beings inside them." He then adds the important cautionary sentence: "But no ET could be like the beautiful people reported by many contactees and abductees, unless they were specially bred from human stock."

Sidestepping any pro-ETH pathway for a moment, could the answer to the humanoid riddle lie in manipulation of the human race not by "ancient astronauts" but by advanced "next door neighbors" from another dimension, who have meddled with humanity since the earliest days of recorded history, and certainly before that? After all, the Sons of God looked upon the daughters of Men and found them fair . . .

Scott Corrales's website: Inexplicata-The Journal of Hispanic Ufology
http://inexplicata.blogspot.com/

UFO Repeaters! Seeing Is Believing - The Camera Doesn't Lie!

Cover art for "Espacio Compartido" (2000) illustrating the Margarell humanoid encounter.

ARGENTINA: CE-3 "REPEATER" IN LA PAMPA

By Quique Mario, CEUFO

Translated by Scott Corrales

A new and gripping CE-3 has allegedly taken place in the Province of La Pampa over recent days, involving a woman who had a previous experience involving a similar type of creature in 2007. The entity was described as very thin and tall, standing approximately two meters tall. Its apparently unexpressive face has sunken eyes, a flattened nose "like that of an ape," and the mouth is described as "resembling a fine line."

The new episode took place on Tuesday, October 20, 2009, shortly after 8 P.M., in a community of 1,500 residents. When the witness recovered from the experience, she phoned her son, who lives a block away, and he in turn notified the Centro de Estudios UFO (CEUFO), which immediately sent a researcher to the location. The details of the case are set forth below and, as has become customary, neither the experiencer's identity nor the exact location are disclosed in order to keep the case from being mishandled by some sensationalist media outlets.

The protagonist was about to re-enter her home after saying goodbye to her grandson when she noticed the strange being's presence in her living room. The woman, 65, gathered up her courage and headed toward an item of furniture with the goal of reaching for a digital camera with which to photograph the intruder. When she turned around to do so, the being placed one of its hands on her forearm. "At that moment I felt myself losing strength and fainting," she said.

According to her family's estimates, the woman remained unconscious between 15 and 20 minutes, after which she was able to phone her son, who rushed over to find her seated in an armchair and experiencing a nervous breakdown. A chair and some elements of the digital camera were strewn across the floor.

When she was sufficiently recovered from the ordeal, she explained that "the being appeared again" – referring to her 2007 experience. Her family immediately notified the Centro de Estudios UFO, which arrived an hour later at the site to ascertain that [the entity] had indeed left strange prints on the woman's forearm when it gripped her.

A small dog [Caniche], the woman's only permanent company, was found cowering under an armchair, showing signs of having experienced considerable fright. The marks on the woman's forearm changed color and appearance as the hours went by. The next day, the largest mark had developed into a considerable blister, and at 11 A.M., the woman reported that the strange being appeared yet again, this time to look at her arm and burst the blister, which produced an abundant quantity of viscous, yellowish fluid. Her relatives corroborated this.

As the days went by, the "marks" took various different shapes until the woman woke up in the early hours of Sunday, October 25, experiencing sharp pains. This prompted her to phone her son and other relatives, who, to their surprise, saw that very bright "metal filings" were visible in plain sight. Photos were taken of this and samples were collected; these, in turn, were submitted for analysis by CEUFO.

OUTCOME

The case requires treatment by medical professionals, without question, and CEUFO advisors have been brought into the case to analyze the elements removed from the scene. Further attention is being given to the protagonist of the event and to making comparisons with the previous experience recorded in November 2007.

ENTITY DESCRIPTIONS

As stated earlier, the odd being stands nearly two meters tall. It is very slender but very strong, as the witness claims "losing her strength" as the creature placed its hand on her. With regard to its features, she said that its eyes "appear sunken into its face," but that they emanate a sensation of "tenderness." The nose was described as ape-like and the mouth as "a thin line" while its skin was greenish or dark gray, and with folds that give the impression of "wrinkles." When asked about the number of fingers on the entity's hands, she had the "sensation" that it had five fingers.

Scott Corrales's website: Inexplicata-The Journal of Hispanic Ufology
http://inexplicata.blogspot.com/

UFO Repeaters! Seeing Is Believing - The Camera Doesn't Lie!

UP WARMINSTER'S CRADLE HILL WITH SKY-WATCHERS BOB STRONG AND ARTHUR SHUTTLEWOOD

By Timothy Green Beckley

IT was in 1981 that I traveled to the UK at the request of my good friend, the late Earl of Clancarty, Brinsley Le Poer Trench, who had arranged for me to speak at the House of Lords in front of a special group organized to get to the bottom of the UFO mystery and to press for "full disclosure," long before the phrase was part of UFO terminology. The group, consisting of roughly one hundred members of both houses of Parliament, included Lord Hill Norton, the former Defense Minister who had taken a combative interest in the subject of our unidentified visitors. Norton and I had a brief chat about Nikola Tesla, whom the Ret. Admiral of the British fleet held dear to his heart because of the possibility of alternative energy sources being sparked by otherworldly life forms.

I arrived in Warminster and had lunch at one of the best Indian restaurants I have ever set foot in – and, believe me, I have eaten in hundreds all over the world. Among those joining me was my buddy, Arthur Shuttlewood, who was the editor of the daily newspaper *"The Warminster Journal"* and whose book "UFO PROPHECY" I had published in the States. The book brought to the attention of the American public the story of an ongoing UFO flap that was taking place only a hop, skip and a jump from Stonehenge. Accompanying Arthur Shuttlewood was his sky-watch companion, a retired RAF pilot named Bob Strong.

While we munched on an appetizer, Strong showed me several scrapbooks filled with literally dozens of photos of UFO craft of all shapes and sizes, from "railroad cars" to huge, bat-like objects. Unfortunately, Strong sadly admitted

UFO Repeaters! Seeing Is Believing - The Camera Doesn't Lie!

Though the typical "flying saucer" was sighted over Warminster, the truth is that the objects there came in all shapes and sizes.

UFO Repeaters! Seeing Is Believing - The Camera Doesn't Lie!

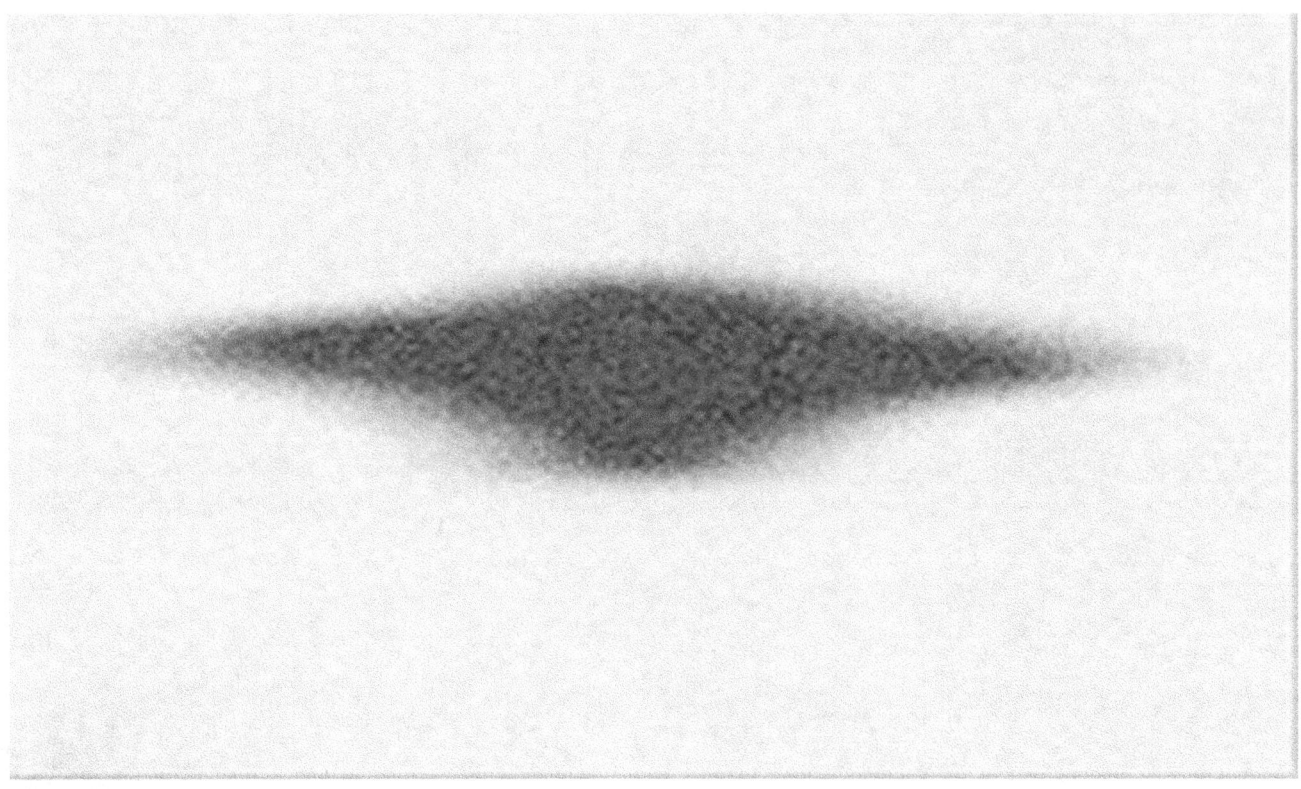

Above: The vast majority of the photos taken of UFOs over Warminster were snapped by RAF pilot Bob Strong.

Below: A "freight train" seems to be shuttling across the night sky.

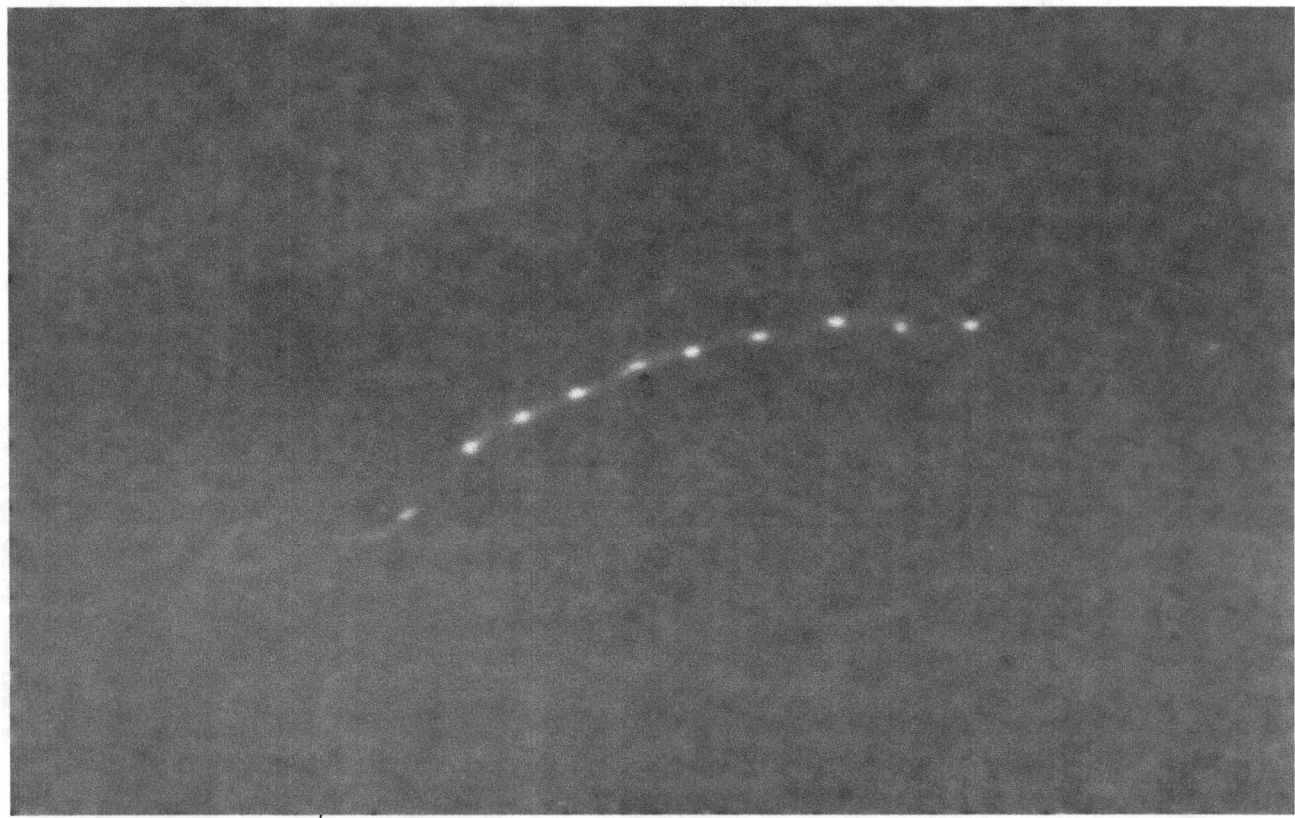

that many of his best pictures had gone "missing" because they had been borrowed by the curious who wanted to copy them but had never returned them as they promised to do. Thus was lost an important part of UFO history that can never be replaced, as well as essential evidence proving the Warminster mystery was not a hoax or based upon faulty eyesight or mushroom-induced hallucinations.

That night, I journeyed with my newfound compatriots to Cradle Hill, a few miles from the center of town, where we gathered with a couple from Scotland who had come on their own after having read about the town's ethereal intruders. They did so without knowing that they would soon be joined by the two gentlemen who had literally put Warminster's "Thing" on the landscape and a traveling "thrill seeker" from across the pond.

At first we saw nothing unusual but were fascinated by several meteors streaking across our line of vision. All that was to change around 10 P.M., when we spotted something unusual fairly high up that seemed to just be hovering or loitering about. To what intended purpose, if any, we had no way of knowing. Cueing us that this was no twinkling star or planet, Shuttlewood went to the trunk of his car and retrieved his trusty, high-powered flashlight. He told us he had used this same heavy-duty torch upon numerous occasions to signal to what he assured us were his Space Brother friends. Arthur then pointed it at the object in the sky and flashed a beam of light several times in its direction. He next offered the flashlight to me, and I also flashed it at the object. None of us knew ship-to-shore or any kind of Morse code, so we just blinked the light on and off like we were playing a game of "close encounters."

The reaction was unexpected and tremendously positive. Every time we blinked at it, the UFO would appear to sort of swing back and forth, like a pendulum. It seemed to be looking down on us. Maybe it picked up our thoughts telepathically. I was told to keep a positive mind because that's what the ultra-terrestrials seemed to respond to the most.

Our sky-watch went on for another 20 minutes or so, and then it started to rain and clouds obscured our view. When we saw nothing more, we retired for the evening.

Had I made contact with a UFO over Warminster? To this day, I still wonder. I will never know for sure, but it did seem as if the object was under intelligent control and was responding to our request to prove it was not just an

UFO Repeaters! Seeing Is Believing - The Camera Doesn't Lie!

While the vast majority of sightings came from Cradle and Starr Hills outside of town, "The Thing," as the objects were dubbed, often appeared over residential areas with impunity.

UFO Repeaters! Seeing Is Believing - The Camera Doesn't Lie!

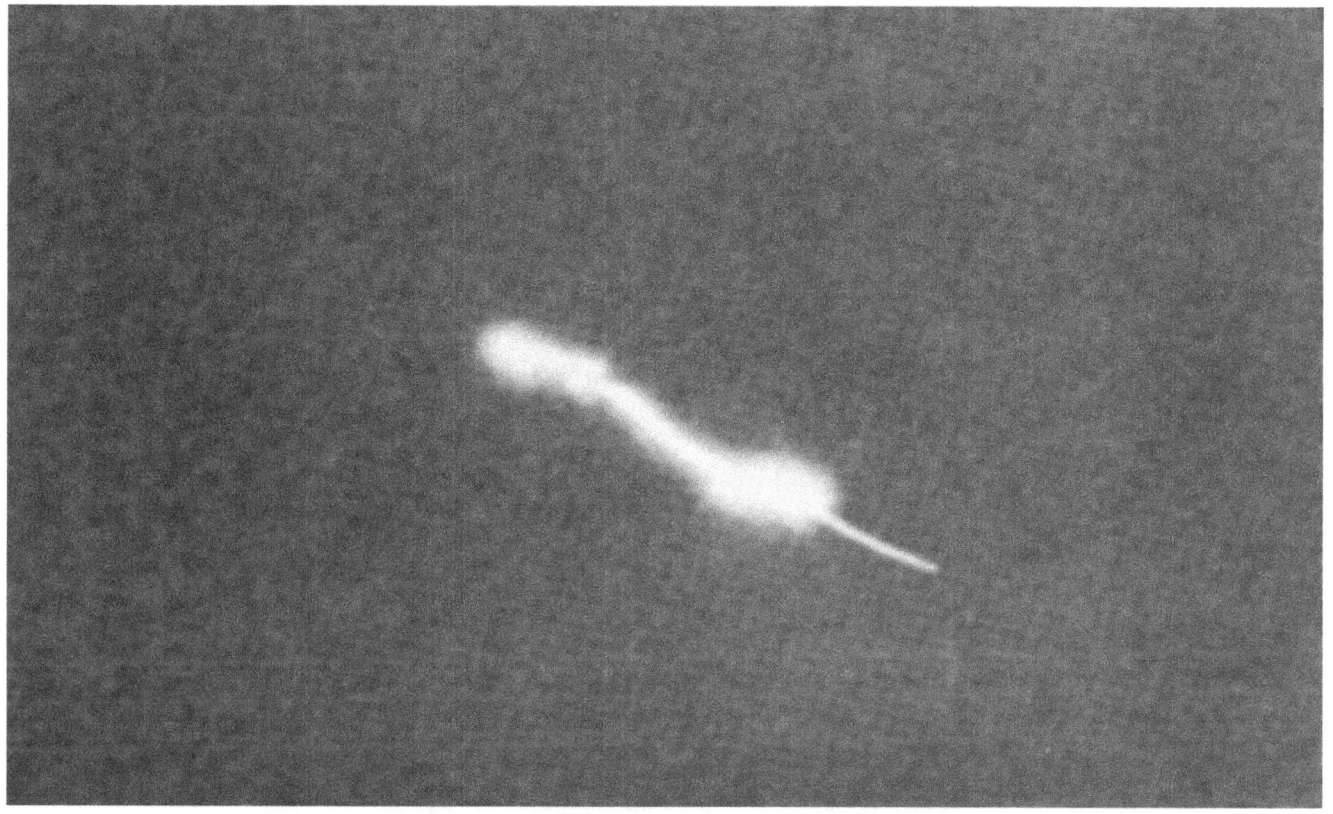

Above: A swift-moving UFO in motion.

Below: A "Hershey's Kiss" from Mars perhaps?

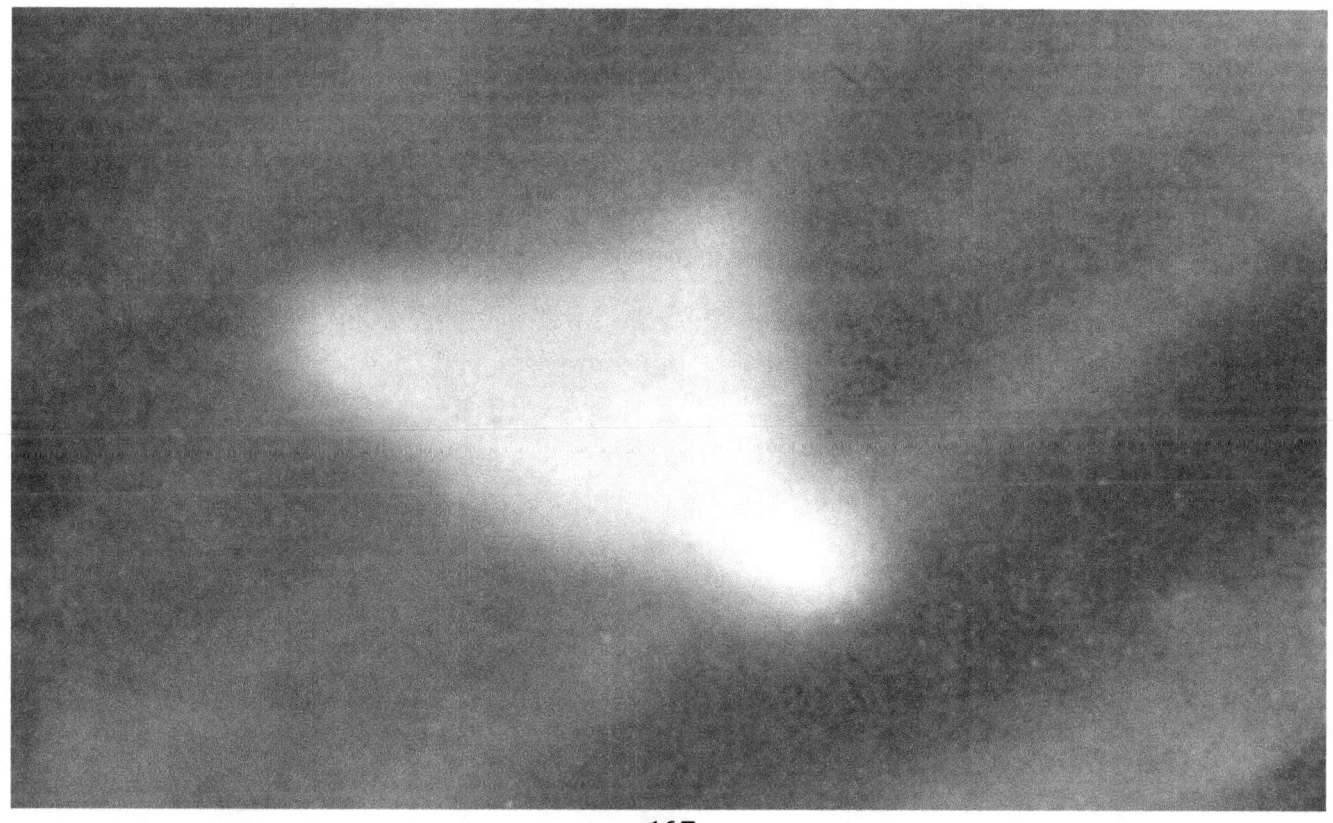

ordinary object in the heavens. Another strange thing: We took several photos of Cradle Hill that night. When developed, one of them showed a strange phenomenon behind two of the witnesses — streaks or bolts of light which were not visible to the naked eye at the time and for which I am mostly certain there is no "legitimate" explanation. There were no streetlamps or houses with porch lights nearby . . . only a vast open field where many a strange incident had taken place over a timeframe of several decades and which still ignite a fire in the hearts and minds of many seeking the truth about the UFOs seen over this locale.

Many had come skeptical and had left the area firm believers. One New York City radio deejay ended up having a multitude of encounters in Warminster over a period of days.

In the book, "**UFOS: KEYS TO INNER PERFECTION**," Bryce Bond's meeting with human looking ultra-terrestrials is described in detail and includes an illustration of the occupants provided by Bryce's close friend for many years, Marc Brinkerhoff.

Bryce reveals many incredible experiences that cannot go overlooked, such as the one he describes first hand for our edification.

"Warminster, at this time of night, even for a Saturday, was somewhat deserted. Only a few people ambled along the narrow streets. I felt that I had eyes on me all the way. It was a most unusual feeling. The small narrow streets, with high brick walls, sky overcast, and the town strangely quiet — maybe a prelude to what I was about to experience that night! After walking a short distance through narrow archways and flower-lined paths, I was amazed how lovely it smelled and how clean it was. On the hill, some of the group had their telescopes set up on tripods; others had binoculars and cameras ready.

"The thing that really struck me was how friendly everyone was. A good portion are very curious, another percentage are thrill-seekers, and the remainder, well, they just enjoyed being there with this warm, loving group of spiritual individuals, sharing stories and conversations . . . UFOs have been here for eons of years. History is filled with reports of strange glowing craft, of landings and contactees. But due to negative programming regarding these ancients, and fear of the unknown being magnified out of all proportion from mouth to mouth, it spread right into modern times. Only in these times we blame television and motion pictures for doing the damage: creating near mass-panic in

UFO Repeaters! Seeing Is Believing - The Camera Doesn't Lie!

Bryce Bond Photo By Phyllis Brinkerhoff

UFO Repeaters! Seeing Is Believing - The Camera Doesn't Lie!

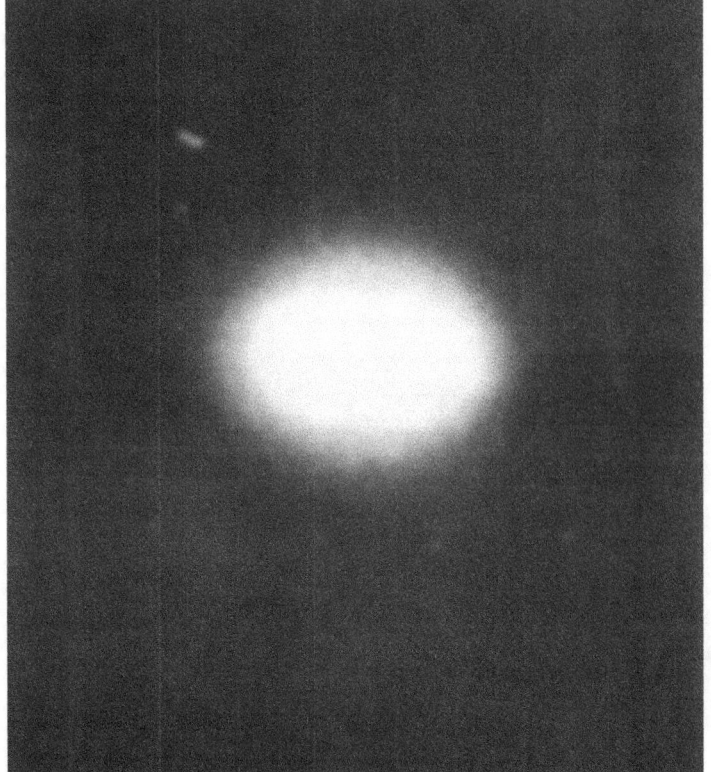

Above: No UFO flap would be complete without a cigar-shaped craft.

Left: This "blob" is similar to the one coauthor Tim Beckley flashed a giant torch light at and seemingly got a response from as the object swayed back and forth.

the mind, showing these UFOs as hostile, coming down from the heavens to devour, murder and rape — and to gobble us up!

"This travesty of beings who are thousands or even millions of years ahead of us in technology, intelligence and spiritual intent. . . . What the masses do not understand, they fear. When they fear, they shoot and run. There are numerous reports that UFOs were shot at, out of panic — even by the military. Put yourselves in their shoes and think: What would you do if you went to their planet, or dimension, or universe, or another period in time? We drove over to Starr Hill, another ancient burial ground area. This sector is where the Romans built upon, with a few of the remnants still in evidence. The location was down in a valley, wheat fields all around and high hills. The sky started to clear, filled with thousands of beautiful stars and still no UFOs . . .

"It was getting awfully late and still I had not interviewed Arthur Shuttlewood. My voice was getting weaker, my head clogged up due to the cool dampness. I got his attention and we crawled into one of the nearby cars to keep warm while I interviewed him. He was telling me that, only a few nights ago, three large entities about eight feet in height were seen down in a little hollow, to which he pointed. While in their presence, people felt a great warmth exuded from them; they were engulfed by it and the scent of roses and violets were very strong. All of a sudden, while Arthur was speaking, his conversation went to a peculiar light that just appeared in the field in front of us. He was somewhat blasé about the whole thing . . .

"Arthur then said quietly: 'I'm very glad you are here tonight, Bryce. There in front of us is a UFO. Notice the triangle shape and colored lights going around? That is a very good sign.' It then started to lift off in a weird pattern — then just disappeared. I was flabbergasted! It was so close. While describing that one on tape for American listeners, another one popped up about 25 degrees along the horizon. This one was very brilliant white, while the other was a blaze of colored lights. The intensity increased as it raised itself very slowly, did a little dance in the sky, then took off and disappeared. But before it did, Arthur jumped from the car, borrowed a flashlight from someone and sent Morse code to it. It in turn sent back the same signal that Arthur flashed out. Then it flew off. This was the highlight of my British trip: a close sighting; yet I honestly felt spiritually close to the lights in the field."

Bryce began interviewing other watchers as to what they witnessed.

UFO Repeaters! Seeing Is Believing - The Camera Doesn't Lie!

Above: Starr Hill

Below: Strange lights were seen dancing across the sky above the area.

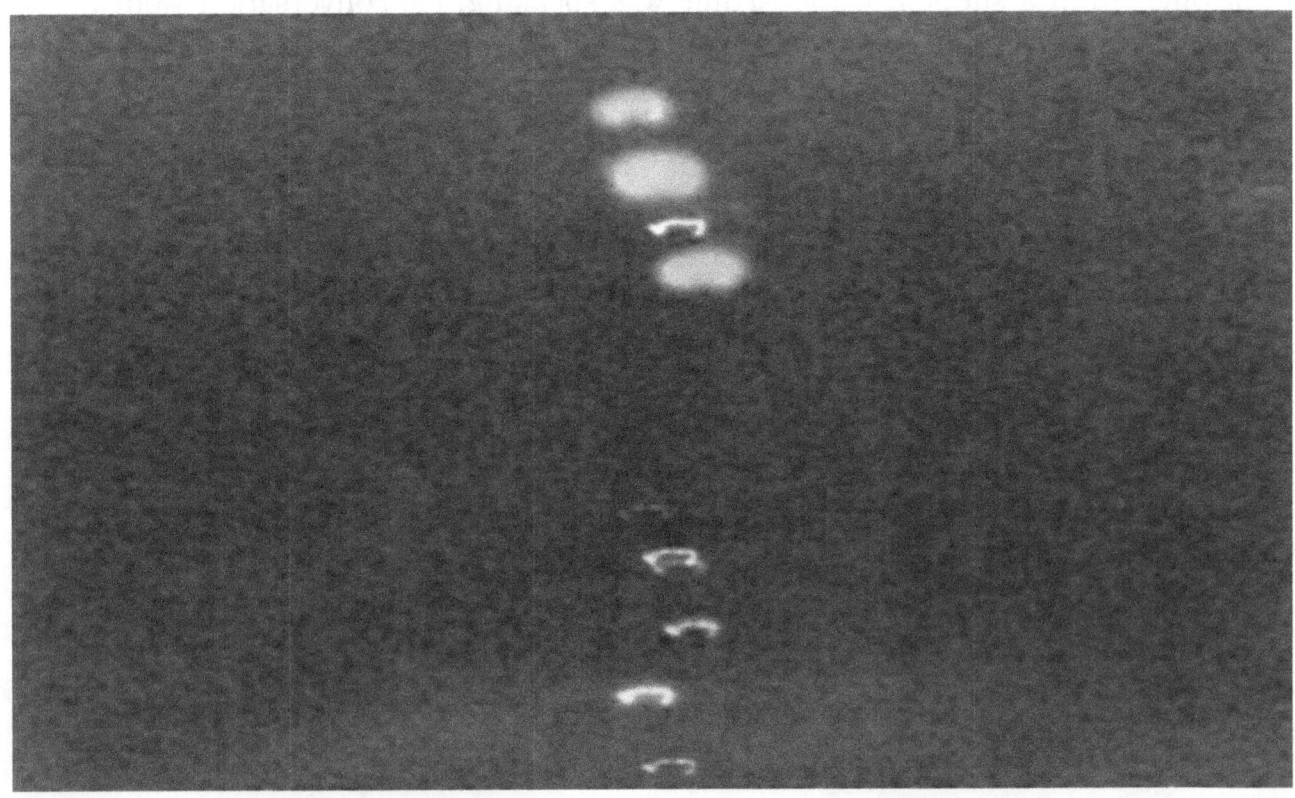

UFO Repeaters! Seeing Is Believing - The Camera Doesn't Lie!

On numerous occasions the transparent outline of eight-foot-tall beings could be seen walking parallel to the fence that surrounds Cradle Hill. They could also be heard moving about. (Artist's impression)

"I turned off the recorder and made a mad dash out into the field, went into a light trance state and asked higher intelligence to make contact again. Leaving the group, I made my way down to the hollow, where two nights before three entities were seen. Again I went into a light trance state for what seemed to be a few minutes only . . . I was awakened by my friends, who thought I had gone. I must have been there for about an hour. I truly do not know what transpired while I was there or in trance. I told my friends I would return shortly and they went back to where the others were standing. I then made my way slowly back to the parked cars and people. Now here is a strange thing: the wheat in the field next to me as I walked back up the dirt road was about waist high . . .

"I walked along the road very close to the fence. Suddenly I heard a noise — like something crushing the wheat down. There was no breeze blowing that night. I looked over. The moon had just come out, shining very brightly — and there, before my eyes, a large depression was being formed. The wheat was being crushed down in a counterclockwise position. It too was shaped like a triangle and measured about twenty feet from point to point. I stood there a few moments and experienced a tremendous tingling sensation — the same sweet smell — being engulfed by warm air. Not fully understanding what had happened, I walked up the road to get Arthur, my host.

"Speaking of the field, Arthur pointed out some landing impressions in the section fronting the farm barn: a circle about thirty feet in circumference, with another depression spotted, but this one in a long cigar shape. All the depressions, recently made and noticed, were in a counterclockwise fashion. After all this, I was very happy and thankful. My mission had been a success," wrote Bryce Bond, who was also research editor of *"Beyond Reality,"* a leading American psychic, occult, metaphysical and UFO magazine. He says some nice but wholly undeserved things about me in his newsletter and describes his trip back to London from Warminster in Reg Bradbury's Kingdom Crusade van. "On the way we stopped at Stonehenge, on Salisbury Plain. With the moon casting its eerie light upon this ancient structure, it was quite awe-inspiring in early morning hours. This whole area is just teeming in legend and folklore, and you begin to wonder who constructed these megalithic giants . . . and for what purpose?"

UFO Repeaters! Seeing Is Believing - The Camera Doesn't Lie!

Arthur Shuttlewood (left) and Lord Mountbatten - who was assassinated by the IRA in 1979 - discuss the many sightings over the British countryside. It is believed that Mountbatten's interest was the result of the landing of an unknown craft on his estate.

2015 is the 50th anniversary of the appearance of "The Thing" over Warminster. The ongoing wave of sightings took on many aspects, as can be verified by reading the literature or watching one of the several YouTube documentaries on Warminster.

https://www.youtube.com/watch?v=y1bzRRg5gb8

SOURCES

http://www.ufo-warminster.co.uk/

https://www.facebook.com/pages/UFO-Warminster/174632342638283

"UFOS: Keys To Inner Perfection," By Bryce Bond, republished 2015, Inner Light/Global Communications

"Our Alien Planet - This Eerie Earth," by Tim Beckley and Sean Casteel, published by Inner Light/Global Communications, both books available from Amazon.com

UFO REPEATERS STILE ITALIANO

By Sean Casteel

THE name Antonio Urzi has become quite well known in the international UFO community. He has produced more than 2,500 videotape recordings of UFO sightings and seems to be a classic example of the Repeater-type experiencer.

A SYMPATHETIC JOURNALIST GETS INVOLVED

Antonio was originally from Livorno, Italy, and later came to reside with his wife in Cinisello Balsamo, a small town bordering the north of Milan. According to Italian journalist Maurizio Baiata, Cinisello Balsamo is "an industrial and residential area punctuated by high buildings, crowded condominiums and some sparse green in a lot of cold cement. Despite these uncanny conditions, almost every day Antonio has been able to capture hundreds of images of UFOs, shooting with his video camera from a small dormer window in a top floor condo."

Baiata writes further that the anomalous objects are apparently willing to present themselves to Antonio in many spectacular ways, patterns and shapes. The craft he has photographed run the gamut from singular balls of light to pairs to numerous spherical luminous objects in swarms or "flotillas" or small fleets. Antonio has also captured images of structured metallic discs pivoting and standing still in the air and dome-shaped craft silently hovering, rotating and shining until they disappear to the naked eye.

UFO Repeaters! Seeing Is Believing - The Camera Doesn't Lie!

Above: A metallic disc flies across the camera lens for Antonio Urzi.

Below: A pair of Urzi's photos for the public's awareness.

Baiata met Antonio and his wife in the late 1990s at a UFO conference in the Italian city of Viareggio.

"Sincerely," Baiata writes, "I was stunned. The couple looked to me to be sincerely wanting to understand what was happening to them, and why. I did not have an answer then and I don't have one now, despite my efforts. I followed the case closely for about five years, and, after a very long video interview that the couple gave me in 2005, I finally reached the conclusion that the case was genuine."

That opinion was mainly supported by the positive results of the video analysis conducted by the British researcher Andrew Fry, to whom Baiata had sent a DVD copy of some of the original videos shot by Antonio. The debunkers of Antonio's videos generally harp on the fact that he has simply produced too many of them to credible and that they are "too good to be true." But Baiata points out that in several instances the sighting and Antonio's ability to film the event occurred in the presence of other witnesses. That includes professional camera operators from the most important Italian TV networks.

"What is really noticeable," Baiata writes, "is that very often wherever Antonio goes to participate in a UFO conference, strange flying objects do appear in the sky at the same time. And this has happened not only in Italy, but in many other locations around the world. The experience continues to repeat itself. All of a sudden, while the Urzis and friends are walking the streets, Antonio points his finger to the sky and the evidence of what he is seeing is often recorded by other cameras. Antonio's sightings are continuous, constantly increasing in number and frequency, and witnessed also by dozens of people. It is understandable therefore that Antonio has become a worldwide sensation."

THE FAMILIAR IMAGE RETURNS

About a year and a half after Baiata's article on Antonio was written, Mexican journalist and TV personality Jaime Maussan reported that Antonio had been taking some test shots with a camera and telephoto lens. Antonio sighted what he at first thought was a flying sphere, but with the telephoto lens he was able to see much more detail. He captured a series of eleven photos that show a saucer-shaped craft with a sphere-shaped object centered on the bottom of the craft and three smaller sphere-shaped objects around the larger sphere. This

UFO Repeaters! Seeing Is Believing - The Camera Doesn't Lie!

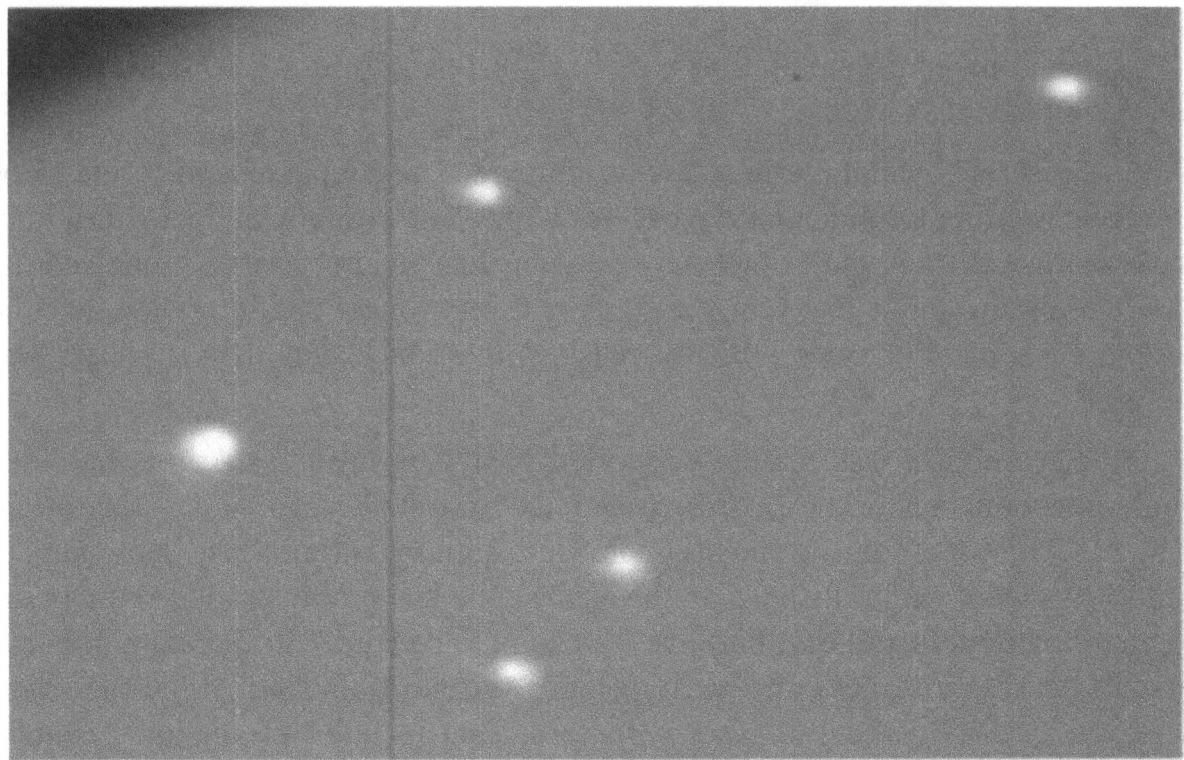

Above: Here they come. How can you dispute Antonio Urzi's amazing claims of repeated UFO encounters?

Below: Big ship and little ship together? Can this be real?

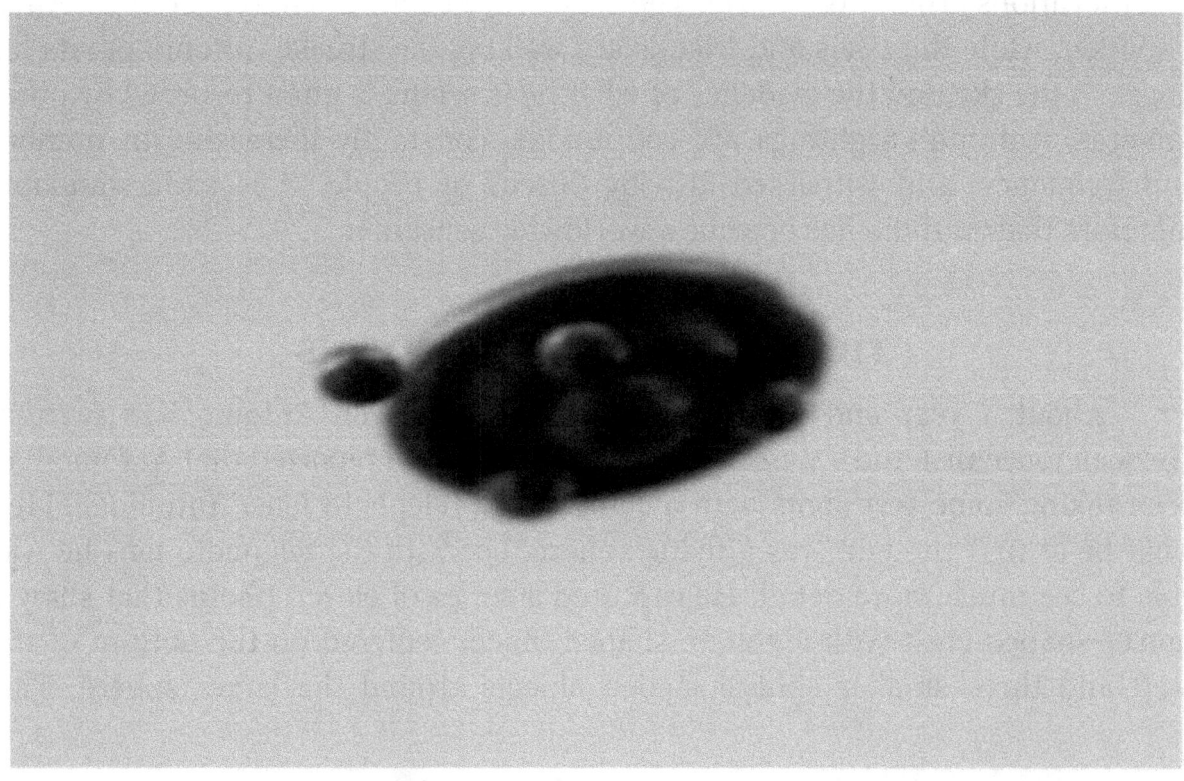

UFO Repeaters! Seeing Is Believing - The Camera Doesn't Lie!

Center Photo Above: Stigmata contactee Georgio Bongiovanni poses with Antonio Urzi (Right) and Urzi's wife (Left).

Urzi's UFOs come in a variety of patterns and forms.

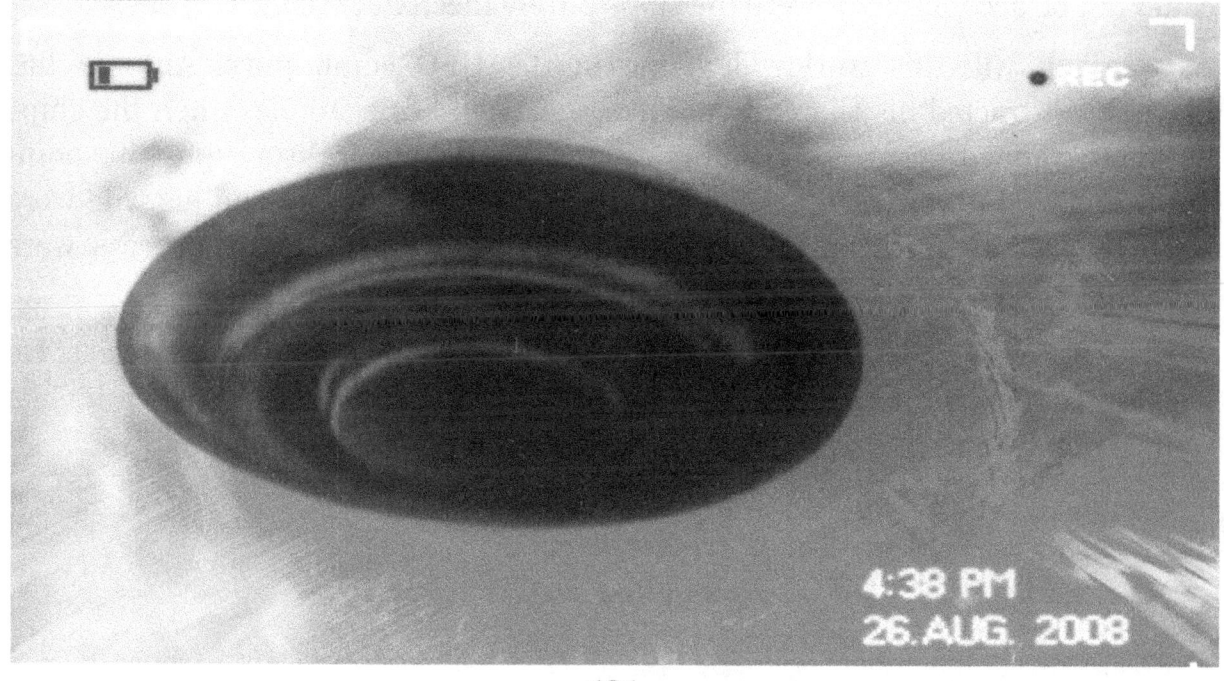

object closely resembles the well-known UFO photo taken by contactee George Adamski in 1952.

The sequence of photos also shows smaller sphere-shaped objects moving around the larger craft. Antonio said that, after snapping the eleven photos, his camera stopped working and the UFO and its spheres disappeared. The photos were submitted to analysis by an Italian UFO expert who then told the Italian media that there was no evidence to indicate that the photos had been altered in any way.

IT'S ALIVE!

In July 2014, Antonio captured an image that came to be called "The Milan UFO." It was controversial at the time and drew the attention of the Italian media as well as garnering some interest from the American UFO community. Researcher and journalist Alejandro Rojas, a radio host for "Open Minds Radio," pointed out that the original title of Antonio's video translates into English as "Unidentified Anomalous Biological Entity."

Meaning that Antonio allegedly believed that what he had photographed was a living organism. Antonio was not the first to offer that speculation. The odd maneuverings and shape-shifting capabilities of certain UFOs has previously led others to see the ships as something beyond a "simple" metallic spacecraft. Their fluid ease in switching from one form to another and strange agility of movement could not be accounted for were the ships purely mechanical contrivances.

Along with his worldwide fame in the UFO community, Antonio has inevitably attracted his share of debunkers as well. For example, when the ships he photographed began to resemble Adamski's, debunkers were quick to point out that they'd never trusted Adamski's photos either. Antonio and his wife were featured several times on popular Italian TV shows and in the process were sometimes viciously attacked by journalists in their native country.

But, says journalist Maurizio Baiata, "Antonio's position is pretty clear. He feels the urge to get his camera, which every day he aims to the sky. Then he just waits patiently and they appear, as if attracted by a powerful human catalyst."

ITALY'S "FRIENDSHIP" CASE

Nearly a half century before Antonio Urzi began making his UFO videos public, a mass contact event was taking shape in and around the Italian town of Pescara. It was the 1950s, when flying saucers seemed to be everywhere in the skies over Italy, sometimes being photographed, sometimes inducing fear and a mild public hysteria. For a long time, the phenomenon of "contactism," or the deliberate encounter, repeated over time, between man and extraterrestrials was believed to involve only a few chosen individuals or "contactees."

But in 2007, that picture would be altered when researcher and author Stefano Breccia published some startling papers that revealed the story of repeated direct encounters between more than 100 people and extraterrestrial beings living in numerous secret bases on our planet.

JOURNALIST PAOLA HARRIS TELLS THE STORY

In the summer of 2013, my sometimes writing partner, John Weigle, and I covered a lecture delivered by Italian-American journalist Paola Harris to the Close Encounter Research Organization in Thousand Oaks, California. (Paola had also been on the scene of and affirmed a sighting by Antonio Urzi.) In her lecture, Paola covered the story of the "Friendship" case in some detail.

The story begins with the aforementioned Stefano Breccia, who first brought the case to light after several of the participants came forward to discuss their experiences with him.

Eyewitnesses to the Friendship case told Breccia about human-looking aliens who spoke perfect Italian, among many other languages. The beings explained that the Earth had been created for a positive purpose but that man was turning everything into evil. The level of human morality was much lower than their own, they said, and they were there to ensure the situation didn't get out of hand. They had not come to conquer, as there was nothing to conquer, but instead emphasized that all things required love and respect and that everything should be done in accordance with these principles. The aliens also said they were familiar with Earth's history and its differing religions.

Breccia was told the aliens had already been here for many years and had lived at secret bases in various places on the planet. They preferred not to reveal themselves publicly because people weren't ready for contact. Breccia himself

UFO Repeaters! Seeing Is Believing - The Camera Doesn't Lie!

Bruno Sammaciccia (left), with Gaspare De Lama, witnesses in the Friendship case.

UFO Repeaters! Seeing Is Believing - The Camera Doesn't Lie!

The aliens in the Friendship Case were said to be giants in comparison to those in the group of Italian experiencers they contacted. This is an actual photograph of one of the supposed aliens.

UFO Repeaters! Seeing Is Believing - The Camera Doesn't Lie!

Above: The objects appeared to fly without any difficulty in a swift falling leaf motion.

Below: The aliens from the group W-56 openly communicated with several representatives of the Italian group.

met with many of the aliens. Some of them were very tall, including one alien who was 15-feet-tall and was photographed towering over some trees in the background.

The aliens were given the name "W-56s" because the year they initially made contact with the Pescara group was 1956. The W-56s are a confederation of different people coming from throughout nearly all of the known universe. To them, the Earth has a mystical meaning because it is among the only fifty Mother Planets where life has been born. But we are not evolved enough, Harris reiterated, to meet this cosmic consciousness in a spirit of complete understanding.

One woman who took part in the contact said, "We were hoping for an experience with teachers who could help us love."

Meetings between the humans and the ETs continued for several months. At one point, the "Friends" started asking for help and wanted industrial quantities of fruits and vegetables of various kinds. After taking delivery of a truckload of produce, the truck driver was lured away by the invitation to share coffee with the humans, at which point the aliens teleported the goods off the truck. The driver was surprised to return and find the truck was already empty.

A BELIEVER WITH NOTHING TO PROVE

Breccia would come to write a book about the Friendship case called "Mass Contacts: The 1950s Contact In Pescara, Italy, With Human-Looking Aliens." When Paola interviewed Breccia for her own book, "Exopolitics: All The Above," he told her that "I do not intend that anybody believes what I have written. It's up to the reader to decide whether I am a fool or not. About the photos, I am the first one to state that the pictures are meaningless. I even present a fake, done by myself. I've included a lot of pictures simply because most of them are totally unknown, up to now. Think of the scout craft formation, seen from above! Or the many pictures shot during a landing. I've never seen anything like that in any UFO book, therefore I believe 'Contattismi di Massa' has been the first one to show such things. There are even two pictures of W-56 people."

According to Breccia, there are bases near Pescara on the Adriatic Coast which he finds difficult to describe because of technology we don't understand. He says, however, there are no fixed entries to them; when necessary, a passageway is opened, then closed, and everything goes back to the "status quo."

UFO Repeaters! Seeing Is Believing - The Camera Doesn't Lie!

Above: A close-up of the craft. You can actually see inside the dome, it would appear.

Below: The object appears in the sky over the trees, indicating that it is fairly close to the ground.

UFO Repeaters! Seeing Is Believing - The Camera Doesn't Lie!

The Friendship Case produced some remarkable films. The reality of these contacts has been attested to by many of those who were involved.

The largest base had a ceiling 300 meters high, and sometimes it rained inside the base.

"A lot of [the aliens] are living among us, interacting at ease with our society, having Earth identities," Breccia said, adding that the beings he had interacted with had left "a very friendly" impression.

Which, much to our relief, seems to be the general pattern among UFO Repeaters. The aliens who return to certain contactees again and again do indeed seem to be trying to establish some kind of "friendship" with that individual, to slowly create an atmosphere of comfort and trust. They even seem to want some of the contactees to meet them with a camera in their hands and are willing to "pose" for a few photos.

Perhaps it's all about creating a "family album" to enable future generations to look back at the early days when contact was still in its infancy?

THE MAN WITH MARKS ON HIS BODY

While the Friendship case dramatically revolves around the idea of Earth's ultimate salvation by way of assistance from benevolent aliens, a more directly religious approach is being promoted by an Italian-born contactee named Giorgio Bongiovanni. For a quarter of a century, Giorgio has been experiencing marks on his body called "stigmata," or wounds intended to replicate the physical injuries Jesus Christ endured on the cross. The stigmata wounds appear spontaneously in some unknown way and are not self-inflicted. The stigmata phenomenon has been reported at least since the Middle-Ages, particularly among priests and nuns; the strange signs on the flesh are said to be confirmation of the sufferers' saintly devotion to Christ.

Giorgio's first experience as a stigmatist happened in 1989 in Portugal, when he was given a message for humanity and received the first stigmatic piercings in his hands. During this encounter, a luminous being revealed the Secret of Fatima and explained to Giorgio that the universe is abundant with intelligent life and that men are visiting the Earth with highly advanced disc-shaped spacecraft. Since that time, Giorgio has had frequent recurrences of stigmata, sometimes on his left side, where Christ was said to have been pierced by a Roman spear, and on his forehead, in reference to Christ's crown of thorns.

UFO Repeaters! Seeing Is Believing - The Camera Doesn't Lie!

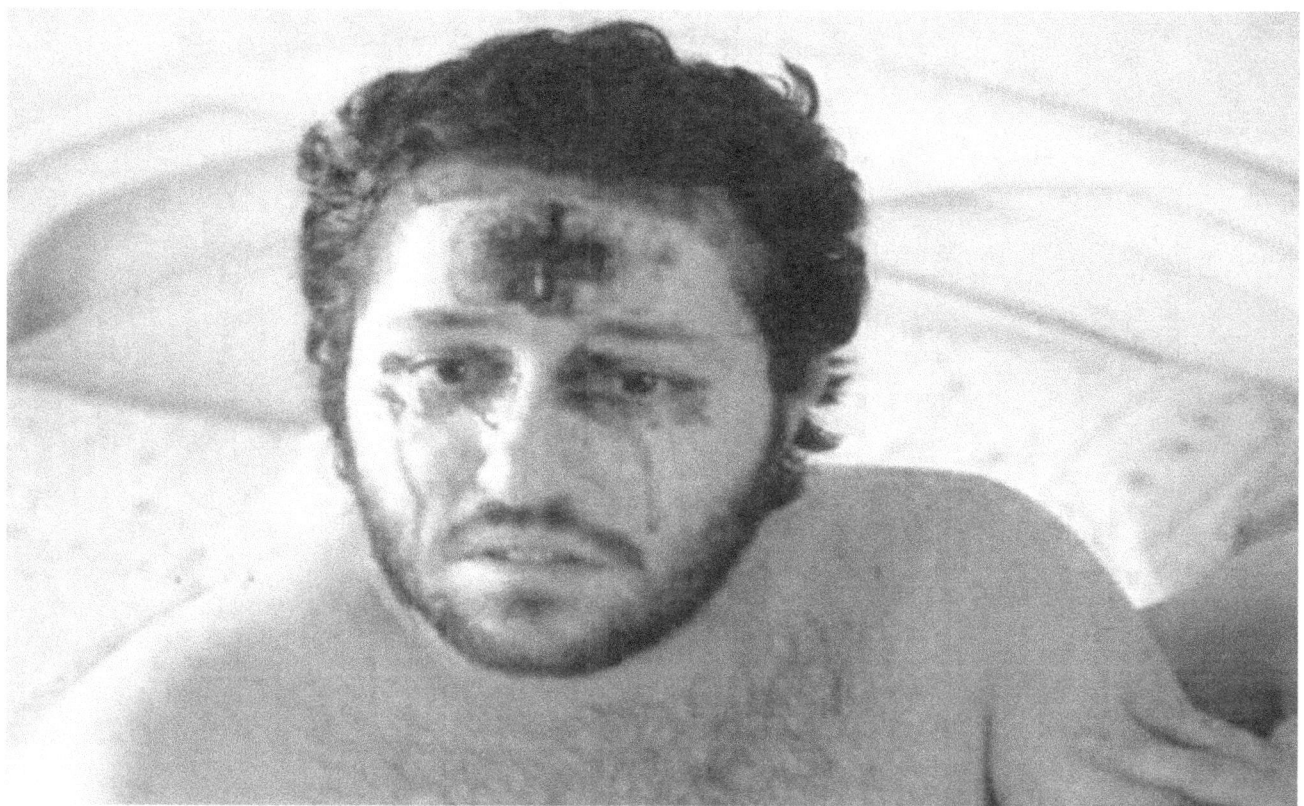

Stigmatist Giorgio Bongiovanni claims to have had visions of the Virgin Mary as well as contact with interdimensional beings. There is hardly any part of Giorgio's body that hasn't bled like the wounds of Jesus on the cross, or so he maintains.

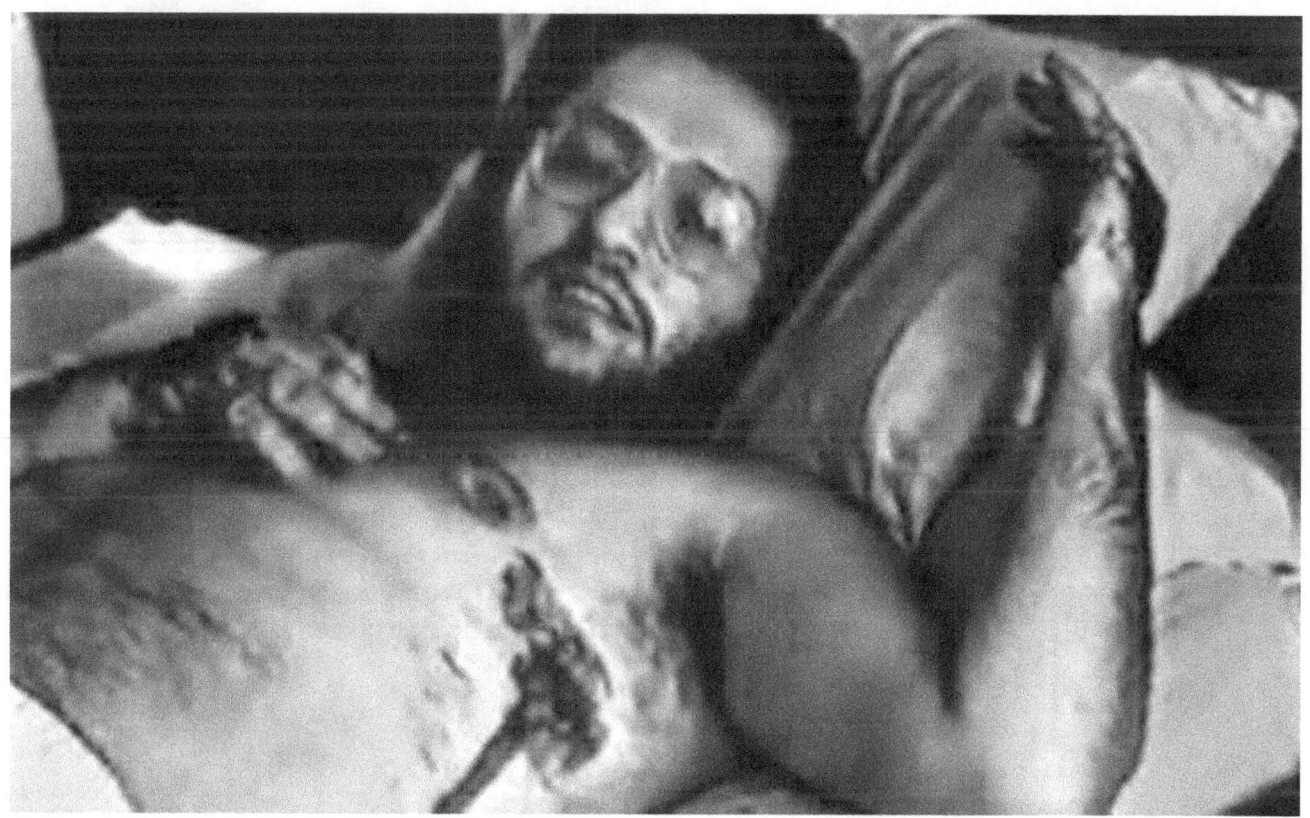

UFO Repeaters! Seeing Is Believing - The Camera Doesn't Lie!

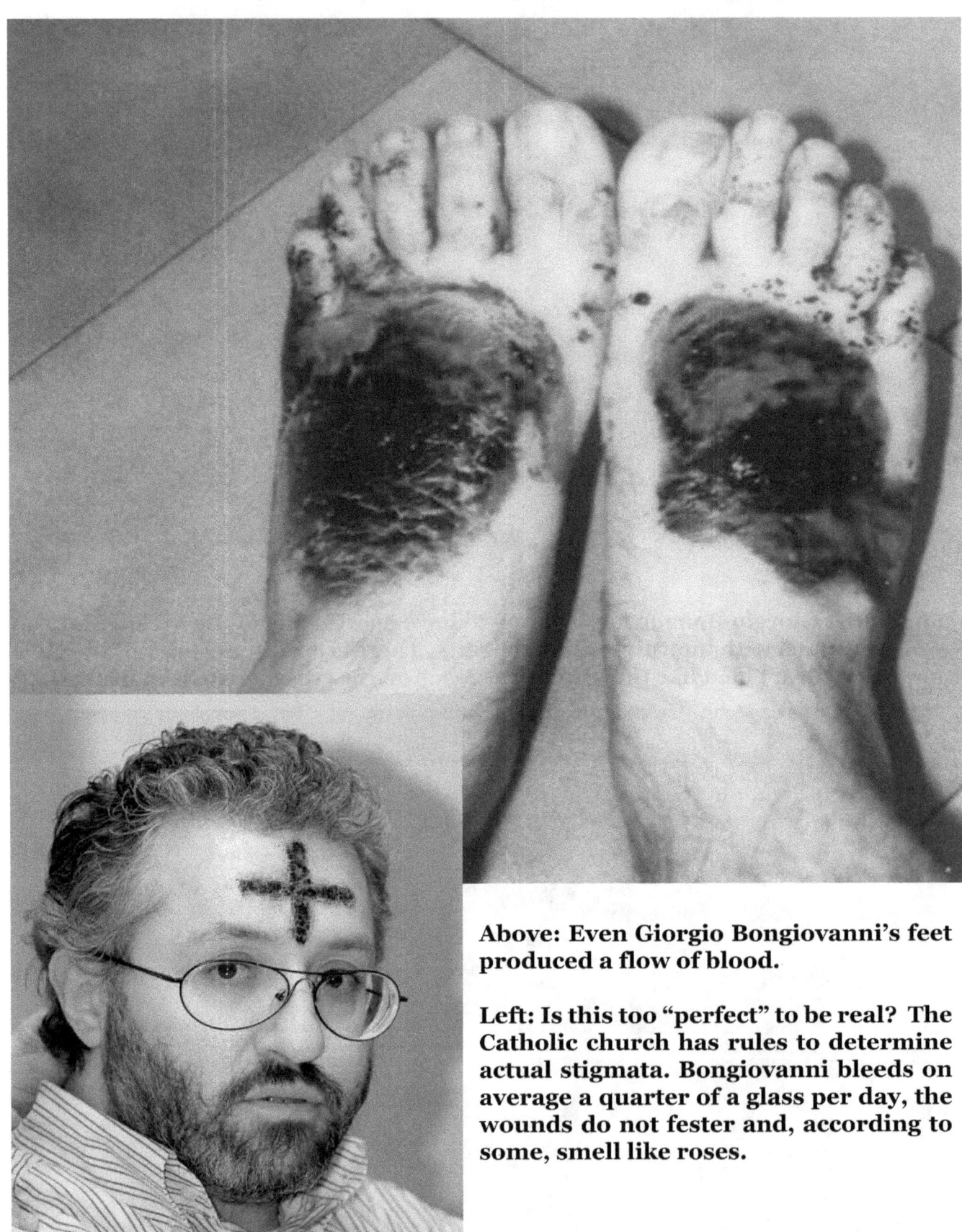

Above: Even Giorgio Bongiovanni's feet produced a flow of blood.

Left: Is this too "perfect" to be real? The Catholic church has rules to determine actual stigmata. Bongiovanni bleeds on average a quarter of a glass per day, the wounds do not fester and, according to some, smell like roses.

UFO Repeaters! Seeing Is Believing - The Camera Doesn't Lie!

The purpose of his stigmata, in Giorgio's terms, is so that the faithful can have a sign they can believe in during the traumatic Earth changes to come. In the years since his 1989 experience in Portugal, he has diligently researched UFO contacts and the messages given to us by beings from another dimension.

Giorgio said in an online interview with journalist Marty Leach that he has been told by these sacred interdimensional flying saucer entities that, "Mankind will face a period of darkness, but all those who have given their lives in favor of life, who have realized universal values in general, independent of which religion they belong to or what beliefs they have, those who have devoted their lives for others and have obeyed Christ's teachings, will be saved."

Although he may not have a stack of UFO photos to show for it, Giorgio is his own kind of UFO Repeater, one whose body bears witness to his contact as he labors to speak a message that is both ancient and urgently needed in the present.

SOURCES

"Adamski-like UFO photographed in Italy," from the website at: http://www.openminds.tv/adamski-like-ufo-photographed-in-Italy-807

"Antonio Urzi, the UFO catalyst," from the website at: http://www.openminds.tv/antonio-urzi-the-ufo-catalyst/3202

"Journalist Paola Harris Lectures On The Importance of Human-Looking ETs," by Sean Casteel and John Weigle, from the website at: http://ufodigest.com/article/human-looking-ets-0822

"UFO Secret: The Friendship Case (2013)," from the website at: http://board.dailyflix.net/topic/95092-ufo-secret-the-friendship-case-2013/

"The Second Coming, UFOs and the future of humanity," by Monte Leach, from the website at: http://themiraclespage.info/encounters/bongiovanni-interview.htm

THE GALACTIC MISSION OF MARC BRINKERHOFF -- EXTRAORDINARY PHOTOGRAPHER OF SPACECRAFT AND ALIEN BEINGS

By Timothy Green Beckley and Harold Salkin

AS the title of this book indicates, in UFOlogical terms, if anyone sees a UFO more than once or claims numerous encounters, they are known as a "Repeater."

Because they feel the odds of meeting up with an ET even once has to be in the millions to one range, most conservative UFO researchers and the various "scientific-minded" investigative groups tend to frown on the claims of such individuals. For the most part, they do not take too kindly to the likes of "Repeaters," though there are always a few exceptions to any rule.

One man, however, started attracting the attention of some sane and sober UFOlogists back in 1977, despite what may have seemed to be "far out" and unproven claims of meetings with extraterrestrials. For not only did Marc Brinkerhoff claim to have established an ongoing relationship with aliens, he also seemed, and still does, to have the uncanny ability to point his camera at the heavens and take photographs of things that have no business being in the sky.

I have known Marc for three decades, I would guess. We, along with his wife Phyllis, have remained good friends, exchanging greeting cards, popping up at the same conferences and on radio shows and podcasts. I guess you could say we are close chums. Now, I can't honestly say I buy Marc's claims that he is a

UFO Repeaters! Seeing Is Believing - The Camera Doesn't Lie!

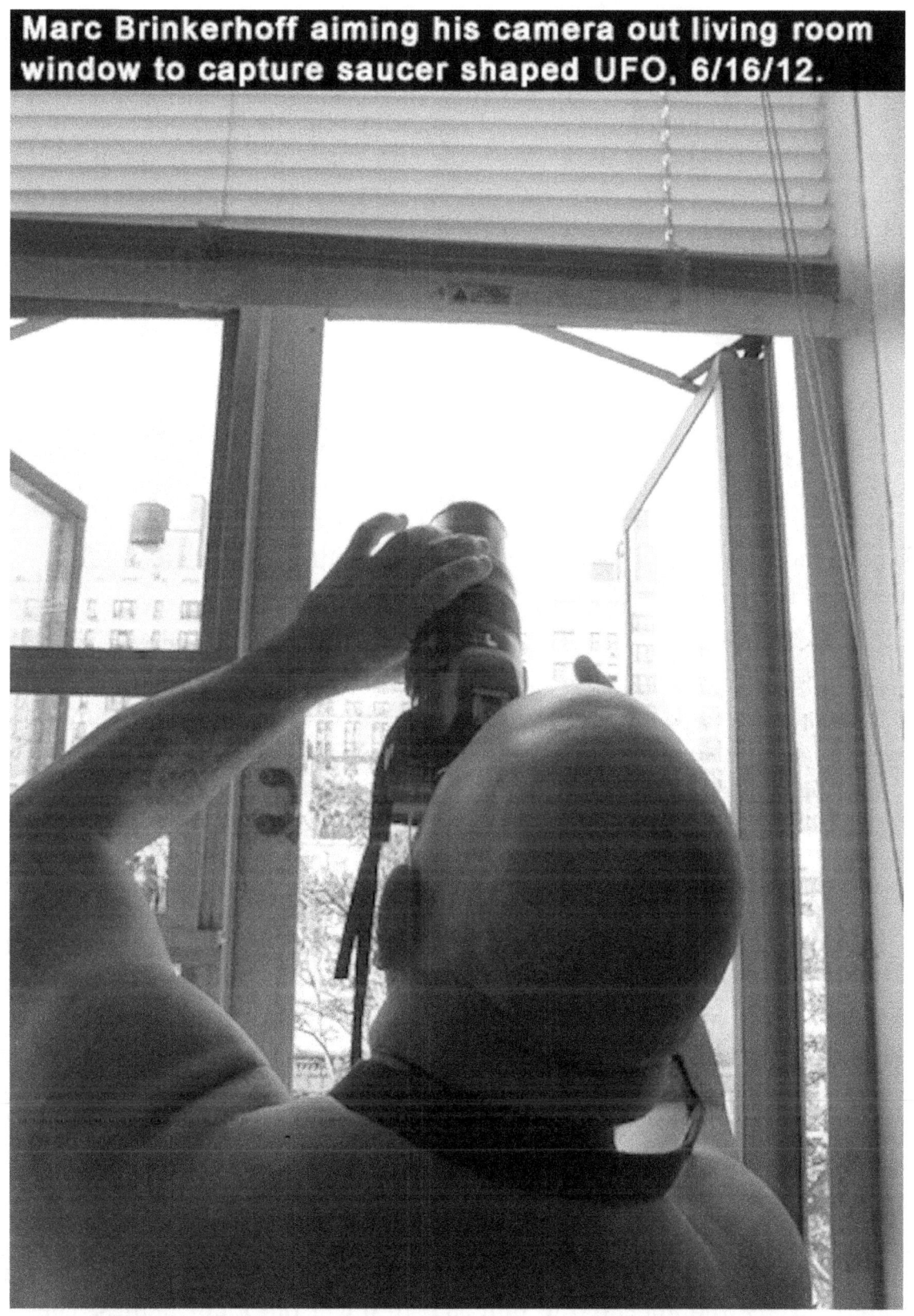

Brinkerhoff spies on the sky, ready to take a picture at any given moment.

Walk-In and conscious channel for 12th dimensional ETs of the "Alsyglion Group" and speaks as their representative on Earth. I do buy that Marc is a fantastic artist who makes the aliens, fairies and wild life he renders come to life on canvas. It's like the creatures, both big and small, are in the room with you. What I also believe is that Marc has the uncanny – almost supernatural – ability to photograph UFOs and possibly their occupants. It's been a long strange trip but it's one that Marc has permitted me to document and one that I do not hesitate to share.

THE EARLY YEARS

Marc's first UFO experience took place when he was just five years old (1958) on an athletic field near the Mahopac, New York, high school. As best as he can recall, it was around 3:00 P.M. when he observed a large silvery sphere, "like the metal ball in a pinball machine. No sound was heard," but he does remember "receiving a feeling of great love from it."

Since that day, Marc contends, extraterrestrials have been contacting him and other humans. Some people say they are programming us to save the world and the universe from possible destruction. He sees the higher dimensional aliens as being benevolent, human-like "Space Brothers" who are here NOT to harm us, but to lead us along the path to spiritual enlightenment and usher in the New Age.

The mild-mannered UFO contactee further believes that in a previous incarnation he lived in other galaxies and dimensions and that his mission in this life is to teach the concept of Universal brotherhood/sisterhood and galactic spiritual evolution to his fellow man. At the time they began telepathically communicating with him, the beings told Marc they came from an area in space near the constellation Bootes and the star Arcturus. Later they explained this information was given so that a child could look it up on a star map. In reality, Marc says his ET family no longer lives on the dimensions of physical planets, but instead on incredibly immense (7th thru 12th) multi-dimensional spacecraft or Arcvannas larger than Jupiter. He says these Arcvannas contain planet-like ecosystems that would boggle the Earth mind. He further declares that he mentally talks to them. On February 22, 1977, Marc met seven beautiful angelic extraterrestrials who appeared to him as 8 to 9 feet tall Light Beings. They had materialized inside a bluish white glowing transparent dome at his favorite

UFO Repeaters! Seeing Is Believing - The Camera Doesn't Lie!

Above: A supremely gifted professional artist, Marc renders a likeness of the late contactee Bryce Bond's meeting with an alien crew onboard a UFO that touched down outside Warminster, England.

Below: This image was taken at Mahopac Middle School field, Mahopac, New York, around 1:30 A.M. to 3:00 A.M. on March 31, 1977, the same night Marc photographed the spacecraft shooting a probe.

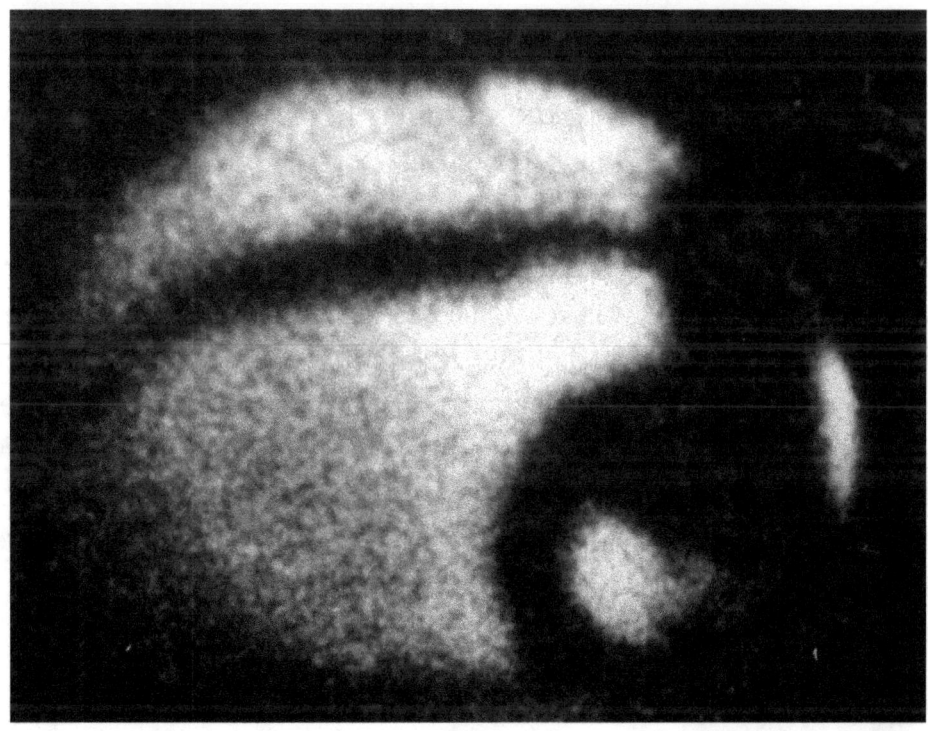

childhood sky-watching location. He says they surrounded him for 20 minutes to telepathically speak to him and infuse him with love until they had to leave, at which point they and the dome dematerialized.

Back then, Marc says, he started taking photos of spaceships from isolated fields in New York State on the instruction of these beings and continued doing so into the 1980s. After a photography hiatus in the 1990s, around 2008, he started shooting his ET friends' spaceships again in New York City, this time with digital equipment. He claims he continued to see the ships and hear from them even though he had stopped shooting for a few years. Marc photographs the UFOs from the street and also outside his 8th floor apartment living room windows on the Upper West Side when the ETs telepathically call to him.

Here is a summation of some of Marc Brinkerhoff's experiences.

1958 - MAHOPAC, NY – AND ALIEN CONTACT

Marc goes willingly onboard a spaceship with very tall (over eight feet), angelic-looking extraterrestrials. He says he recognized them as his 'friends and family' from his time before when he lived in space (past life). They take him for a ride behind the moon out to Saturn and back before they place him back down in the school field four hours later.

1961 - CANADA - NOVA SCOTIA

Marc was eight years old. During the summer, he was with his family waiting in the car at a motel.

It was a few miles from where they would have to go wait for a ferry to take them to Prince Edward Island the next morning. Marc stayed in the car while his parents went to see if there was a vacancy. Marc was leaning outside the back driver's side open window, just looking at the stars, when suddenly there appeared a huge cigar-shaped UFO making a loud humming noise, like a swarm of bees. It was eleven inches long at arm's length in the sky. The UFO glowed white and appeared to swoop downwards from the night sky, heading to the deep forest behind the motel. The UFO dematerialized before hitting the trees. Marc knew intuitively that the UFO teleported to another dimension. The time was after 11:00 P.M.

UFO Repeaters! Seeing Is Believing - The Camera Doesn't Lie!

MARC BRINKERHOFF
UFO Photographer ~ Contactee ~ Artist ~ Author
IntergalacticMission.com

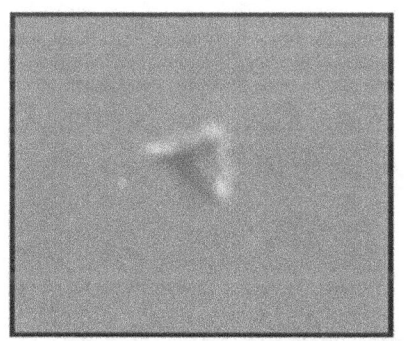 

7 morphing UFOs captured while in MOMA Sculpture Garden, NYC with 3 witnesses on Aug. 23, 2012. They moved too fast to catch much more.

3 UFOs traveling in formation captured outside my living room window on the Upper West Side of NY, Nov. 13, 2010.

UFO Repeaters! Seeing Is Believing - The Camera Doesn't Lie!

1964 - 1966 - MAHOPAC, NY

While watching the stars at night, in his backyard, Marc spotted a "moving star." He claims he had telepathic contact and it stopped overhead for 20 minutes. After that, he says, the UFO would come back any time he asked. Marc was constantly seeing UFOs, sometimes with his father and friends and also a few times at a local drive-in movie theater. Many times he would be called telepathically to look out a window and a UFO would appear and hover. A few times he would be awakened at 3:00 A.M. to go to a window and a UFO would fly by and sometimes stop and teleport away. Many times the UFOs came in the form of a large, bright, glowing star that would maneuver extremely high in the sky with actions such as right angle turns, zigzags and breathtakingly fast departures. Marc also saw silver spheres, white spheres, mirrored spheres, oval and football shaped spaceships. He tried to help his father and friends get answers from the UFOs occupants. Marc would hear the ETs answer him telepathically, but his friends did not hear the messages telepathically. He asked his space friends in the UFOs if they could answer questions for his friends by moving up and down for a "yes," or left to right for a "no" answer, and his space friends agreed. The UFOs would also demonstrate incredible maneuvers for him and anyone who was with him at the time.

1967 - MAHOPAC, NY

One very cold winter night on February 10, 1967, around 7:00 P.M., two glowing white enormous UFO disks hovered silently about 125 feet over Marc's backyard. His whole family witnessed the sighting.

The shape of the UFOs looked like the top third of a sphere with a flat bottom. Marc said that the UFO on the right side of the yard sent an off-white beam of light to the ground for about 20 seconds and then pulled it back into the spaceship. Then the UFO that was over his house on the left suddenly opened a window where Marc and his father could see six silhouettes of people from the waist up! The being on the left waved to them. Marc told his father, "That is my friend!" Suddenly, the spaceships became much brighter! They were so bright that his family had to turn their eyes away. However, for some reason, Marc's eyes were not disturbed by the glow. He said, "To me, it looked like a car headlight that was on regular and then someone just turned on the bright lights. I never even had to look away."

UFO Repeaters! Seeing Is Believing - The Camera Doesn't Lie!

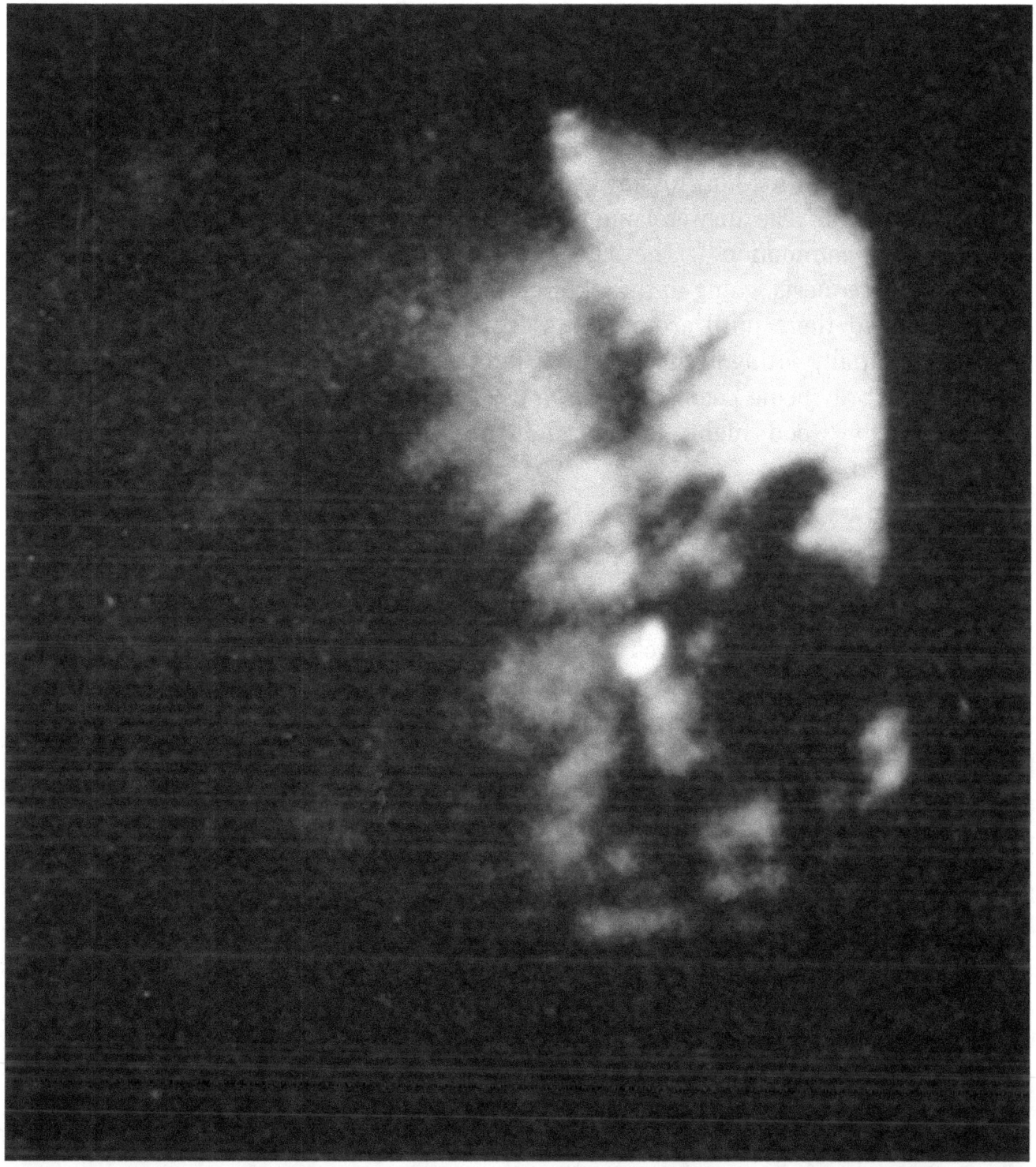

Marc says, this photo "shows a spaceship window which is a square with slanted corners. (Or an eight-sided, square-shaped window.) Two space beings are silhouetted against an amber/orange background. The figure on the right appears to be sitting, while the tall, darker silhouetted figure on the left is standing. There is a ceiling-like structure and other background images as well. However, I also noticed the white spot in the center and was told that it represents the point of manifestation onto the film with their energy."

The two spaceships started moving to the school field 30 seconds away from Marc's house and waited, hovering over the high school for him. "My father drove my dog and I up to the school field and the UFOs moved to hover over me in the football field. My father stood by the car for about 10 minutes until it became too cold for him to stay. I telepathically asked the space people, 'Why don't you land?' The answer came back, 'We are too large. A landing would cause too much commotion.'" The UFOs then maneuvered according to Marc's telepathic requests, going to the right and to the left and backward and forward. "I remained there until around 9:45 P.M. with my dog (approximately 2 ½ hours), actually sitting in the wet snow, but feeling perfectly comfortable because of the heat ray being beamed down on us. The spaceships then sent a telepathic message of 'Good night' to me and zoomed straight up in the sky and disappeared."

OCTOBER 1971 - CROTON FALLS, NY

At around 8:40 A.M., Marc was driving to the Croton Falls Train Station to drop off a female friend going back to New York City. They were driving on Croton Falls Road and Marc had just told her about some of his past telepathic experiences and contact with friendly space people and UFOs when he heard telepathically, "Look up!" Slowing the car down to almost a stop, Marc looked up to the sky from behind the windshield. To his and his friend's amazement, a "double" object, like two footballs fastened together at the middle, appeared and floated silently just over the pine trees lining the road. It flew over the car and out of sight. It was as big as a large plane. The apparent size was 12 inches at arm's length.

JUNE 1976 - MAHOPAC, NY

While walking near his old school in Mahopac, Marc, his cousin and a friend all looked skyward to witness a mirror like silver sphere, silently traveling slowly overhead at several thousand feet up.

UFO Repeaters! Seeing Is Believing - The Camera Doesn't Lie!

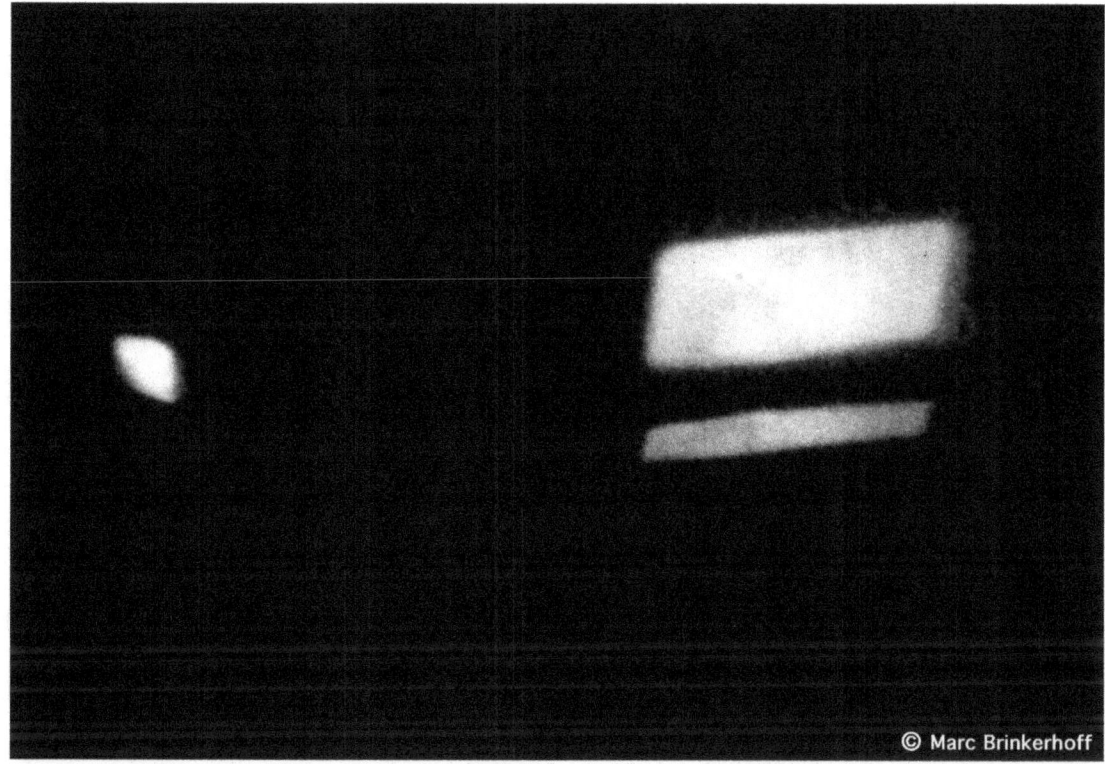

Above: Red scout spaceship and hatchways to a mother ship: This image was taken at the Mahopac Middle School field in Mahopac, New York, after 9:00 P.M. on Saturday, September 17, 1977.

Below: This is an image of part of the under-flange of a spaceship (UFO) that is shooting a probe disc with a light beam trail.

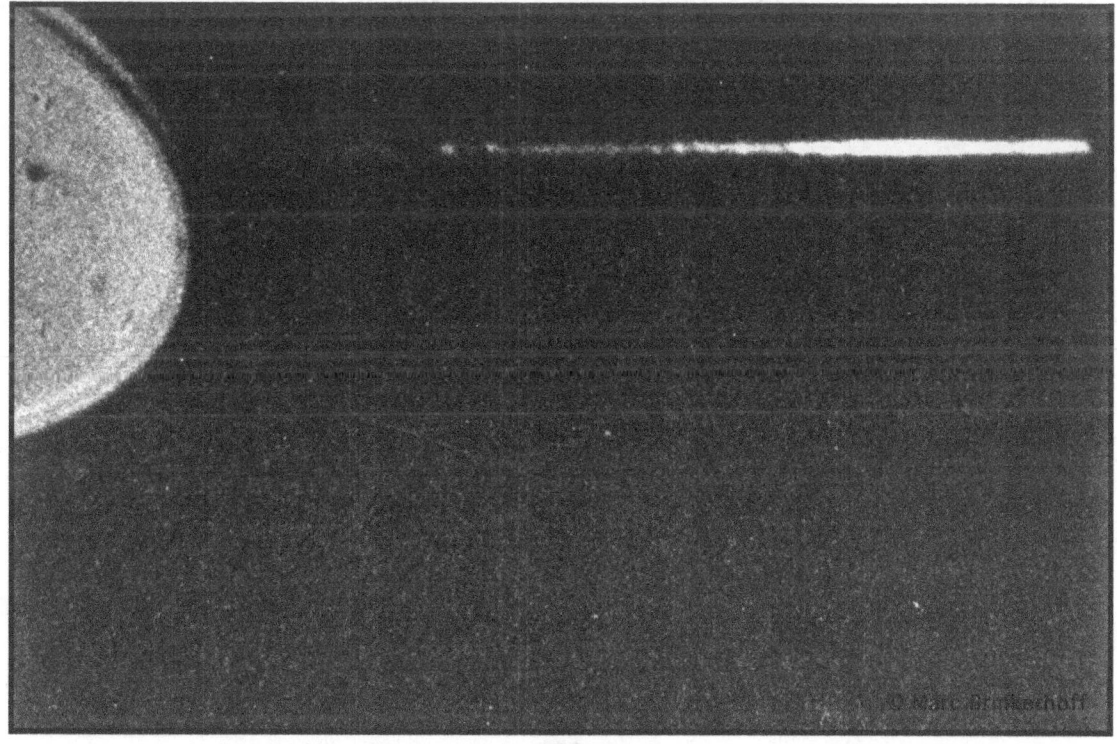

UFO Repeaters! Seeing Is Believing - The Camera Doesn't Lie!

PHOTOS TAKEN BY MARC WITH ARGUS 257 INSTAMATIC CAMERA

MARCH 31, 1977 – MAHOPAC, NY

Marc was at the Mahopac school field around midnight, following his usual procedure: pointing his camera as directed telepathically. The results were two frames numbered 3 and 6 in the 126 camera film roll. After the film was developed, frame 3 showed a circular light on a dark background. It was about 1/8 inch diameter. This was enlarged many times, until it became visible to the eye. It was a circular, lighted area, yellowish in color, with a humanoid figure silhouetted in front and to one side of center. The head, arm and part of the body can be seen. Marc said this was the porthole of a spacecraft with a spaceman shown in the silhouette. It was the same night Marc also photographed a spaceship shooting an analyzing light disk probe on Frame 6.

MARCH - OCTOBER 1977 - MAHOPAC, NY

Marc would often go to the Mahopac school field between the hours of 11:30 P.M. to 4:00 A.M. He followed his usual procedure of aiming his camera at a part of the sky which he felt, telepathically, was what the space people wanted. Though no UFO was visible to his eye, he snapped the shutter when he felt the impulse to do so, and when the film was developed, a picture was seen. Most of his pictures during the late 1970s were taken this way.

MAY 1977

Six shots taken during different months show a green, crescent-shaped streak of light. Marc says he telepathically asked if the space people could send a spaceship to the area.

JUNE 30, 1977 - MAHOPAC, NY

Marc photographed, around 12:00 A.M., an orange-red UFO that left an ionization trail.

UFO Repeaters! Seeing Is Believing - The Camera Doesn't Lie!

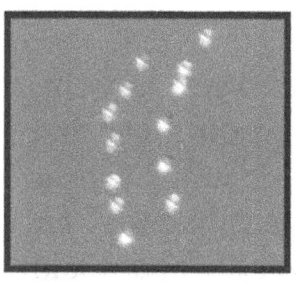

Formation, Upper West Side, from living room window, NYC Nov. 1, 2010

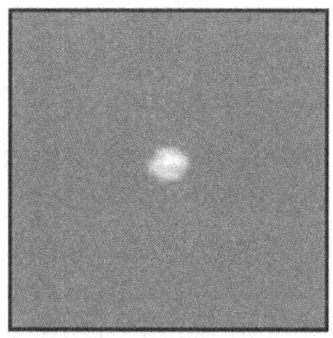

Golden Saturn UFO, Upper West Side, from living room window, NYC June 29, 2011 - movie film.

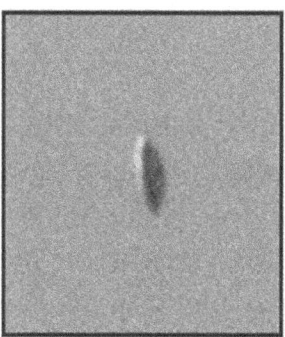

This classic saucer shape UFO flipped over and tilted at me while I captured it outside my living room window on the Upper West Side, NYC July. 16, 2012

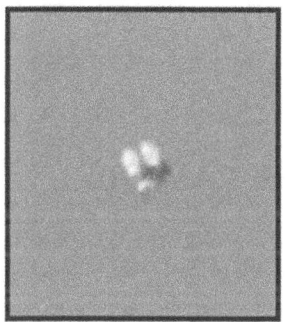

Morphing orbs with saucer shape UFO shot on Upper West Side, NYC, from living room window, Aug. 14, 2010.

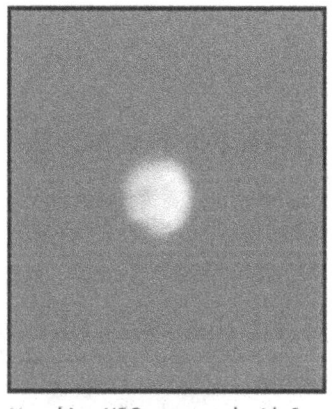

Morphing UFO, captured with 3 witnesses in Canaan, NY, July 27, 2011.

My wife shot this photo of me capturing the saucer UFO on July 16, 2012.

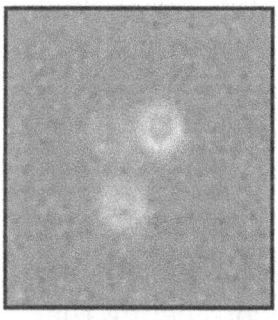

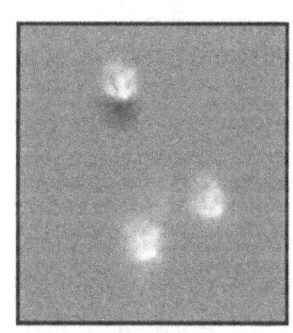

Morphing saucer shapes shot from Cooper Union, NYC, on way to visit my friend, Ingo Swann on my birthday, May 18, 2012.

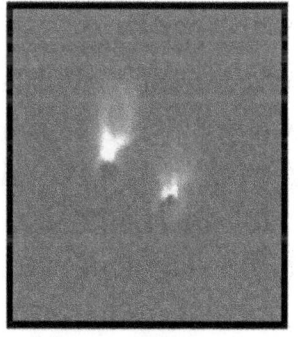

UFOs captured while visiting New York Botanical Garden, NY with 2 witnesses on April 19, 2012. They changed into a variety of shapes before disappearing.

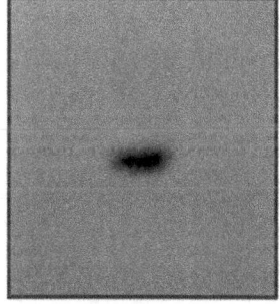

Saucer shaped UFO NY Botanical Gardens, NY June 8, 2012.

Morphing cylinder shape UFO Lexington & 86th bus stop, NYC, May 6, 2012.

MY PROCESS:
Often I am telepathically called to the window in my Upper West Side apartment to capture the ships. When I am walking outside, I am called to 'look up' in a particular direction and I will see them. Sometimes they come when I pray for them, but not always. I see way more than I am able to capture.

Marc's UFO photos over New York City. Seeing is believing!

OCT - DEC 1977

Different UFOs throughout these months would fly over Marc wherever he went. Usually the UFOs would come after 12:00 A.M. until around 4:00 A.M., and some would stop and hover. There were also many spaceships that would appear as a bright star, like Marc had seen in the 1960s. Marc called them "Rovers" for "Roving Stars." They would stop overhead, make right turns or zigzags and would answer verbal and telepathic questions if he had friends with him. The spaceships would go up and down to answer a "yes" question and left to right to answer a "no" question. Marc is still followed by UFOs who will telepathically call to him to "look up."

MOVIE FILM TAKEN BY MARC - GAF SUPER 8 MOVIE CAMERA

MARCH 1978 - MAHOPAC, NY

Bright, orange-colored disc was filmed in action over schoolyard in Mahopac. Marc calls it a "scout ship." The UFO appears on the movie film for 3 or 4 seconds, or about 20 frames before teleporting away.

APRIL 1978 – WARMINSTER, WILTSHIRE, ENGLAND

Marc was visiting Warminster, Wiltshire, England, and walked alone towards a field, which was away from some friends with him on a sky-watch. The sky was dark, the stars were visible and the night air cool. Marc had a good feeling that night and felt peaceful energy in the area where he stood. Intuitively feeling to aim his GAF Super 8 movie camera to the sky, he let the film roll along as he telepathically sent prayers and words of oneness and love to his space friends. When Marc went home to the United States, he had the film developed and, amazingly, it showed fifteen off-white, light, amber-edged glowing UFOs and a blue arc flying in formation. They flew across the movie screen a few times, changing their formation patterns.

JUNE 1978 – MAHOPAC, NY

Marc went to the Mahopac Middle School field near where he lived after 2:00 A.M. with his GAF Super 8 movie camera. He aimed the movie camera at the night sky and intuitively moved it to different areas in the sky. Marc would telepathically call to his space friends and ask if they could put something on the film. After developing the film and watching it, Marc found he captured three blue-white, glowing light beams moving upwards in the film and disappearing. They resembled the glowing beams on the underside of a UFO that was leaving the area. These images were studied by scientists and proven to be solid light objects on the film.

JULY 1978 – MAHOPAC, NY

Marc aimed his GAF Super 8 movie camera at the night sky under intuitive guidance from his space friends and said that, if they wanted to put anything on the film, they could. When the film was developed, it showed an elongated, white, glowing rectangular UFO that appeared as a bent light object moving across the screen.

Marc's films, negatives, GAF Super 8 movie camera and Instamatic cameras, were taken for analysis by the Scientific Bureau of Investigation in 1979. All were sent to three different organizations that run in-depth tests on cameras and film. The tests included checking cameras and film for light leaks or other ways of hoaxing film. All of Marc's cameras, negatives and movie films were found not to be flawed nor to exhibit any signs of tampering. The bent light image on the GAF Super 8 movie film was the one that stunned the ex-NASA scientists and other investigators the most because they could not replicate the bending light in any way onto film.

COMMUNICATION BY FLASHLIGHT WITH UFOs – ALSO ET CONTACT

MAY 18, 1978 - MAHOPAC, NY

While Marc was staying with a UFO group in Warminster, England, for a month, he asked if he could have a "25th year birthday sighting." His space contacts told him to be back home by May seventeenth. Excited by what might happen, Marc drove up to the Mahopac school field alone with his white German shepherd dog around 12:00 A.M. The night was misty and cool and it was raining heavily. Carrying his shoulder bag with a flashlight, one pair of binoculars, a GAF Super 8 movie camera and his Argus 257 Instamatic camera, all the while holding an umbrella, made it difficult to set up for sky-watching. Walking to a hill overlooking the field, Marc was experimenting with thought control over the rain. Several times he asked mentally for the rain to "speed up," and it did. He also asked for a "slowdown," and this also occurred on cue. Then the rain stopped for a few minutes. Suddenly, a bright pink glowing sphere flew horizontally about five feet over the treetops near the woods behind the school field! There was a faint pink light trail following behind it before it flashed off. The sphere traveled about 20 feet and looked about three feet in diameter. About ten minutes later, a white glowing sphere flashed on over some trees, hovered and then flashed off.

The rain began to come down in a steady flow while Marc held his umbrella, trying not to get any cameras wet. He took his flashlight and sent five flashes, on and off in a dot and dash pattern, towards the clouds. Instantly a light beamed from behind the clouds and sent back the same flashing sequence!

Marc tried to film it, but could not hold the umbrella, flash the light and hold the movie camera at the same time. He was intuitively told to look at the field. There appeared to be a heavy mist forming into a fifteen-foot high and roughly almost ten-foot wide dome shape on the ground. As Marc walked towards the smoky purple dome shape, the rain suddenly stopped and he was aware of an eight-foot tall male humanoid space being about four feet in front of him. The space being was standing near the center of the purple gray mist. The space being seemed to be comprised of a substance much denser than the ground mist but not totally "solid." No sound or words were heard, but a beautiful heavenly scent of garden flowers permeated the air around Marc. There were no flowers near the field and he remembered the floral scent seemed to manifest when his space friends were near.

Marc intuitively understood the being was an ultra-dimensional ET friend sending peaceful, loving energy towards him. Marc could see a few facial features clearly, too. The being was human-looking, with large, elongated eyes, hair to his shoulders, golden-bronze skin tones, wore a medium blue spacesuit and looked like one of the ET friends Marc met on a spaceship in 1958. Telepathically, he sent peaceful energy and a feeling of oneness, love and light towards the space being. A few seconds later, the benevolent ET telepathically sent a message to Marc, saying "Thank you. We all send love and blessings to you always." Soon after, the spaceman said he had to leave and in seconds faded away as the dense dome mist disappeared, too. He thanked his ET friends for making his birthday special. A few minutes later a light rain started to fall. Still feeling elated after meeting the alien, Marc and his dog walked back to the car and arrived back home around 2:15 A.M.

JUNE 2, 1978 - MAHOPAC, NY

At 1:20 A.M., Marc and Phyllis were on the Mahopac school field and asking telepathically for a contact. Marc flashed his flashlight and a white light appeared in the sky. Marc flashed three times, and the UFO flashed the same sequence back. It moved to the left and flashed three times, then diagonally upward, then back to the original spot, flashing three times at each point in an equilateral triangle it formed the sky.

***

Marc professes to have been receiving telepathic material, which he has written down in longhand in several notebooks. In 1977, he had collaborated with several people in this upstate area who have gotten similar data. One experiment, to verify the material, was this: Marc would sit in one room of his house with a collaborator in another room. Marc would ask a question mentally, and the collaborator would telepathically receive both the question and the answer. The nature of the answer was such that it was judged to be coming from the "Mother Ship" that Marc strongly believes he is in communication with.

Marc is also an extremely gifted artist and has created many paintings of spacecraft, scenes from other planets and unicorns, many of which have become commercially successful posters. And, while Marc is not shy about recounting his experiences in public, he has been extremely selective about doing certain radio and TV shows, telling his story only to those in the media who seem sincerely interested in finding out the truth about UFOs.

Does Marc actually have the ability to take photos of spaceships, or is something else equally strange going on? Does he, as some parapsychologists might suggest, have the ability to psychically imprint certain shapes and forms

UFO Repeaters! Seeing Is Believing - The Camera Doesn't Lie!

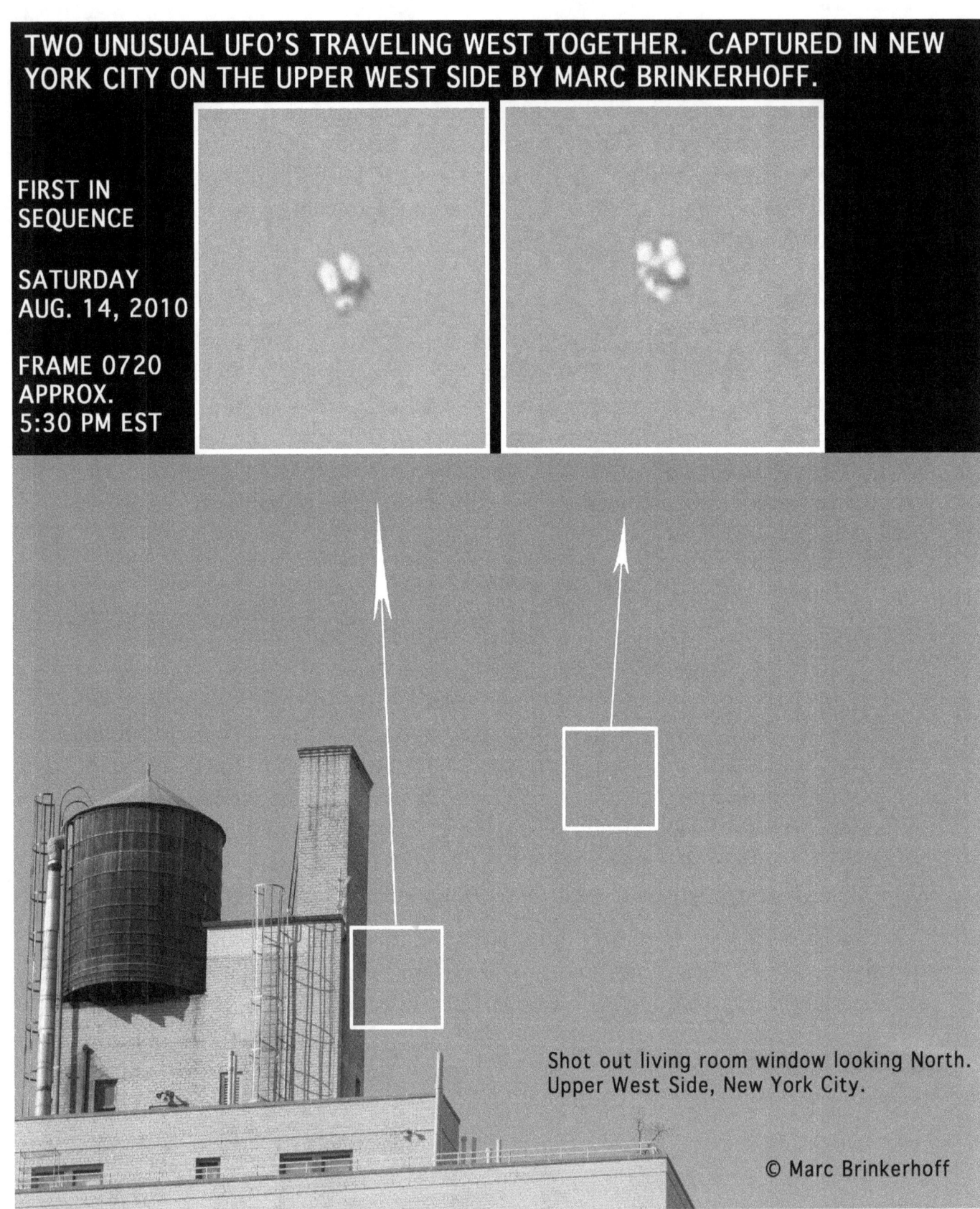

210

onto film, giving the impression that they are authentic UFOs, when, in fact, they might be a form of mental projection? There is, naturally, no proof that this is what is transpiring, though certain "gifted" individuals, such as Uri Geller and Ted Serios, seemed to be able to perform such feats of mental manipulation which go beyond the accepted fringe of science. Or is it possible that Marc is who he claims to be? Is it possible that he is a sort of a "Walk-In" who has arrived for spiritual purposes to help heal the wounds of humankind? Frankly, there are more questions than we have the answers for. But the fact remains that Marc Brinkerhoff has photographic PROOF that something is just "not right," and, hopefully, with proper investigation, we can reach some reasonable conclusions.

UFO "FOOL FOR THE CITY" – WITH HOMAGE TO JOHN LENNON

If you asked me, I would think that most readers wouldn't hesitate to accept Marc's multiple sightings and photographs. What we have related so far in the way of his experiences all seem to have taken place in rural areas, out of the way of prying eyes and smart-assed non-believers. If you're on a rural road or in a schoolyard, chances are no one is going to notice you or disturb your quiet demeanor as you go about scanning the sky and popping off a photo here and there. Since the ships are silent, it's not like a loud boom is going to wake you from your slumber or make you scan the heavens should you be taking the garbage out or walking your dog (he might notice before you anyway!).

But, hey, now we are about to visit sacred ground – because most of Marc's sightings in recent years have taken place in the middle of Manhattan, near Central Park, in broad daylight, where anyone could peer skyward and see what he is seeing – and photographing.

Now, mind you, these are not just lights in the sky. These are large, single objects and entire "fleets" putting on a show for Marc's benefit – and, I would assume, for ours as well. Look over the photos in this section and you cannot help but be AMAZED!

At least on some occasions, it's as though the objects are right outside Marc's apartment window.

So just how close do they get?

"Some of the spaceships I have seen were about 200 to 1000 feet up. One time two UFOs seemed to be right at the level of some buildings (which may be 20 stories high) a few blocks away that are directly across from my 8th floor living room window. When spaceships (UFOs), show up that close, they do not stay for very long. They usually teleport and flash off in the sky or slowly dematerialize. We have seen spaceships show up really close for just a few seconds and then disappear right before our eyes. This does not lend itself to being able to capture a photograph when that happens."

As to whether they are showing up to please him or are making merely "random appearances," Marc has this to say: "I would have to say, yes, they know I am inside or outside and often call telepathically to me to look out the window or look up if I'm outside. Many in New York City are pretty high up and I can only get a good glimpse with my binoculars that I keep right by the window. When I am in the country, the spaceships have appeared much closer, but I may be driving or I do not have a camera on me at the time. I never know when they might show up. I'm just told when they are visible, and sometimes they come when I pray and call to them, but not always. Sometimes when I am outside or in the country, I may get an intuitive feeling my ET friends are overhead in the sky invisibly in a spaceship. I would 'feel' to look up at the sky and suddenly a spaceship would fly into view! It is one of their ways; they have liked to give me a surprise since I was very young."

In October 2010, there was a rash of sightings in New York City that made the front page of the tabloids and was the talk of the town on radio and TV. I even did a half-hour "play by play" that week on Coast to Coast AM with George Noorey asking me pointed questions about the Big Apple UFO flap.

The sightings were in the neighborhood where the Edgar Cayce group, the Association of Research and Enlightenment, were holding a weekend-long seminar on the crystal skulls. There were approximately 500 people in attendance and at least a dozen skulls. A lot of those present said they could feel the energy and could not dismiss the fact that a number of UFOs showed up over the nearby buildings in the Chelsea section of Manhattan. The ships appeared in formation and sat motionless in the sky for what seemed like hours, belying the notion offered by skeptics that they were balloons that had lifted off from a graduation party upriver in Westchester County.

A few days before, I had met Marc at a social gathering organized by UFO promoter Michael Luckman in Greenwich Village. Marc had with him several snapshots of UFOs hovering near his apartment building. I thought perhaps there was a connection with these seemingly "coincidental" events.

"Since I was not there," Marc told me, "I cannot say for sure what people were seeing in Chelsea on October 13, 2010. However, after researching the event and checking with my ET crew, this is what they told me: The ETs from the Ashtar Command took advantage of the opportunity to 'hide in plain sight' among many balloons and knew the ships that were not balloons would be seen as a sign to the people who attended the October 10, 2010 Crystal Skull event here in New York.

"Regarding UFOs and sky events, " Marc pointed out, "there have been times during airplane shows or when there are skywriting planes flying when some people have reported seeing the planes being trailed by one or two shiny silver or colored spheres. I actually saw a silver sphere hovering in the sky near some clouds soon after I had seen skywriting planes go by many years ago. The orbs or spheres are not always UFOs with people in them. Many times a small sphere can be a monitoring probe sent to observe an area. Most of the monitoring probes are sent by benevolent space beings to observe the Earth. The spheres can be any size, color or shape as well; even small disks shaped like plates with domes or small oval objects have been seen in the sky. Some monitoring probe spheres or orbs can be from 5 to 8 inches in diameter on up to 3 feet to 20 feet in diameter. The monitoring spheres can see a lot of detail from high up, many times better than our own satellites. The monitoring probes are usually directed by either a giant starship (which is usually vibrationally shrouded to appear invisible and is very high up in the sky) or by cloaked or camouflaged spaceships that may also come from a dimension near our physical one. Many benevolent ETs from the Ashtar Command are observing and monitoring areas in cities and towns all over the Earth."

We wanted to know if his friendly visitors from afar are in contact with him via mental telepathy as they "hang out" nearby in the sky opposite his apartment window. "Yes. I can see through my Over-Soul's eyes as they see through mine when my ET friends connect telepathically to me. It feels like I am in two places at once in my thoughts and having clear, colorful visions of deep space travel. Many times it is like I am seeing a movie in my Third Eye area. I can intuitively see and feel what my Over-Soul is doing and where my ET friends (who I have long called the Upstage Crew since the early 1970s) are flying to when they are traveling in a spaceship. Many times I have seen amazing nebulae and breathtaking galaxies through their eyes in a telepathic vision."

And would they put on an even stronger show of power if they were able to? "The ETs I am in contact with are all benevolent and are Space Teachers and Ascended ET Masters. They do not wish to show force or power, which could be misinterpreted and appear as a mass UFO takeover. If that happened, it would NOT be The Ascended ET Masters from my group or the Ashtar Command. The benevolent ETs would rather be invited by the leaders of a planet to come and work together to find solutions to global problems, but they would not choose one government over another."

But is he the only one to see these UFOs, or are there other witnesses – perhaps friends or neighbors – whom the benevolent aliens take within their visual sphere of reference and reveal themselves?

"A few of our friends Marie, Diane and others have been witnesses in recent times when I have telepathically called in UFOs and filmed them," Marc replied. "On July 27, 2011, our friend Marie was thrilled to witness a UFO for the first time in her life, after I telepathically called to my space friends and Ashtar's crews to stop by if they were in the area. When we were at the MOMA Sculpture Garden in New York City on August 21, 2012, our friends Diane and Myrna all witnessed seven UFOs that came a few minutes after I telepathically prayed and asked for a sighting. One of my doormen witnessed a UFO and has seen them after I told him how the ETs call telepathically for us to 'Look up.' He was called a few times as well to 'Look up' in front of our building and saw a white, glowing sphere hovering above him. It stayed for a while and then would move a little and flash off."

And what – if any – plans do the ultra-terrestrials have in store for humankind? Are we soon going to find ourselves in the midst of mass sighting waves all over the planet, as some UFO Repeaters and contactees have predicted? Marc hedges his bet a bit on this when he answers: "As I mentioned earlier, the groups I'm in contact with would NOT be responsible for a mass sighting. However, I feel there may be more group sightings of UFOs around the world in the coming years, including with UFO formations as well. The more frequently people see the spaceships, the more the masses will undoubtedly realize ETs exist. This will eventually open up a possibility for dialogue with our ET brothers and sisters. But, again, I'm talking about my higher dimensional ET friends and family who take the 'prime directive' seriously."

UFO Repeaters! Seeing Is Believing - The Camera Doesn't Lie!

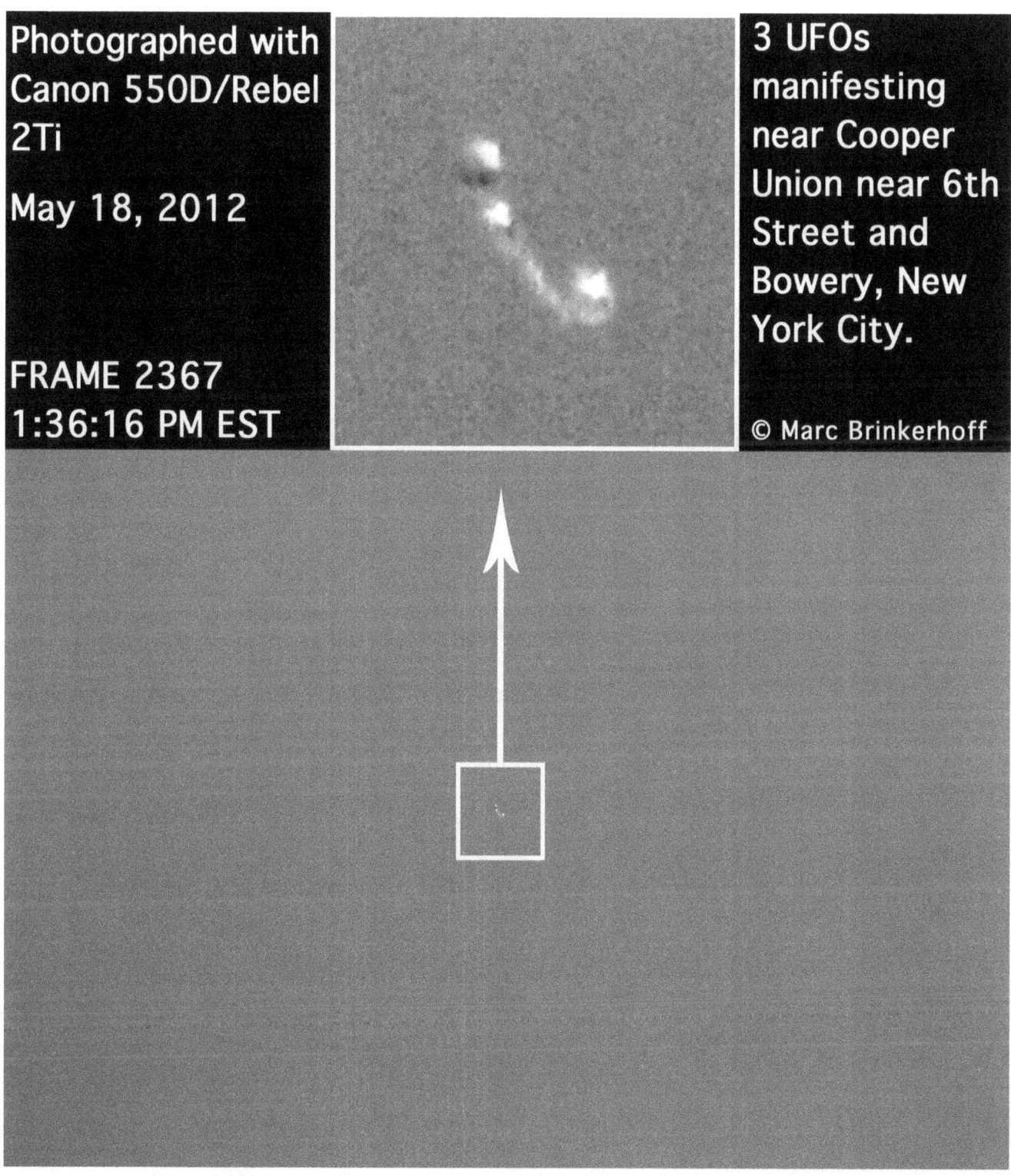

UFO Repeaters! Seeing Is Believing - The Camera Doesn't Lie!

Marc updates his web sites frequently (www.IntergalacticMission.com / www.MarcBrinkerhoff.com), and by typing his name in on YouTube you will find various workshops and lectures he has given. His ET contact and ability to photograph UFOs continue to this day. A recent on-air interview I did with Marc can be found at www.TheOuterEdgeRadio.com and is certainly worth a listen. And so excuse me while I grab a pair of binoculars and join Marc as we look out over the Manhattan skyline. To quote what John Lennon sang on his "Double Fantasy" album:

Nobody told me there would be days like these.

Nobody told me there would be days like these.

Nobody told me there would be days like these.

Most peculiar, Mama

There's UFOs over New York and I'm not too surprised.

Sources

www.marcbrinkerhoff.com

www.intergalacticmission.com

UFO Review

UFO Universe

UFO Repeaters! Seeing Is Believing - The Camera Doesn't Lie!

TOM DONGO, SEDONA AND THE BRADSHAW RANCH

By Timothy Green Beckley

JUST about everyone knows that there is something about the town of Sedona, located in the red rock country of Arizona that is mystical and magical. It draws 4 million visitors a year like a magnet. They come from all over the world to hike, rock climb and attune themselves with nature. They take part in vision quests, meditate with crystals and dream-catchers and, above all else, look for UFOs. And some of them are very lucky – some more than others. Perhaps one man most of all.

If you go to my YouTube Channel – *Mr UFOs Secret Files* – and watch the video *"Invisible Aliens 'Invade' Town – Underground Bases Exposed,"* you will get an agreeable, pleasant view of the town's supernatural underpinnings as experienced by a gentlemen who seems to be trailed by all that is unexplained and decisively strange.

Tom Dongo runs the ultimate and most illuminating jeep tour of Sedona. He knows the continuum of this place like the back of his hand as well as its incredible geology. And, if you want to go on a UFO Sky-Watch, you've picked the person who knows his alien lore – from the location of possible underground bases to secret canyons where UFOs have been known to hide.

On a recent visit to Sedona, when Tom came to where I was staying, he didn't arrive empty handed. Under his arm he had two hefty photo albums, the

UFO Repeaters! Seeing Is Believing - The Camera Doesn't Lie!

Above: The nature of Tom Dongo's various experiences in Sedona are highly unusual even for a UFO Repeater.

Below: Three UFOs meandering about over Sedona on an unknown mission.

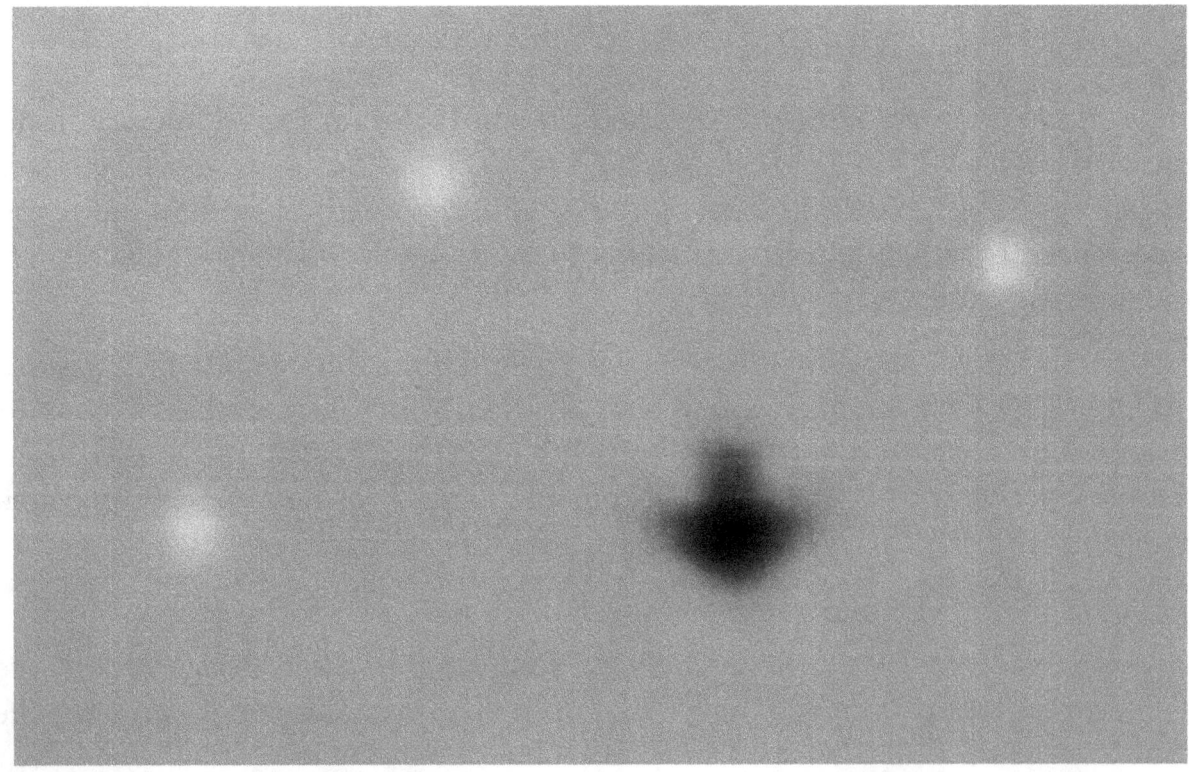

kind with glossy pockets that you can place 8.5x11 prints in for protection so that they don't get fingerprints all over them or have drinks spilled on the one-of- a-kind pictures.

Seated on the couch, my associate Charla Gené and I bombarded Tom with questions for an hour or more as he thumbed through the albums, selecting prime photos to show us which offer "nonrefundable" proof that Sedona is "up there" when it comes to high-strangeness UFO cases. There were orange orbs, entities that showed up in pictures when they were not visible to the human eye and weird machines nestled back among the red rocks like something out of a science-fiction backyard. Sedona is known for its various vortexes, including one near the post office and one located on the road to the small community airport. Here again is an instance where the UFO shenanigans seem at least partially to do with a specific local – i.e., Sedona a known portal or UFO "window area" – but are centered on one or possibly a number of UFO Repeaters as the primary impetus.

Tom Dongo would certainly fit that category as he waxes about the topic philosophically. "I find the whole subject of UFOs and ETs, as well as anything connected to that subject, to be absolutely fascinating – even some of the attributes of the phenomenon viewed by some with a measure of fear and loathing or even terror. I think the reason for the fear is, in part, that many people fail entirely to grasp the actual magnitude of the presence of alien beings here on our planet.

"I feel that the existence alone of these ET entities, as well as the almost inconceivable technology and mental abilities they must possess, is an opportunity for us to learn from them. It is a chance for us to break away finally from the railroad track-like rut we have been in for so long. Look, for example, at some of our social, economic and religious belief patterns. Some, if not all of them, should have been tossed in the junk pile decades ago. Worst of all, like obedient sheep, the common man has been manipulated into position by greedy and power-hungry individuals for thousands of years.

"This is a good chance to make a new start – a clean, fresh start. Will it take something like bizarre-looking space aliens to jolt humanity out of our subservient, materialistic lethargy? Humanity surely needs to begin to work cooperatively together to create heaven on earth and to preserve what was given us to cherish."

UFO Repeaters! Seeing Is Believing - The Camera Doesn't Lie!

Above: Tim Beckley strolls about near the red rocks of Sedona.
Photo by Charla Gene.

Below: After spending several days socializing and interviewing Alan Benz, the former librarian for the long defunct Aerial Phenomena Research Organization (APRO), Beckley motored on to Sedona with associate Charla Gene. Upon leaving the Coffee Pot Cafe and returning to their vehicle, they noticed the "unusual nature" of the license plate on the rear of the car parked immediately next to them. The plate's initials spelled out APRO, an organization once based in Tucson which hasn't existed in over two decades. A mere coincidence? Not in Sedona, where synchronicities are an every day occurrence.

UFO Repeaters! Seeing Is Believing - The Camera Doesn't Lie!

Gloria Reiser took this strange photo in Boynton Canyon in 1990. Behind her is a "machine" that looks like something out of a bad sci fi movie. "Kronos" comes to mind.

And while UFO sightings and encounters have not been confined to any one locale around Sedona (a tall, translucent being was even seen crossing the road in traffic a few years ago) one spot has generated more reports over the course of time than anywhere else in this community known for such natural landmarks as Bell Rock and Cathedral Rock.

Though once privately owned, today there is a fence that runs all around the Bradshaw Ranch, keeping out interlopers and the curious who have heard of its reputation as a portal opening into another realm.

Renowned investigator William Hamilton III filed this written document with me while I was editing the nationally distributed "*UFO UNIVERSE*" magazine. It carefully lays out his research on Sedona and the Bradshaw Ranch, using UFO Repeater Tom Dongo as the focal point for the long list of strange phenomena.

THE RANCH ON THE EDGE OF FOREVER:
THE BRADSHAW RANCH

By William Hamilton III

There are places of mystery in the world. Strange things are seen and bizarre events unfold in these mysterious places. Sedona, Arizona, is such a mysterious place. Visitors flock to this Arizona New Age capital to view the striking red cliffs and rocks that highlight the verdant growth of pine and juniper as well as to feel the uplifting energy of Sedona's vortices. Conservative people think the vortex believers are a little short of a full deck. After all, if the vortex is invisible, how does one know that a vortex is on one sight and not another. Even if people rightly claimed that they could feel the energy of the vortex, why didn't it just twirl them around?

There are other visible mysteries that occur in the Sedona region. There are UFOs and strange orbs of light that move through the back canyons, notably Long and Boynton Canyons. A mysterious military or para-military presence has been reported in Boynton Canyon, Secret Canyon and Sycamore Canyon. Back in 1991, I traveled to Sedona to visit a man who lived in Long Canyon. John was a caretaker on an old housing project. He had sighted a large boomerang traveling from the direction of Secret Canyon in the north to the edge of Sedona in the

UFO Repeaters! Seeing Is Believing - The Camera Doesn't Lie!

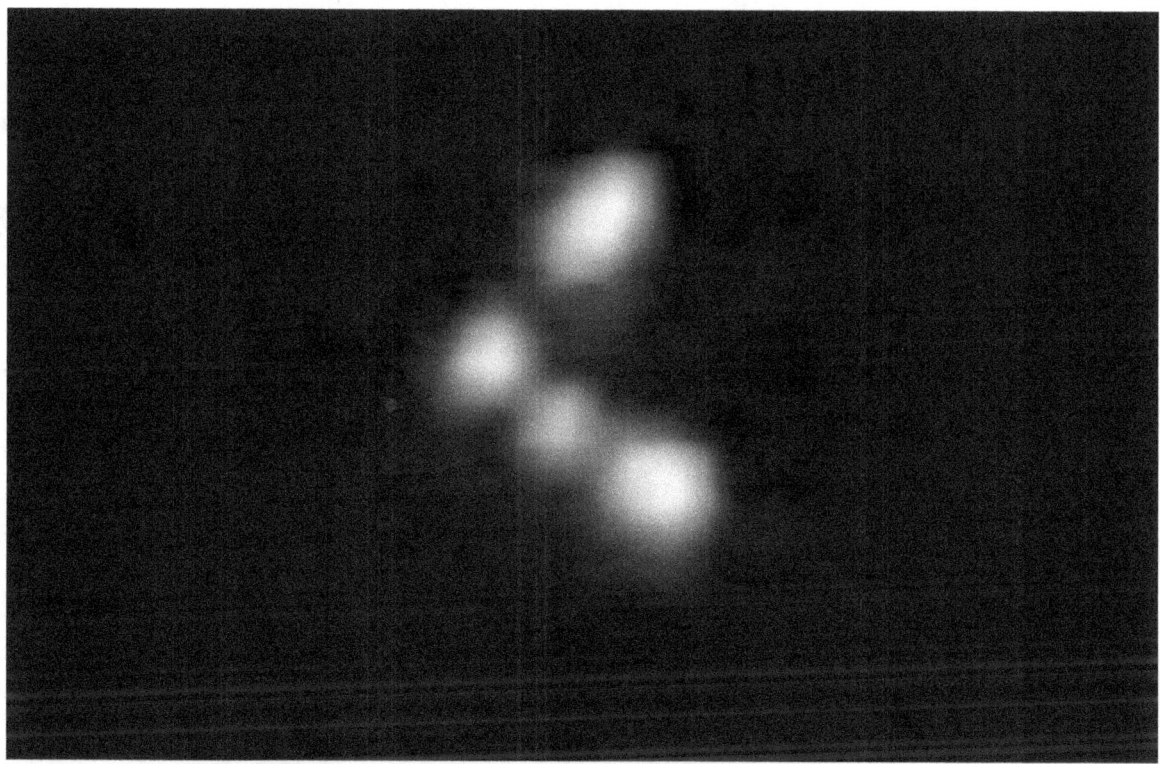

Above: A spectacular UFO in the heavens of nearby Cave Creek, Arizona.

Below: No photo collection would be complete without at least one rod or cigar-shaped object such as this one in the MUFON files.

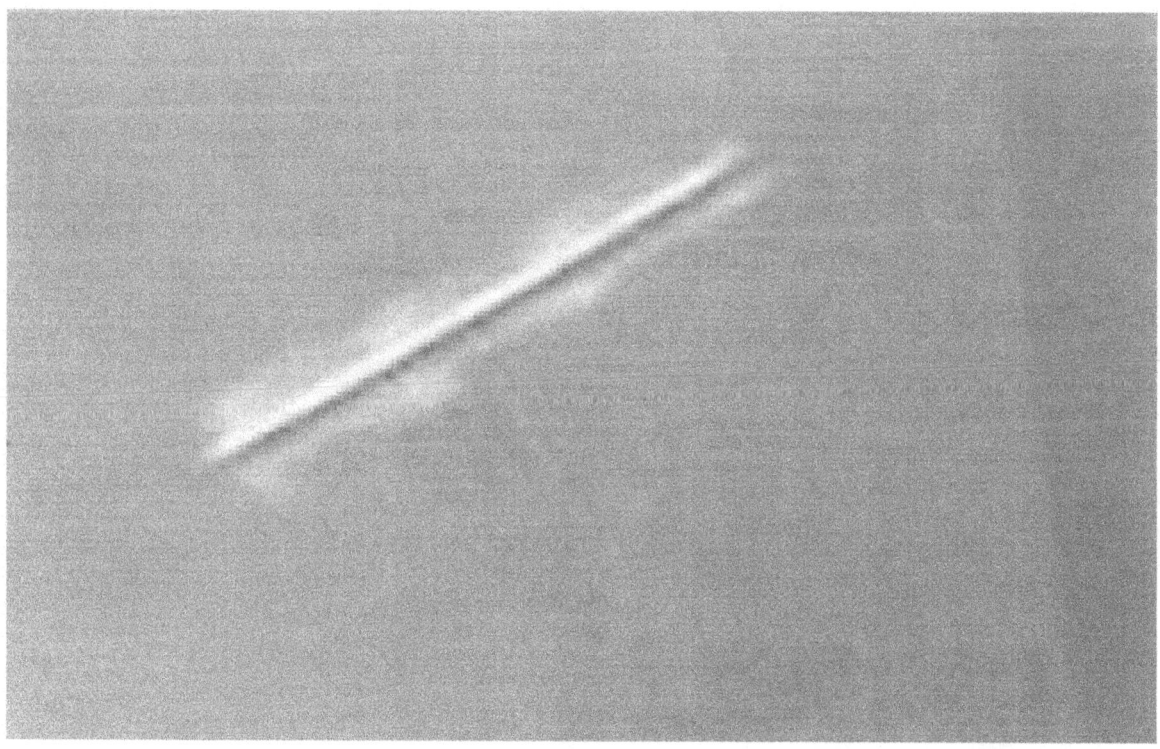

UFO Repeaters! Seeing Is Believing - The Camera Doesn't Lie!

One would be hard pressed to find an "ordinary" explanation for this disc in the sky.

south. The remarkable thing about this very large vehicle was its attitude of flight: it was flying on end and leaving a sparkling trail!

Strange, unmarked helicopters had been seen coming from the direction of Secret Canyon and flying south, the same direction as the boomerang flew. That day when I was in one section of Long Canyon I could hear the whooping blades of a helicopter behind the mountains to the north. Shortly, an olive drab helicopter flew low over the trees after taking off from somewhere within the canyon. Once, a fellow investigator tried to hike back to Secret Canyon around one o'clock in the morning when he heard the whooping swish of helicopter blades. Attempting to follow the trail back into the canyon, he was stopped by a voice that emanated from a loudspeaker warning him to go no further. Thinking the speaker was there to ward off hunters, he proceeded further until he was stopped again, this time by a laser-targeting light moving around his chest. From the direction of the laser's source, he heard another voice telling him that he had entered a restricted area and that he was to turn around at once.

Field investigator and researcher Tom Dongo has spent his last few years living in the Sedona area, interviewing witnesses and chasing UFO sightings, abductions and other paranormal phenomena as well as trying to track down the reports of a secret military presence in the canyons. He has written books on his findings. He kept searching for a focus for the phenomena and found three; one was on a 90-acre ranch off the Boynton Canyon back roads in an isolated canyon between Red Canyon and Loy Butte.

Our friend Kim had moved to Sedona to raise her children and attend Northern Arizona University in Flagstaff. We introduced her to Tom and she started going on nightly sorties with Tom out to the ranch in this isolated canyon where all manner of things were happening. Tom always brought his camera loaded with 400 ASA film and a time exposure trigger. Kim brought her own camera. They would shoot one, two or three rolls of film just pointing and shooting whenever they felt moved. The owners of the ranch are Bob and Linda Bradshaw. Bob was a freelance photographer as well as a rancher and his beautiful photos of Arizona landscapes have been published in books and magazines. Linda seems to be the contact point between worlds. Her experiences of the paranormal go back to childhood.

My wife and I were invited to go out on a sortie and meet Linda. We gathered our cameras, video camera, binoculars and tri-field detector and headed north for Sedona on October 7, 1995. I was prepared to meet the unknown.

UFO Repeaters! Seeing Is Believing - The Camera Doesn't Lie!

Tom Dongo and Tim Beckley on Schnebly Hill Sedona

In keeping with the theme of this chapter, when photographer Charla Gene went through her album of photos of Tom and Tim in Sedona, these two weird "clouds" appeared in the sky over Schnebly Hill where they were skywatching.

UFO Repeaters! Seeing Is Believing - The Camera Doesn't Lie!

We rendezvoused at Kim's house in Sedona. Tom arrived, bringing photographs that he had taken at the ranch. These photos mostly showed a variety of inexplicable light phenomena. In one photo, a randomly-laced trail of variously-colored light hovered over the ground. Other photos showed light streaks, orbs, and, in a few cases, structured objects. Tom did not see most of these lights and orbs, but they registered clearly on his film. I was eager to travel out to the ranch site before sunset so I could get a look at the surrounding terrain.

We traveled in two vehicles, Tom in his van and the rest of us in Kim's trans-sport van. We piled jackets and cameras in the back. The road was rough and rocky in places and riding in the van gave me the feeling of riding in a nineteenth-century stagecoach. The last mile or two along the ranch road was the roughest surface we had yet encountered. We managed to arrive as the sun was setting, and I could still get a good daylight view of the property. The main house and two other buildings sat squarely at the bottom of a little valley surrounded by trees and bushes. We were far away from city noise. Linda and her dogs came out to greet us as we disembarked from the vans, making us feel welcome and invited. We went into a well-decorated house that had all of the accouterments one would expect to find in an urban house and sat around the kitchen table. Linda served us coffee and handed us a large photo album filled with the strange pictures of paranormal light phenomena. The sheer number of such photos was remarkable. Others have taken similar photos, but not in such quantity. Linda told us parts of her story as we sat looking through her fascinating photo album.

Linda tells us that she has experienced strange phenomena all her life, but, after moving onto the ranch, the frequency and strangeness of the experiences increased. One night while she and her husband were sitting in the kitchen they heard a noise that sounded like shattering glass come from inside their kitchen space, but nothing was seen and no shards of glass were ever found. She has heard footsteps both outside and inside the house when nobody could be seen. To further compound the mysterious events, some unknown agency would lift her camera at night and snap pictures around various parts of the house. One picture showed the light over the kitchen table, yet the area surrounding the light was completely dark! Another picture taken by the unknown agent showed the yard as seen through one of the kitchen windows, but it wasn't quite the same yard, as a portion of the scene seemed blocked off by a mysterious illuminated border.

As it was getting darker and a full moon was rising in the east, we decided to gather our coats and equipment and go for a walk around the property. Linda

UFO Repeaters! Seeing Is Believing - The Camera Doesn't Lie!

Above: An orb conspicuously sitting on a tree branch.

Below: Large orange orb photographed at the base of the Bradshaw Ranch.

first took us to the horse corral. There were many nights when her horses were spooked by something that left tracks in the dirt. These large three-toed tracks were not identifiable as belonging to any of the known wildlife in the canyons. Linda indicated a trail that we could walk toward an old Western movie set that had been erected some time ago. She said that we would find more tracks as we walked into the Old West town. Most of the buildings were just facades. Linda said we should look for the tracks of Big Girl, a Bigfoot that both she and her son had seen on occasion and which had left evidence of its presence at nearby locations.

I was told that if I tripped my camera flash in the dark that I would see that the air was filled with an unusual sparkling energy. I deliberately flashed my camera in the dark while looking through the viewfinder, and, indeed, I could see glowing particles filling the air. Seeking a conventional explanation for this spectacle, I surmised that particles of dust must be suspended in the air, and that my flash simply reflected off these numerous particles of dust. But, as I continued the experiment, I noticed that the glittering particles did not move around as I have seen dust move but rather seemed to be suspended or frozen in the air.

As we continued walking, I noticed from time to time that a tiny light would flicker on in distant bushes then extinguish. I asked Tom about this and he said that he noticed this on all of his frequent excursions out there. They appeared to be like the fireflies I used to watch at my uncle's house on Long Island when I was a young boy. But fireflies were not known in Arizona.

Tom kept looking around the horizon for the lights of UFOs. He claims that the frequency of UFO sightings over the canyons had picked up lately. He then proceeded to pull night-vision binoculars out of his pack to scan the horizon more closely for signs of movement. I could see a number of aircraft lights off in the distance to the south and east of us. When we came to the movie set we turned our flashlights on the ground and could make out some unusual tracks. One track looked exactly like those I had seen published of alleged Bigfoot tracks. I photographed it. Other tracks were of the large three-toed variety akin to those made by large birds or small dinosaurs.

At the end of the trail sat a platform made into a gallows. It was an ominous sight to greet in the light of the full moon. The women climbed the stairs to sit on the platform followed by one of Linda's dogs. Tom and I walked around, scanning the horizon for any faint movement. The air was still and silent. Occasionally, Tom would raise his camera and shoot on a seeming whim. When

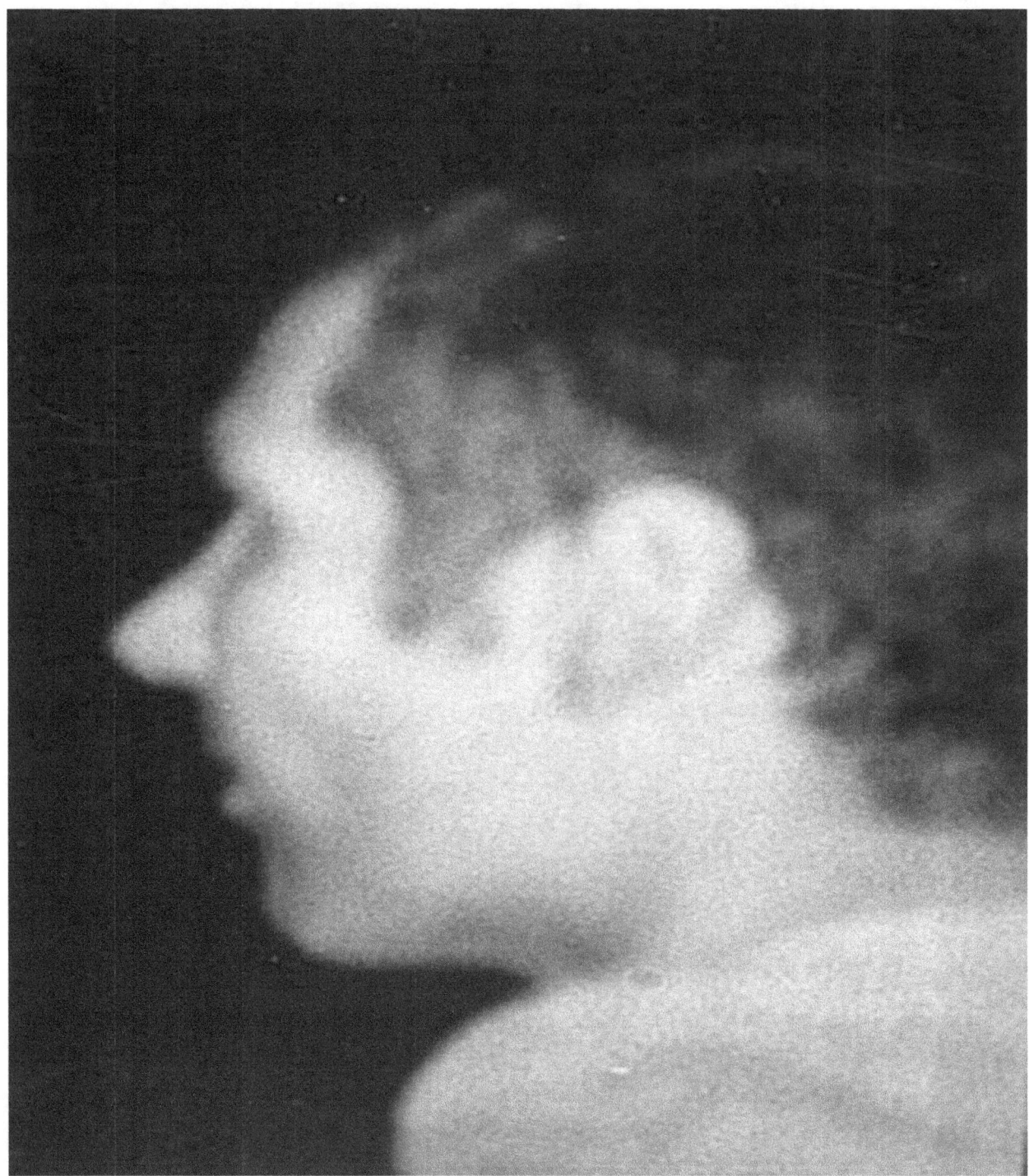

The "Blue Haired Man Of Sedona" was not seen at the time the photo was taken. Noted Tom Dongo: "Linda (Bradshaw) and I were standing side-by-side when she took the Blue Haired Man photograph. We were the only ones in the vicinity. The only thing that really strikes me as uncanny is the angled forward V-shaped sideburn. Here's why. The sideburn is in all ways identical to the sideburns worn by James T. Kirk and the Enterprise crew from the original 'Star Trek' series. This makes me wonder if Gene Roddenberry was privy to certain information before anyone else."

the camera flashed, I could see the strange glitter in the air, but nothing else seemed out of place or mysterious.

After standing around for a half hour or so, we headed back to the ranch. When we all got cozy in the kitchen, Linda served coffee and I started to ask more questions. Linda told me about her son Victor's experiences. Victor had taken a hike back in the canyons one day and stumbled upon some white trucks and men in white suits. One flat-bed truck carried a wingless craft on its bed. Victor felt that he was being observed. He had his video cam at the ready and was scanning the scene below his position when he thought he heard a noise in the bushes behind him. When he turned to look, he saw a creature peering back at him and then ducking out of sight. This creature looked like a typical gray alien. On another hiking expedition into the canyons, he had become lost. He was walking in one place in daylight; then he found himself in an unknown location and it was suddenly night!

Tom had also seen a creature, but it was right near the ranch. One night while Kim and Linda were talking, he saw a small humanoid in a brown suit dash across the field near the juniper tree. The dogs gave chase, barking and running after the entity. As it neared the fence line, it seemed to vanish into thin air, and the dogs quite suddenly gave up the chase. Tom had never seen anything like this and was startled after the entity vanished from sight.

Linda gave me a copy of the book that she and Tom had published, titled "Merging Dimensions." It is replete with dozens of photos. Unfortunately, the photos are reproduced in black and white and one misses seeing some of the startling colors that are visible in the original photos. Each of them are accumulating more anomalous photos every week. Anomalies have also appeared on some of Kim's photos.

Pamela and I went back to the ranch for a second visit on December 7, 1995. The night was even colder than the first night's visit. After nightfall, the stars sparkled like jewels. Tom set his camera up on a tripod with a timer attached to the camera to get long exposure photos of distant moving lights. Tom and Linda had been seeing "a ship" that would characteristically pop up behind some far hills to the south and west. Pamela had loaded her camera with 400 ASA film. We did see some unusual moving lights that night, but they seemed too far off to classify them as UFOs. Sky-watching is a game that involves a lot of patience.

UFO Repeaters! Seeing Is Believing - The Camera Doesn't Lie!

MERGING DIMENSIONS
THE OPENING PORTALS OF SEDONA
TOM DONGO AND LINDA BRADSHAW

Tom Dongo's book, "Merging Dimensions," contains some of the most stunning photographic images taken of unknown aerial objects in and around Sedona.

UFO Repeaters! Seeing Is Believing - The Camera Doesn't Lie!

During a break in our watch, I went inside to get warm and convinced Linda to show me the video that Victor had pieced together from several different shoots around the canyon. This fifteen to twenty-minute video was shot in daylight and darkness. On it I saw some of the most peculiar "things" flitting around near the ground. One segment focused on a low-flying airplane which was blocked out by a brilliant orb of light that flew across the plane's path. The video was compelling. Very strange things were happening on this ranch.

I kept asking Linda for details about the photograph of the window or gateway taken near the juniper tree. She had only seen a bright rectangle of light, yet the developed photo looks like a window into another world. Unless Tom, Linda and now Kim were in collusion on a magnificent hoax, I would have to think that the photos are untampered with and show what they purport to show. While it is true that they have not been subject to expert analysis, it still leads one to speculate about the happenings on the Bradshaw Ranch.

There seem to be three significant elements to the Bradshaw events: 1) The Gateway Window; 2) the ever-present orbs; and 3) the sparkling energy in the air. The presence of humanoid entities, mysterious craft and mysterious animals seemed tied into the elements offering clues to the mysterious world that was intersecting our familiar world in this remote canyon beyond Sedona.

Looking at the Gateway photo reveals a number of things. The scene inside the window area is in daylight. A structure that looks exactly like a telephone pole with the cross struts and insulators is on the right. A third of the way down from the top of the window one can see a dark oval object that looks like a flying saucer. At the bottom left corner is a jumble of indistinct objects that could be foliage or even a humanoid figure. What is even stranger is an embossed area to the left of the phone pole that looks like a light, round object with projecting lines and the number 39 raised up to the right of the round object. There are two photos of the window taken in rapid succession before the window closed down. There are no telephone poles on the ranch property and there are certainly none stuck in the ground next to the juniper tree. If one wanted to come up with a hoax scenario, it would have to involve snapping a picture in daylight and superimposing it over a picture taken at night in another location. Of course, then one would have to explain how the daylight photo was taken of a hubcap or some other plain object thrown into the air to simulate a flying disk. Photo experts could examine the negatives for signs of double exposure or superposition. I, for one, would like to see the photos analyzed, but, for the sake of argument, let us

Above: Could this be an Ultra-terrestrial in the middle of shape shifting?

Below: Orb photo taken on a Tom Dongo UFO and Orb tour June 2009.

examine the implications inherent if the photos were taken as described by the witness. Additionally supporting the authenticity of the photos is the fact that photos taken by Kim and Pamela also show anomalous images.

A little research on photographic film reveals that it is essentially a thin plastic base coated with an emulsion. The emulsion is composed of gelatin within which tiny particles of light-sensitive salts have been suspended. Because of the silver halides in the emulsion, all light-sensitive photographic emulsions are sensitive to the blue, violet and ultraviolet end of the visible and invisible spectrum. There are emulsions that make film sensitive to infrared frequencies and, of course, film made sensitive for x-rays. Objects beyond the range of sight could register on various types of film. No special film or filters were used by Tom or Linda to capture the invisible energies around them.

Some percentage of abductees have reported seeing glowing orbs. These orbs will appear in the abductee's house and pass right through solid barriers. In Brian Scott's case, he reported seeing an orb pass in front of a dresser mirror without reflecting in the mirror. Others have reported seeing orbs float above the ground without reflecting light off the ground even when the orb appeared brilliant to the observer. Orbs have appeared of various colors and from baseball to basketball-sized. An orb is a good candidate for a hyper-dimensional object. Not all of the orbs photographed are visible yet they appear on film as translucent objects.

Even when orbs are visible, they are capable of passing through a solid wall or closed window. Their light emission may excite the optic nerves in humans and animals yet may not reflect off surrounding surfaces. In actuality, the light-band frequencies of radiation may pass through a material object because they cannot be fully absorbed or re-radiated by atomic electrons. And yet their radiation will affect film because of radiation at ultraviolet frequencies. The impression made on the film shows variations in photon density between different orbs appearing in the same image. We can only surmise that there exist stages of progressive materialization of hyper-dimensional objects where they can appear only as a ghostly glow or become a fully objectified source of light. The evidence viewed in this way gives strength to the idea that the hyper-dimensional parameter is a frequency dimension and not an extra-spatial dimension. In other words, the orb is moving into and out of this dimension by shifting its frequency and perhaps its phase.

According to physicists, subatomic particles are composed of wave packets, and these matter waves can pass through a small slit and show evidence of wave-like interference. Most of the matter waves we can see absorb and reflect photons within a narrow band of frequencies. Suppose objects composed of higher frequency wave packets, and out-of-phase with our normal mundane sensible world, were to approach a mundane material barrier composed of everyday protons and electrons. It would probably look just like a ghost passing through a wall. The wall would offer it little or no resistance. If a hyper-dimensional cesium atom would be compared to a mundane cesium atom in normal dimensions, we would probably measure a faster rate of time and the space the cesium atom passed through would be isolated and separate from our normal space. There could be various levels of dimensional states. Without a more rigorous data collection and analysis, this remains only a speculative hypothesis.

We might also consider that the "glitter" seen in the air around the ranch property is caused by radiation from another dimension causing excitations in atmospheric molecules. Some of the molecules of oxygen and nitrogen could be absorbing radiation from the other side of the dimensional barrier, causing random photon re-radiation in the air. The "glitter" appeared static. These glittering particles did not seem to be moving.

The implications of these phenomena require a reassessment of the nature of physical reality. If our scientists are studying only a portion of physical reality and basing theoretical models on the data collected from only one frequency dimension of the universe, then we may be harboring a very narrow view of this all-encompassing universe. Other worlds peopled by other beings might not only be found in the far reaches of intergalactic space but in the near reaches of extradimensional space.

A phenomena that resembles the orbs is ball lightning. Ball lightning usually appears during thunderstorms. The ball is usually bright, fuzzy and orange-yellow in color. Ball lightning has been seen that was up to 16 feet in diameter. Ball lightning has been seen to materialize inside enclosures, even an all-metal aircraft. How it accomplishes this feat is unknown. If we could produce ball lightning in a laboratory, we could probably experiment and record its weird behavior and antics and gain some insight as to how the orbs materialize inside of homes.

The typical view is that a parallel reality exists along a fourth-dimensional spatial axis; however, it is possible that a parallel reality exists along a fourth-dimensional temporal axis or energy axis. If space and time are fundamental dimensions, then it is possible that universes exist in other dimensions of space and time. The real hint comes from the energy expended in moving from a point in our world to a point in some adjacent world. But until some scientists take this phenomena under serious study, we are not likely to demystify these bizarre happenings.

Some UFOs may be someone else's spacecraft from an extra-solar planet in our Milky Way galaxy, but some UFOs may be visiting us from points of space that cannot be seen. I remember a conversation that I had with my informant, Charlie, about objects that had completely disappeared from the surface of the Earth, some of which he acknowledged were known about and others that were classified as military secrets. According to Charlie, not all UFOs come to Earth from outer space. Some tunnel here from another space-time dimension. He told me that some of the recovered crashed discs had a unit that we called a "trans-spatial resonator." These resonators could open portals and allow the craft to pass from one dimension to another. Maybe Charlie is telling the truth. After visiting the ranch on the edge of forever, I not only think of Sagan's billions and billions of stars but also the possible billions and billions of universes that are out there somewhere.

P.S. Linda sold the ranch and now lives in Montana. I moved from Arizona back to California.

Bill Hamilton Executive Director Skywatch International, Inc.

WHY TOM DONGO?

But the fundamental, unanswered question remains – why Tom Dongo? Why, out of all the honorable folks living in and around Sedona, would he seem to be the main focal point for all these strange occurrences? He admits that he isn't quite sure.

"A hundred times I have said – why me? This stuff has been going on for over 25 years now, and I have written six popular books regarding many of these inexplicable occurrences. Why is it that I have such strange paranormal happenings around me, sometimes on a continuous basis? I don't understand it. I don't have a clue. I have had many borderline-psychotic explanations from, usually, well-meaning people as to the reason behind this activity. Such as: Recently, I did a presentation at Sedona MUFON. There were about a hundred

UFO Repeaters! Seeing Is Believing - The Camera Doesn't Lie!

Charla strokes the "crystal ball of landing" hoping they will perhaps land while we are visiting Tom Dongo in Sedona.

UFO Repeaters! Seeing Is Believing - The Camera Doesn't Lie!

people in the room. I noticed while showing some UFO-type slides that a number of people were acting very uneasy in the audience. It wasn't until after my talk that someone told me that two blue, basketball-sized spheres of light with little lightning bolt flashes in them came through a high window and were sitting about five feet above my head. Then another sphere came out of one of the first two and flashed across the room. At that, the three of them blinked out and did not return. This sort of thing has been going on for a long time now. Maybe I will never know why!"

* * * * *

And maybe none of us will – but we can almost guarantee that we haven't seen the last of unexplained UFO phenomena in and around the red rocks of Sedona. You can bet your Venus-bound Mother Ship on that!

Editors Note: All photos in this chapter are from the Tom Dongo Collection. Copyright by the individual photographers.

SUGGESTED READING
BOOKS BY TOM DONGO
AVAILABLE FROM AMAZON.COM

MERGING DIMENSIONS: THE OPENING PORTALS OF SEDONA

UNSEEN BEINGS, UNSEEN WORLDS

EVERYTHING YOU WANTED TO KNOW ABOUT SEDONA IN A NUTSHELL

MYSTERIOUS SEDONA

MYSTERIES OF SEDONA: NEW AGE FRONTIER

MERGING DIMENSIONS

WEBSITE: www.TomDongo.com

STRANGE CRAFT WITH OCCUPANTS PHOTOGRAPHED OVER TURKEY

"The objects in the footage have the structure of a specific material that is definitely not made up by any kind of computer animation, balloon, prop, model or special effects used for simulation in a studio."

I would tend to remain very skeptical about this series of UFO photos – stills, actually, captured from video footage – taken on several different occasions over the coast of Turkey along the shores of the town of Kumburgaz. If it wasn't for the fact that one of the witnesses present was the eminent "UFO Doctor," Dr. Roger Leir, I would have dismissed the case wholeheartedly as being a mirage or a large vessel coming into port, two of the explanations that have been given by the usual horde of skeptics. Not only do we have photographs of the object itself, but we are able to look inside and see who is at the helm of the craft – and they certainly don't look human!

On the popular Coast to Coast AM radio talk show, host George Knapp tried to pin down Dr. Leir as to why the video(s) could not have been hoaxed. Leir said there was a full moon out and that there was an excited crowd present and that they all saw the craft coming closer and closer. Leir says that no way in hell was this a hallucination or a trick of the lens. "We saw what we saw!" he proclaimed without hesitation. Furthermore, the noted podiatrist, who has been

UFO Repeaters! Seeing Is Believing - The Camera Doesn't Lie!

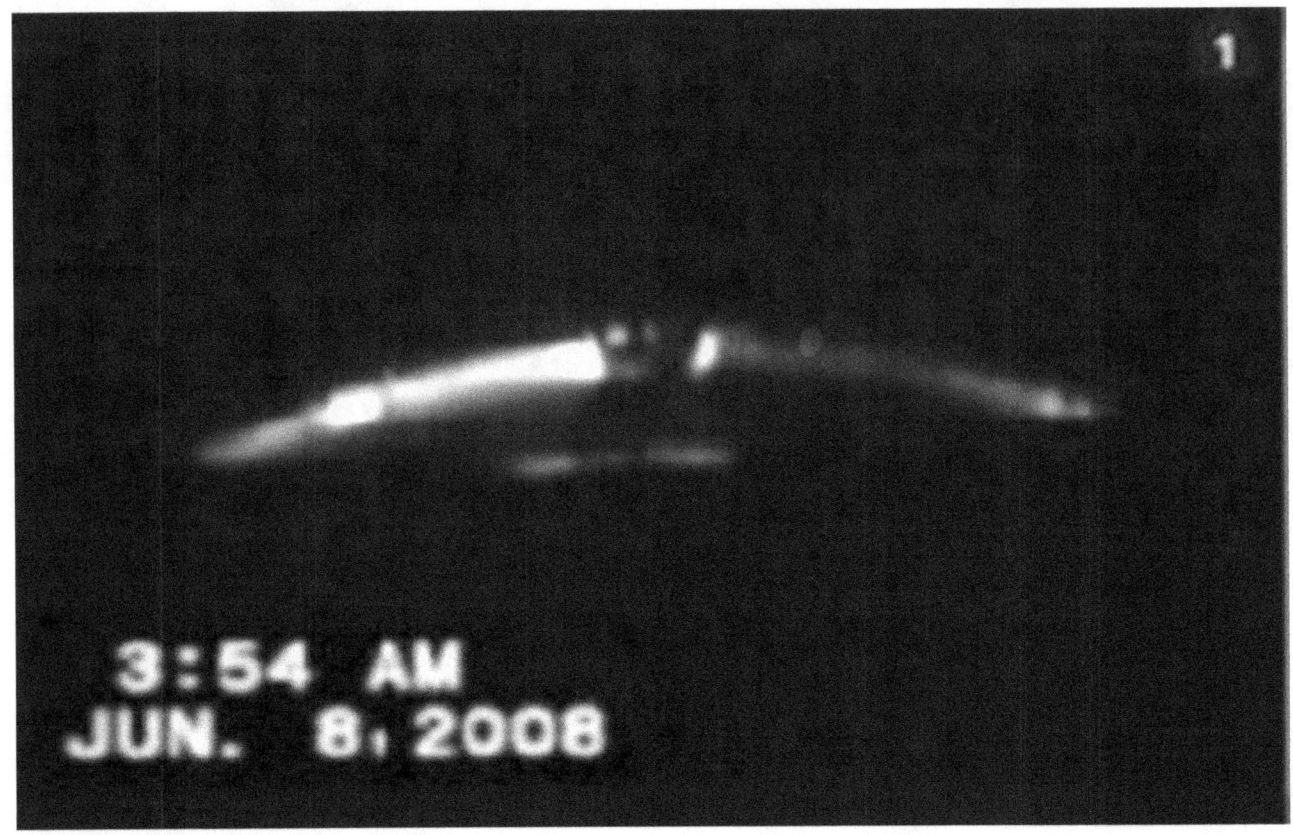

Photos 1 and 2 are referred to in video analysis by Chilean expert.

responsible for removing more than a dozen alien implants from UFO abductees, said, "We were on the beach and filming out over the water. The moon was the size of a dime. The object was the size of a flashlight. The camera that we were using had a 400mm lens with an electronic 'doubler.' When we focused on the craft, it became clearer and clearer. I was astounded when I saw the video. Optical physicists have gone over the video with a fine tooth comb and they say it is the real McCoy."

Behind this series of astonishing aerial photographic events is a Turkish security guard, one Yalcin Yalman, who on several occasions between 2007 and 2009 (maybe later?) scanned the heavens and apparently knew when the craft were going to appear – although we have not heard him say this, not understanding the Turkish language. But how else can you explain what he has accomplished?

The following is a photo analysis report filed by expert Mario Valdes of Santiago, Chile, on behalf of the Board of Turkey's National Council For The Study Of Science And Technology (TUBITAK):

Tuesday, April 24, 2012

GRAPHIC ANALYSIS ON THE VIDEOS REGARDING UNIDENTIFIED FLYING OBJECTS FILMED OVER KUMBURGAZ, TURKEY BETWEEN 2007 AND 2009 (SUMMARY) - ANALYZED BY MARIO VALDES SANTIAGO - CHILE

Original Raw Videos: 2007-2009 Original Videos - Entire Case Background: More Information

SUMMARY OF THE CASE

THIS case developed in the location of Kumburgaz between the years 2007, 2008, and 2009. Its main witness was a night guard named Yalcin Yalman, who while on duty registered video of strange objects that appeared at sunrise to be floating or changing while in flight over the sea on the coast of Marmara. Yalman was able to film many video segments, some during the day accompanied by witnesses with whom he spoke while he was filming.

UFO Repeaters! Seeing Is Believing - The Camera Doesn't Lie!

Above: UFO sighting makes headline news in Turkey.

Below: The man behind the amazing UFO videos, security guard Yalcin Yalman.

244

One singularity of this case was that the images were made with a camera that had an adapter for close-ups of 200X optical, capturing a great amount of detail of the objects.

At first, the videos were analyzed and made public by the SIRIUS UFO organization, directed by the researcher Haktan Akdogan. This case made big news in Turkey and in other countries as well. It also started a great debate between the official members of the Turkish scientific community. Specifically the NATIONAL COUNCIL FOR THE STUDY OF SCIENCE AND TECHNOLOGY (TUBITAK) got interested in analyzing the original footage, with the intention of determining that the video was nothing more than a hoax, gambling on the idea of scale models, toys, or CGI.

The original tape was handed to the TUBITAK representatives on live TV in their own headquarters. Once the analysis was concluded, they gave an official report, from which we took the following fragment: (see video on YouTube). Some editing and paraphrasing had to be done for purposes of clarification and space. Admittedly, some of the photos referred to may be out of sequence but they can – hopefully – easily be spotted and picked out as the reader goes along

"The objects observed on the images have a structure made of a specific material and are definitely not any kind of CGI animation or by any means a type of special effects used for simulation in a studio or for video effects. So the conclusion of this report is that the observations are not a model or a fraud." The last part of the report declared, "It's concluded that the objects observed have a physical structure and are made of materials that don't belong to any category of airplanes, helicopters, meteors, Venus, Mars, satellites, artificial lights, Chinese lanterns, etc. and that the objects mostly fit in the category of UFOs (Unidentified Flying Objects of unknown origin)."

Other analyses were done by video specialists and special effects companies from Japan, Russia and Turkey, all reaching the same conclusions. In Chile, I asked Professor José Atenas, an expert in graphics and video with more than 30 years of experience in television, to examine the videos. Atenas also concluded that the images are authentic.

So far, nobody has been able to demonstrate that the recordings are the product of tricks or some type of manipulation. Therefore, the debate has concentrated more on the nature and origin of the objects filmed by Yalcin Yalman.

SOME CONSIDERATIONS

To be honest, at the beginning my idea was to analyze the videos hoping to find some elements in them that would be evidence of a possible fraud, taking into account that the spectacular manner in which the case was labeled (announced that for the very first time a UFO was videotaped with its occupants precisely visible inside one of the objects) was not a minor issue for those of us who are obsessed with these themes. It was from skepticism, and why not say it, with a quota of prejudgment that I decided to take some time and check out the fragments of the movie. You could say that my expectations were to "find the string of the puppet."

To make the analysis, I used electronic copies of the original videos given to me by the Turkish investigator Haktan Akdogan, who picked up this case first-handed. I met with Haktan personally to confer about this incident and I was very grateful to him for handing me a copy of the original tape with which I could accomplish this work.

The analysis will be related in a chronological and sequential way, in the same order that the research and results came.

Finally, what I present here is only a portion of all that was extracted from the videos and from the image analysis. It is a lot of material and, when the moment comes, I will complete this publication with more findings.

FIRST APPRECIATIONS RELATED TO THE VIDEOS

There is always a first impression, and it can even be subjective, and, by the way, preliminary.

At first look, it called my attention to the honesty of the takes. That is, you can't observe any kind of tendency or intention of hiding something. It is clear that the cameraman does everything possible to configure his camera the best way to capture the objects; he makes constant changes in light entry and zoom, trying to show as clearly possible what is happening while he films. He also worries on registering different reference points and at the same time making very powerful close-ups.

Even if at first the appreciation can be subjective, as I mentioned before, it must be considered in the context of an attitude and disposition of total openness

UFO Repeaters! Seeing Is Believing - The Camera Doesn't Lie!

Above: A close-up of the object.

Below: Experts find it hard to dispute the reality of these incidents over Turkish coastal waters.

by the witness, who has shown his face and delivered all the background of this case, including the video camera and the original tapes.

My first look at the components of the tapes (IMAGE: film grain, illumination, close ups, and reference points; also AUDIO: ambient sound, narration, and witness attitude) agrees totally with an authentic recording of objects at a great distance, filmed at nighttime (the ones used in this work). There are also daytime recordings with interesting details, but in this analysis will be only the night ones.

Having these observations in account, plus the reports from TUBITAK and the opinion of professor José Atenas, I am willing to do and expose the following graphic analysis.

THE BEGINNING OF THE ANALYSIS AND THE FIRST OBTAINED PHOTOGRAMS

As I mentioned before, the objective of this review was to find elements that would reveal a fraud or a setup in the sequences of the video. For this I carried out an exhaustive observation of the images, with a considerable close-up and frame-by-frame process. The video segments used in this part correspond to the June 8th, 2008, and May 13th, 2009, dates. (1 and 2)

Given that the most spectacular aspects of the case rest on the alleged presence of UFO occupants in the footage, the observation point was centered primarily in the center zone of the object; that's where, according to the witness, there was "someone," what has been interpreted as the occupants or crew. In summary, the records of the case indicate that in the center of the object would be found some type of door or window that at times remains opened and from where it's possible to see two "heads," which would correspond to the slippery occupants.

A short time after reviewing, I could observe a couple of photograms that caused me strangeness and amazement. My first reaction was to say "Bingo! Here there's something." After a second view of the fragment, I was able to isolate a sequence that seems, to say the least, interesting. Not just because of the clarity of the takes, but also because the investigation started to turn more complex from the point of view of the different explanations and theories possible. In fact, at this point is where a series of questions appear that later on I will comment about.

In concrete, the sequence shows with acceptable clarity the moment in which one of the figures, apparently of humanoid characteristics, raises his head and then looks – and it remains for a fraction of time looking right at the front. The appearance is that of a head with two relatively big and dark eyes. Also it is possible to interpret what part of the body of the figure is left to see as a body or small torso in relation to the head. (3 and 4)

After checking uncountable times this photogram sequence (5), I got the conviction that the figure in question is not static; on the contrary, it is in permanent movement, in general, with the "view" looking down, with the exception of this segment, in which the figure happens from this position to look fixedly at the front, to then lower the "view" again.

In the following close up sequence, (6) it's possible to see that the "humanoid" figure is visible even without the need to apply zoom.

SOMETHING IS MOVING IN FIRST PLANE

As I indicated previously while analyzing the first sequence of stills the following detail raised my attention. Something moves in the first plane, almost in front of the figure in study. To try to solve this questioning, I returned to check the complete video, at different speeds and levels of close-ups, centering the observation only on this zone. (11) You can check the sequence of video and identify the zone to which I refer.

What moves in front of the figures that we saw previously seems to be a third figure. This one has characteristics different from the previous ones. In concrete, it's a figure with an "insectoid" aspect in his form and movements. If I had to describe it or classify it somehow, I would say that it looks very close to a praying mantis. It has a brown color, his head is not as big as that of the previous ones and is of triangular form. It has two very big and dark eyes, located on the sides of the head and in ascending form. It seems to have a long neck and a very thin body. Having checked the videos carefully, it is possible to distinguish his arms stretching in a similar way to what the mantis does. His position in the scene is of profile orientated towards the left side of the image, his body remains sloping or curved, moving the head and the arms, and simultaneously inclines forward.

UFO Repeaters! Seeing Is Believing - The Camera Doesn't Lie!

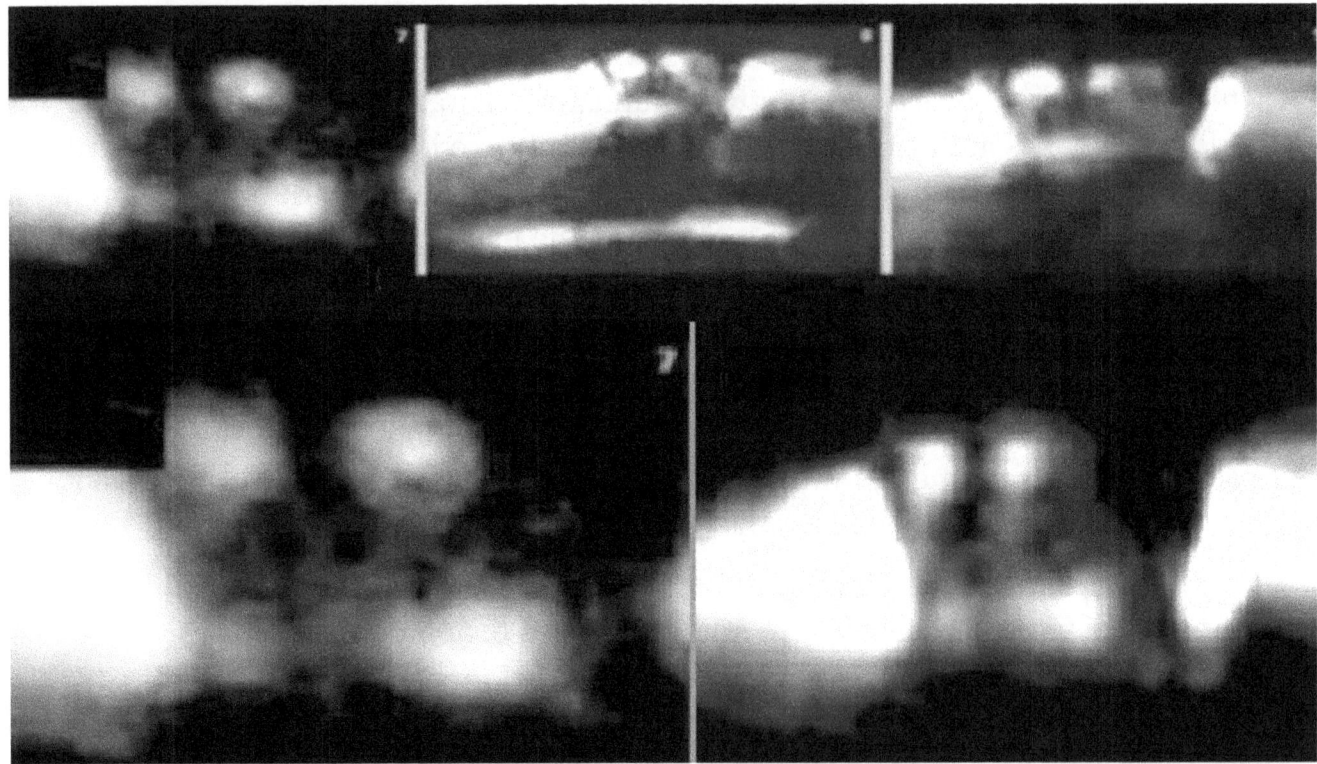

Above: A close-up view of the possible occupants of the UFO.

Below: Here we see the actual heads of what some believe to be the crew of the Turkish UFO.

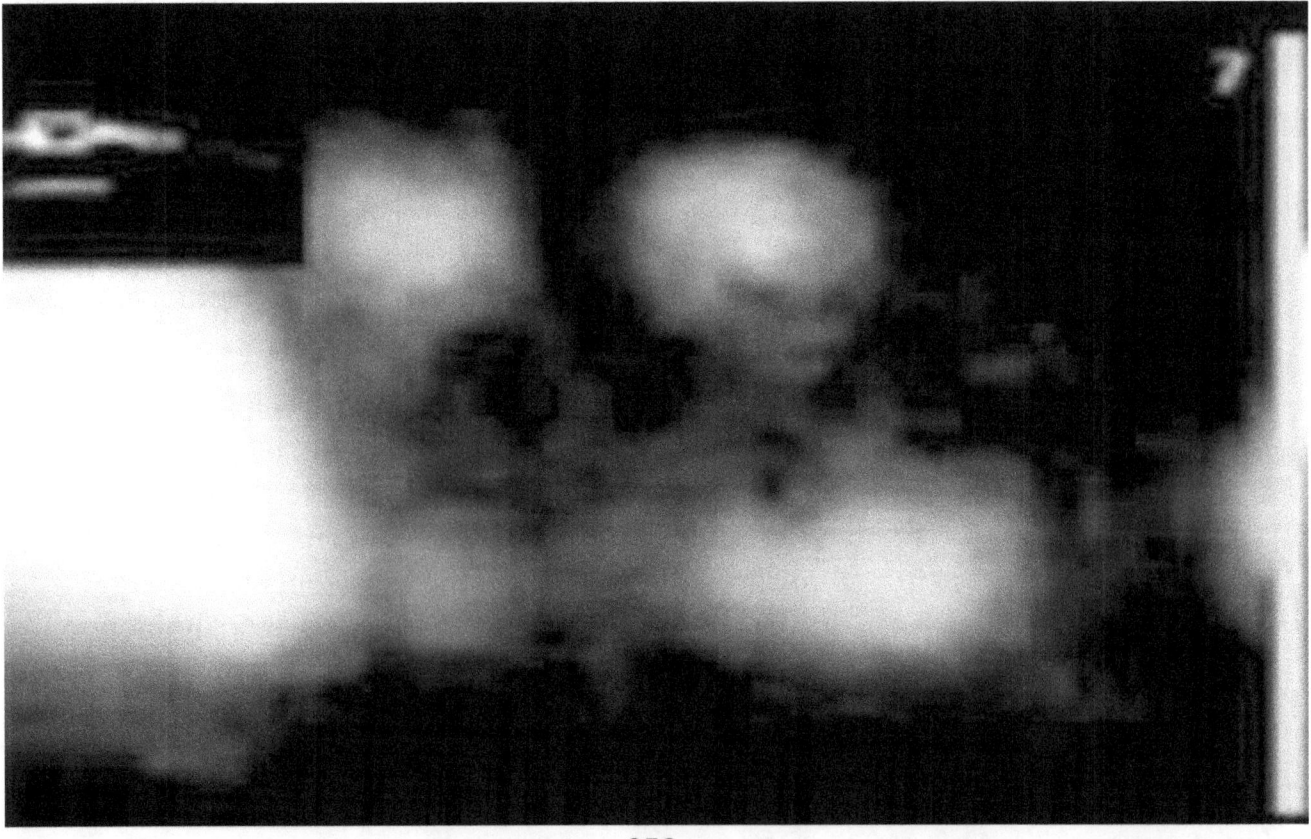

WHAT ARE THEY DOING?

The three figures seem to be interacting between themselves. Seemingly, they are occupied in some concrete action, located specifically in the lower half part of the scene, since in general they seem to be looking down. In fact, the "insectoid" figure displaces his arms repeatedly towards this zone of the image. To try to verify what they can be doing, I did a new review of the videos, analyzing carefully this time the zone in question.

The three figures seem to be manipulating something in the mentioned zone. We can perceive movements that can be assumed to be the hands moving in this space. At this point I exposed some stills that can support this idea. Nevertheless, after studying this zone of the scene, I could find a worrying enough image which might begin to give indications of what these three enigmatic figures might be doing.

GENERAL CONCLUSIONS

During this investigation it has not been possible to find indications of manipulation or tricks used for the production of the videos. The objects caught in the tape do not correspond to static figures.

Only by lowering in a considerable way the speed of playback is it possible to identify the figures and determine their movements. Even a frame-by-frame observation is necessary.

In my opinion, it's about live recorded images. They are not generated by computer animation and not 3D renderings.

Neither do they seem to be filming puppets or scale models. This possibility is improbable, among other reasons, because of the movement and gesticulating that is observed in the figures found in this analysis. Also, according to my examination in relation to the size and the proportions of the objects, they might be like the size that you would have in a light aircraft or a yacht with its crew members, filmed distantly and increased with a powerful enough zoom.

None of the images or theories here exposed have been found nor published previously, with one to three years passed since the events. Obviously, they have not been exploited somehow, neither by the witnesses of the case, nor by the investigators who analyzed or announced it, nor by speculators of the UFOs topics. It is improbable that someone has plotted a fraud with these characteristics without the most controversial and polemic images having gone out into the public light.

To make a few images or scenes as those that appear in these videos, one would need, to my understanding, a great quantity of time, resources and know-how in the area of special effects, which does not mean that it would be impossible. What really turns out to be a strange absurdity is that, even if this has happened, the realized work has been mastered so completely with a playback speed so rapid that it makes almost impossible to notice its presence in the tape. Consequently, nobody would see it, since it has not been discovered until now.

I consider these details of great importance since they impede furthermore the conventional explanation.

Just as I have not found elements to affirm that the figures and forms that appear in the images are computer animations or scale models, there is also no concrete evidence that the figures that appear here have some origin or certain nature that could be demonstrated.

My conclusion is that this case is, up to the moment, a real event of high strangeness, with the characteristics here exposed, that does not have a conventional, convincing and demonstrable explanation and that therefore, to my understanding, is kept unidentified.

Mario Valdés. ©

02 de Agosto de 2010

valdesmario@hotmail.com

* * * * *

UFO Repeaters! Seeing Is Believing - The Camera Doesn't Lie!

Report By: Haktan Akdagon SIRIUS Space Research

This extraordinary series of incidents took place in a compound in Kumburgaz/Istanbul, was witnessed by many residents and filmed repeatedly by the same night watchman, one Yalcin Yalman, in 2009, 2008 and in 2007. The images captured are expected to have a tremendous worldwide impact and be hailed as "the most important UFO/extraterrestrial images ever filmed."

During the months of April and May 2009, many UFO sightings were reported nationwide from different cities in Turkey, some of which were filmed and photographed and the images broadcast on television. Within that same timeframe, these objects were witnessed by the residents of Kumburgaz/Yeni Kent Compound and caught on video several times by Yalman. His footage has been called the most closely detailed and significant images of UFOs captured anywhere.

In this amazing UFO video footage, ships with metallic structures are clearly visible. What's even more important is that, in close-ups of some of the frames, "entities" can be distinctly made out.

Here at Sirius UFO Space Science Research Center, we did a detailed analysis of the complete footage with the participation of members of our board of scientists. We have enlarged the video images of the footage, checked the pixels and examined all the footage frame-by-frame. After doing all the necessary analysis, which went on for a week, we came to the definite conclusion – with no doubts – that the footage is 100% genuine!

The objects captured in the footage are definitely not the result of any kind of computer animation nor are they made by any form of special effects used for simulation in a studio. Therefore it was concluded that the sightings were neither a mockup nor a hoax. The objects have physical and material structures that do not belong in any known category, such as: planes, helicopters, meteors, Venus, Mars, satellites, fireballs, Chinese lanterns, weather balloons, natural or atmospheric phenomena, etc., but instead fall into the category of UFOs. Also, nationally known special effects experts Tarkan Ozel and Cem Ozel (www.ozelfx.com) have also analyzed the video footage and reached the same conclusion, that the footage is genuine.

Respectfully,

Haktan Akdogan - Chairman

http://www.siriusufo.org/

UFO Repeaters! Seeing Is Believing - The Camera Doesn't Lie!

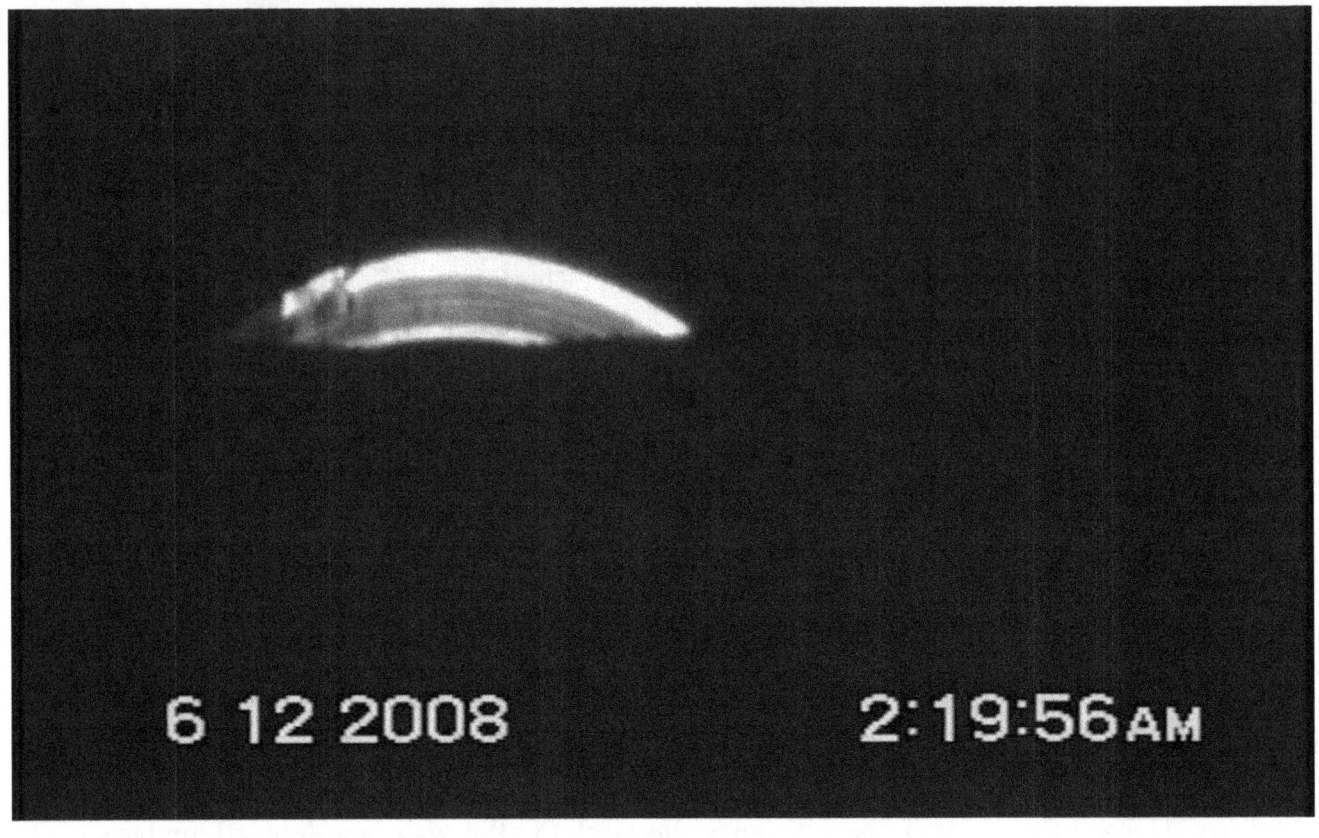

What could this thing in the sky actually be? And will it return?

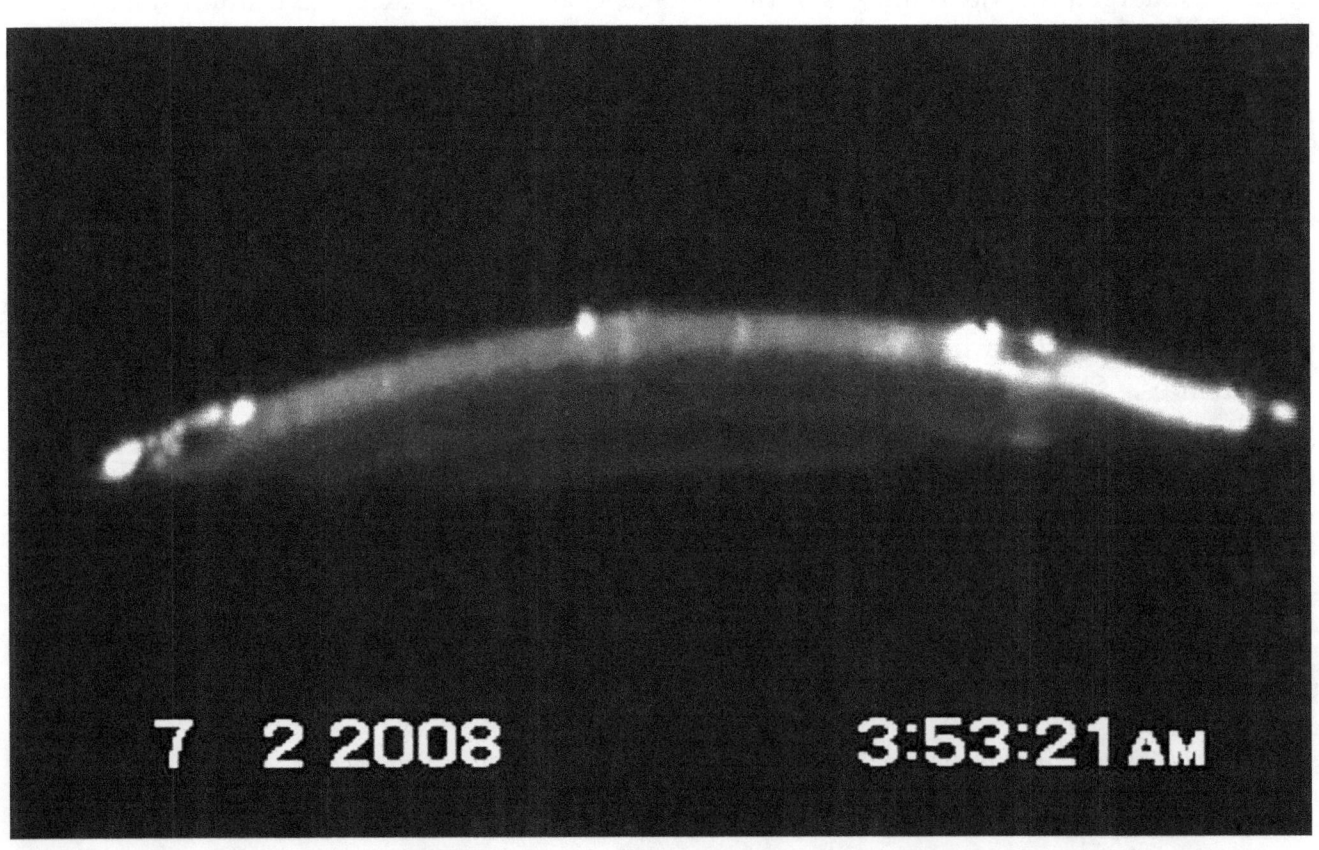

We have a feeling this case has not come to an end . . . that there will be more revelations as time passes. No doubt the skeptics have not finished their badmouthing of the case which, to our way of thinking, is indeed controversial and needs to be studied further. We are eager to know more about the background of Yalcin Yalman, the case's chief UFO Repeater, and the other witnesses. It is unfortunate that the late Dr. Roger Leir is not around to investigate further as he remains the most impressive authority to have been involved in the case.

SOURCES

"Graphic Analysis of the Turkey UFO," by Bear, from the website at: http://alienscalpel.com/updates/graphic-analysis-of-the-turkey-ufo

"Turkey UFO Incident," from the website at: http://turkeyufocase.blogspot.com/

ROB HARTLAND OF AUSTRALIA

AUSSIE Rob Hartland says he has taken more than 20,000 digital photographs of the daytime sky in his Perth home, and a small percentage of them reveal possible extraterrestrial spacecraft when enlarged. His photos received media coverage in both his hometown newspaper, "Perth Now," on April 27, 2013, and on the "Open Minds" website here in the U.S. two days later.

"It began when he was taking photos of clouds to test out a new camera," the Perth newspaper reported. "He noticed a 'smudge' that, when enlarged and enhanced, 'had some structure to it, suggesting it could be some sort of craft in the sky.' He says since then he has identified a dozen different UFOs, including round, square and saucer-shaped craft, posting the photos on his website – wispyclouds.net – for extraterrestrial buffs and skeptics to ponder."

Hartland explained some of his methodology, saying that he usually focuses the camera on the edges of mid- to high-altitude clouds.

"I take about 30 shots at a time," he told the Aussie paper. "In ten to fifteen minutes, I'll take 300 to 400 images. Then I connect the camera to the computer. I zoom in and enhance any little thing I note on the images and you get these craft in anywhere from two percent to twenty percent of the shots.

"Some of them appear to have transparent canopies," Hartland continued, "and in some shots it looks like there could be occupants inside. I always say 'could' rather than 'is.' There is always doubt. But UFO stands for 'unidentified flying object,' and, as far as I'm concerned, these aren't identified. It's possible

UFO Repeaters! Seeing Is Believing - The Camera Doesn't Lie!

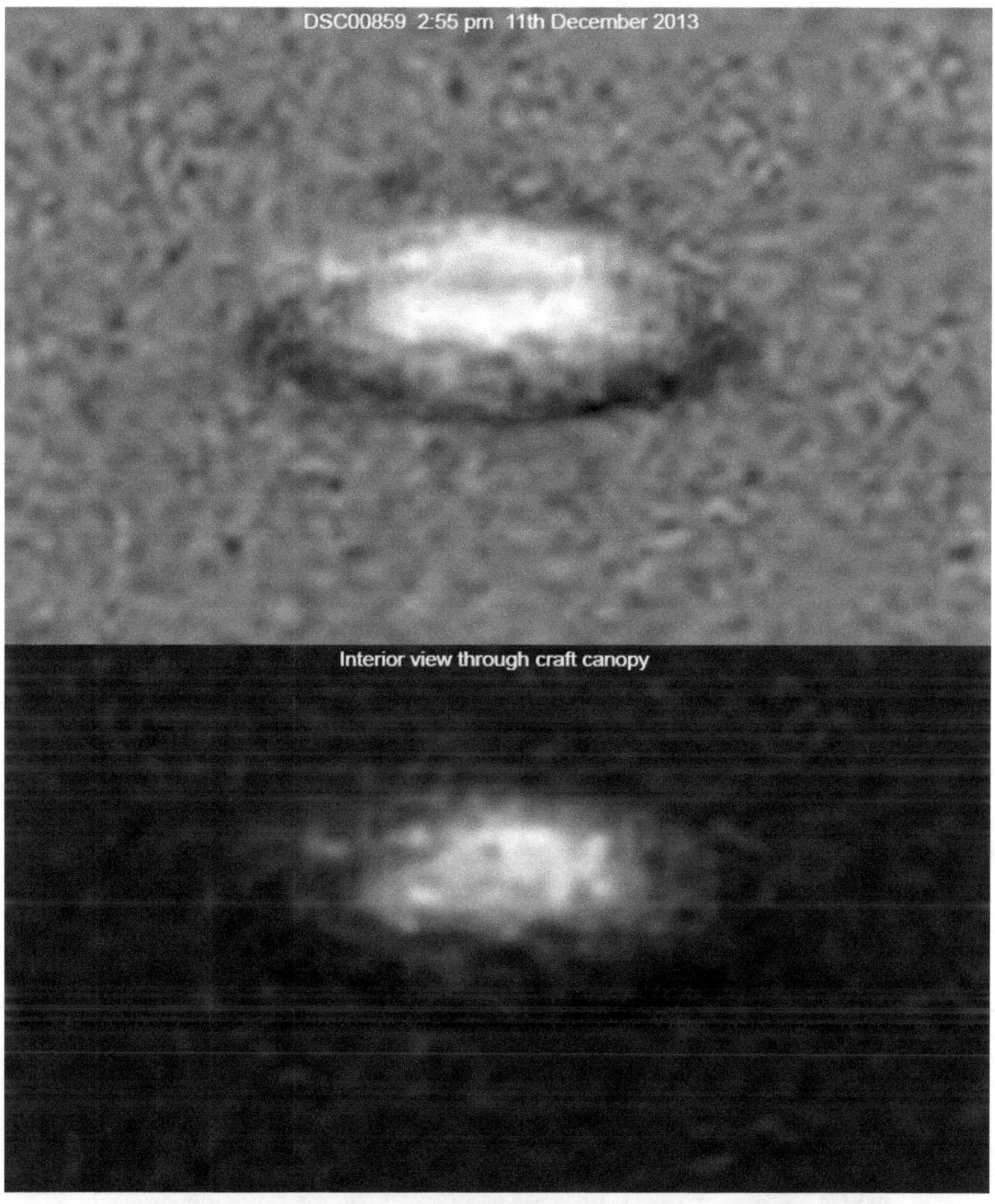

Hartland says that he has been photographing UFOs over his house in Darlington in the Perth hills of Western Australia since early November, 2012.

UFO Repeaters! Seeing Is Believing - The Camera Doesn't Lie!

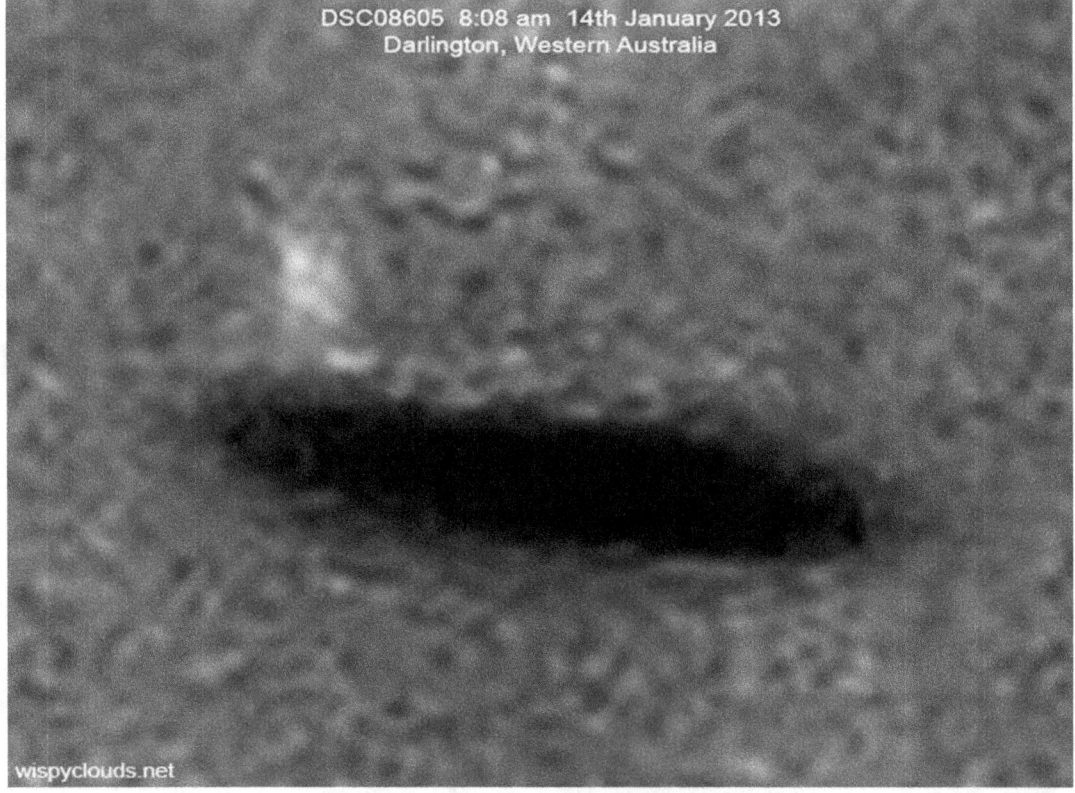

The UFOs are not seen with the naked eye, but afterwards are detected on the digital images and enlarged using a computer.

UFO Repeaters! Seeing Is Believing - The Camera Doesn't Lie!

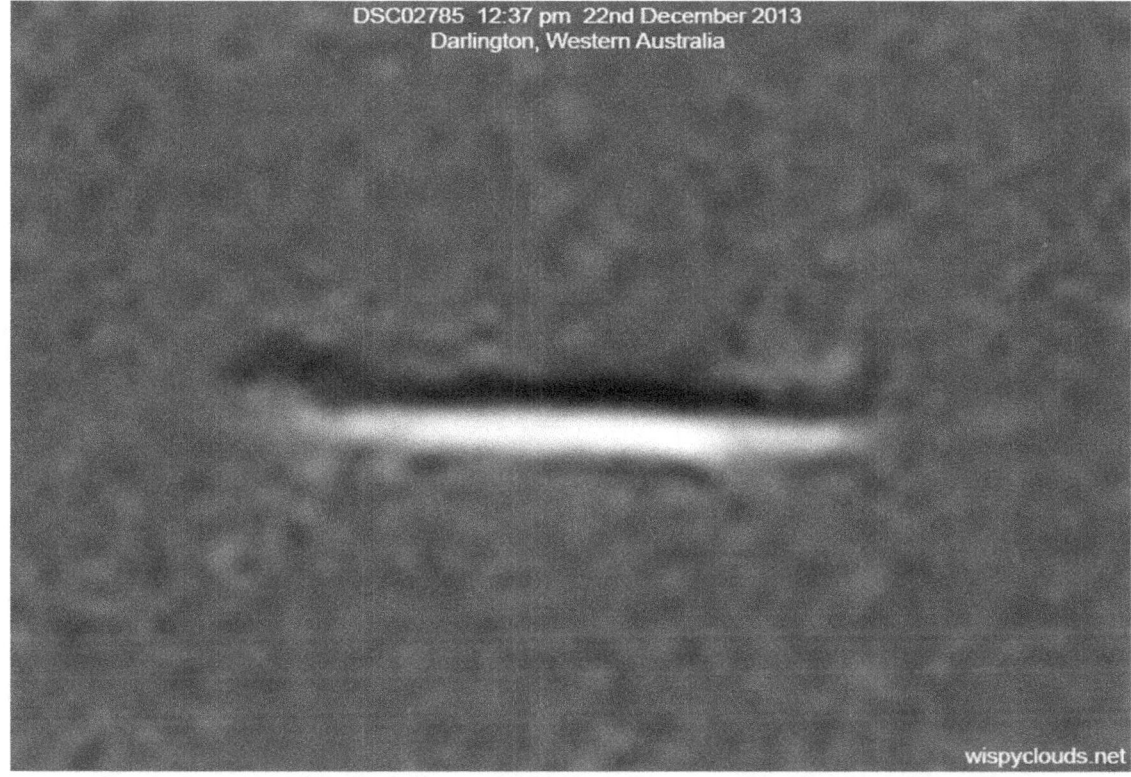

Hartland says that the craft/UFOs that he has photographed vary enormously in shape and size, and it seems that they are always present, usually flying overhead at high speed.

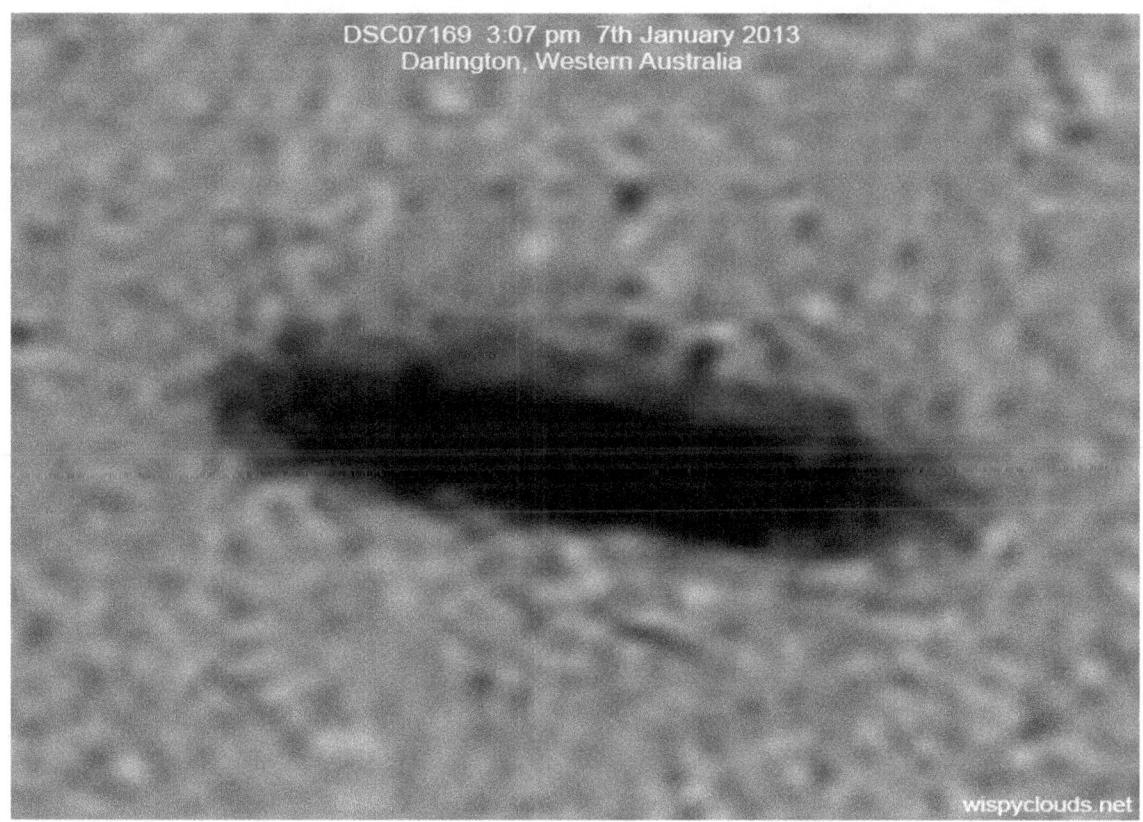

some are manmade, but I don't think they all are. There's no way it is a bird or insect or plane. They look totally different and these craft move much faster."

Hartland began taking his photos in November 2012 using a new Sony Cybershot DSC-RX100 camera. According to Jackson Flindell, the picture editor of another Aussie paper, "The Sunday Times," Hartland's images "did not appear to have been tampered with, but dust on a digital camera's image sensor could cause anomalies in digital photographs, while powerful magnification could also distort images in some cases."

Hartland holds a Ph.D. in biochemistry and said he had no history of mental illness or drug abuse. He insists that he never alters his photos, though he acknowledged many people would find his claims hard to believe. As is frequently the case with individuals who are able to repeatedly photograph UFOs, Hartland's initial photos were captured quite accidentally. But a routine eventually developed in which the ships seem to "obligingly" show up as he photographs the clouds around his home.

SOURCES

"Hundreds of UFO pics captured over Perth by Darlington," by Trevor Paddenburg, from the website of the Australian newspaper "The Sunday Times" at: http://www.perthnow.com.au/

"Man photographs hundreds of UFOs in Australia," from the website at: http://www.openminds.tv/man-photographs-hundreds-of-ufos-in-australia-992/20464

Rob Hartland's photos available online at: WispyClouds.net

THE UFOS POSE FOR PAUL VILLA
By Sean Casteel

LIKE the legendary Swiss contactee, Billy Meier, Paul Villa was an unassuming gentleman of modest means who happened to capture some striking UFO photos. Villa had no axe to grind and no desire for publicity or fame. As so often happens in the world of UFO encounters, Villa did not find the flying saucer phenomenon; it found him.

Villa told UFO investigators that he would receive a telepathic message telling him to be at a certain location, usually somewhere near his home in Albuquerque, New Mexico. When he arrived at the designated place, the alien ships would essentially "pose" for him while he took photos with a Japanese-made camera and standard Kodak film.

The result of those efforts is a beautiful series of full color photos depicting the flying saucers in all their glory. Inner Light/Global Communications has previously published a book called *"The Secret Life of Paul Villa"* that includes 20 pages of the very convincing photos as well as a fascinating background text written by veteran UFO researcher Wendelle Stevens, who followed the Villa case closely for several years. Stevens makes a very strong argument for the authenticity of the photos, noting the following features:

1. They are quite sharp, compared to most saucer photos seen up to that time, which was the 1960s through the 1970s.

UFO Repeaters! Seeing Is Believing - The Camera Doesn't Lie!

Albaquerque, New Mexico, 1966

UFO Repeaters! Seeing Is Believing - The Camera Doesn't Lie!

UFO Repeaters! Seeing Is Believing - The Camera Doesn't Lie!

Paul Villa

2. The image size of the saucers is large enough to show good detail without the extreme graininess that comes when enlarging other UFO photos of less quality.

3. There is a series of photos, instead of just one photo, which provides more details for examination.

4. Villa's truck is in the foreground of some of the photos, providing a known object with which to compare the size of the saucer and to judge its distance away.

5. The degree of sharpness of other objects in the near foreground and clouds and trees in the distance indicates that the object had to be very large in order to achieve the depth of field observed to exist in the photos, thereby ruling out the possibility that a small model may have been used to fake the photos.

THE MAN HIMSELF

Paul Villa was born on September 24, 1916, in Albuquerque, of Native-American/Spanish descent. While he did not complete the tenth grade, he had a good working knowledge of mathematics, physics, electricity and mechanics and was particularly gifted at detecting defects in engines and generators. His wife, Eunis, was a "war bride" from Germany; the couple met when Villa was serving as a sergeant in the U.S. Army occupational forces after the war. He brought Eunis back from Europe, and they settled in Southern California.

COMING TO KNOW THE SPACEMEN

Villa said he first spoke with spacemen in 1953 when he worked for the Department of Water and Power in Los Angeles. While on the job one day in Long Beach, he had a strong urge to go down to the beach, a feeling he did not then understand. There he met a man about seven feet tall. Villa's first impulse was to run away, but the man called him by name and told him many personal things about himself.

"He knew everything I had in my mind," Villa said, "and he told me many things that had taken place in my life. He then told me to look out beyond the reef. I saw a metallic-looking, disc-shaped object that seemed to be floating on

UFO Repeaters! Seeing Is Believing - The Camera Doesn't Lie!

UFO Repeaters! Seeing Is Believing - The Camera Doesn't Lie!

UFO Repeaters! Seeing Is Believing - The Camera Doesn't Lie!

the water. Then the spaceman asked me if I would like to go aboard the craft and look around. I went with him."

For Villa, the aliens were entirely human-looking, though more uniformly attractive than Earth people and definitely more refined in face and form. They took Villa on a tour of the saucer and confided in him that the whole galaxy to which Earth belongs is a grain of sand on a huge beach compared to the unfathomable number of inhabited bodies in the entire universe. They said their craft are constantly active over our planet and that they are here on a friendly mission to help Earth people.

THE PHOTOS BEGIN

The extraterrestrials spoke to Villa in his native Spanish but also spoke English fluently with him as well. They told him they had been observing the development of our "dubious civilization" from observation platforms on our Moon, Mars and Venus. As his contact experiences continued through the years, Villa was eventually invited to photograph the ships, and the aliens began to actually "pose" for that purpose. They flew their craft slowly and hovered as Villa snapped away.

Villa's photos first came to light when some of them were published by Gabriel Green, a controversial contactee in his own right, in Green's "UFO International Journal" in October 1965. At the time, the photos were greeted with some suspicion, even within the UFO community. Coral Lorenzen, who cofounded, along with her husband, Jim, the now defunct Aerial Phenomena Research Organization (APRO), visited Villa at his home and asked him pointblank how he had faked the photos.

Villa responded, sarcastically, "Well, my dear lady, you just make yourself a model and toss it in the air and photograph it."

Wendelle Stevens later wrote that such a deception is not easily carried out. In fact, he tried doing it himself and, by the third photo, his model was ruined. It was also impossible to get the model in the correct attitude and angle simply by tossing it up in front of the camera.

The photos Villa took are breathtaking to look at and do appear to show actual flying saucers set against lovely desert scenery. There are different types of ships from photo to photo, which is consistent with UFO witness accounts since

UFO Repeaters! Seeing Is Believing - The Camera Doesn't Lie!

Photo taken June 16, 1963. The occupants of the UFO "permitted Villa to take photo's of their ship which posed and hovered close to the surface between 2 and 4P.M. while he took various shots of the craft framed by the trees in the foreground. He used a Japanese-made Rokuoh-Sha camera with an f4.6, 75mm lens loaded with 120 Kodak film."

UFO Repeaters! Seeing Is Believing - The Camera Doesn't Lie!

the 1940s and has led some analysts to think we are being visited by several different alien races and civilizations. That theory accounts for the many types of occupants reported, from the grays to the reptilians to the blonde, human-looking Nordics.

AN UNHAPPY CASE OF FAME

The notoriety that came with being "chosen" to take the photos did not make life easy for Villa, however. He suffered many instances of harassment, including an incident that happened when he stopped off at a local tavern on his way home from work. As Villa was sipping his beer, a complete stranger walked up to him and said, "So you're the nut that said he is talking to spacemen?" The stranger next punched Villa in the nose, drawing blood.

Villa never forgot that moment of genuine violence. He was often forced to move his wife and household to new locations after such incidents, which included neighbors attacking his mobile home and even some very frightening visits from the dreaded Men-In-Black. People who found him in Albuquerque, where he had relocated his family from Los Angeles after the photos appeared in the "UFO International Journal," took things from around his home for souvenirs. The thoughtless interlopers infuriated him and the incidents necessitated another move, this time to an obscure small town in the remote desert south of Albuquerque.

Villa died of stomach cancer in 1980 at age 64 and was buried in Santa Fe. Some of his photos were never made public, including a series that was reportedly taken on another planet. Wendelle Stevens writes that he had lost touch with Eunis Villa and appealed to readers of **"The Secret Life of Paul Villa"** for any information they had that would enable him to contact her and get a look at those rumored, long lost photos. We may never know everything the UFO occupants revealed to Paul Villa, but the idea that there is further photographic evidence to be seen is certainly a tantalizing one.

SOURCES

"The Secret Life of Paul Villa," by Lt. Col. Wendelle Stevens (Ret), Inner Light/Global Communications, 2009.

UFO Repeaters! Seeing Is Believing - The Camera Doesn't Lie!

274

WHERE HAVE ALL THE SPACEMEN GONE?

By Tim Swartz

IT used to be, in the good old days of UFOs, (June 24, 1947 to 1973) that the strange craft were piloted by a wide range of flying saucer folk. There were little people, big people, blond blue-eyed space brothers, monsters, robots, saints and demons from the sky and many more.

It seemed as if we were being visited by every inhabited planet in the galaxy. The Earth must have been the Disneyworld of the universe to account for all the different types of space people dropping in to check us out.

Today, that has all changed. Instead of a nice, diverse mix of UFOnauts, we are stuck with the same boring old big-eyed grays. What has happened to all the others? Has the Earth been shut down for economic reasons? Have we been auctioned off in a celestial eBay to the highest bidders, namely the grays? Where have all the spacemen gone?

ALL SHAPES AND ALL SIZES

Unidentified flying objects have been zipping through the skies of Planet Earth as long as there have been people around to watch them. Ancient writings, folklore and religious texts are full of tales of unusual, glowing airships and the weird creatures contained within them. And, much like the UFOs, the strange

UFO Repeaters! Seeing Is Believing - The Camera Doesn't Lie!

Above: Bruno Ghibaudi, a scientific newspaper journalist, took photographs of strange UFOs over the beaches of Pescara along the Adriatic sea in April 1961.

Below: Photo of UFO taken off Catalina Island near Los Angeles around 1963. Courtesy Tom Dongo - http://tomdongoufoparanormalblog.blogspot.com/

beings inside come in an amazing and prolific range of extraordinary shapes and sizes.

For someone whose only knowledge of UFOs comes from the popular media, this may seem perplexing. After all, anyone who has watched television or gone to the movies in the last twenty years knows flying saucers are spaceships carrying little gray men from outer space. The gray alien with large black eyes has seemingly supplanted the hundreds of other weird beings reported over the last sixty years by UFO witnesses. However, the gray alien stereotype is a relatively recent addition to the pantheon of "aliens" that have interacted with mankind throughout history.

GODS FROM OTHER WORLDS

The Philistine deity, Dagon, who was one of the four sons of Anu, the lord of heaven, was said to have a human face and hands, but a portion of his body resembled a fish. Dagon flew down from the sky in a ball of fire and taught mankind the ways of the plough and agriculture.

As well, a history of Mesopotamia written in the third century BC by Berossus, a Babylonian priest, states that ancient man lived in a lawless manner like the beasts of the field. In those days there appeared a creature whose name was Oannes, or Ea, meaning the "fish of heaven." Oannes' body was like a fish, and under the fish's head he had another head, and connected to the fish's tail, he had feet similar to those of a man.

Oannes taught mankind writing and math and he is credited by the Sumerians for giving civilization to man. Oannes was said to return to the sea every evening, but, when he departed for the last time, he flew up into the sky and returned to the heavens.

The creation myths of the Australian Aborigines say that their creators came a long time ago in "shining boats" which "flew above the sea." Some say that the gods came in a "flying canoe" with "great wings clasped tightly to the side."

Aborigines from around the Ayres Rock say that in the distant past a large, red "egg" fell down to Earth. Out of the egg emerged white-skinned beings, followed by their children. The adults had problems breathing the air and died, but the children managed to survive. In time, the egg slowly rusted away and unified itself with the soil, creating the red soil of Central Australia. After many

UFO Repeaters! Seeing Is Believing - The Camera Doesn't Lie!

Above: Rock art of strange figures wearing what appears to be helmets with antenna. Found in Sego Canyon, Utah. Paintings are estimated to be over 7,000 years old.

Below: Cave painting found in the Hoshangabad district of the state of Madhya Pradesh, India. The ancient art depicts a humanoid figure along with circular objects that look like modern depictions of UFOs.

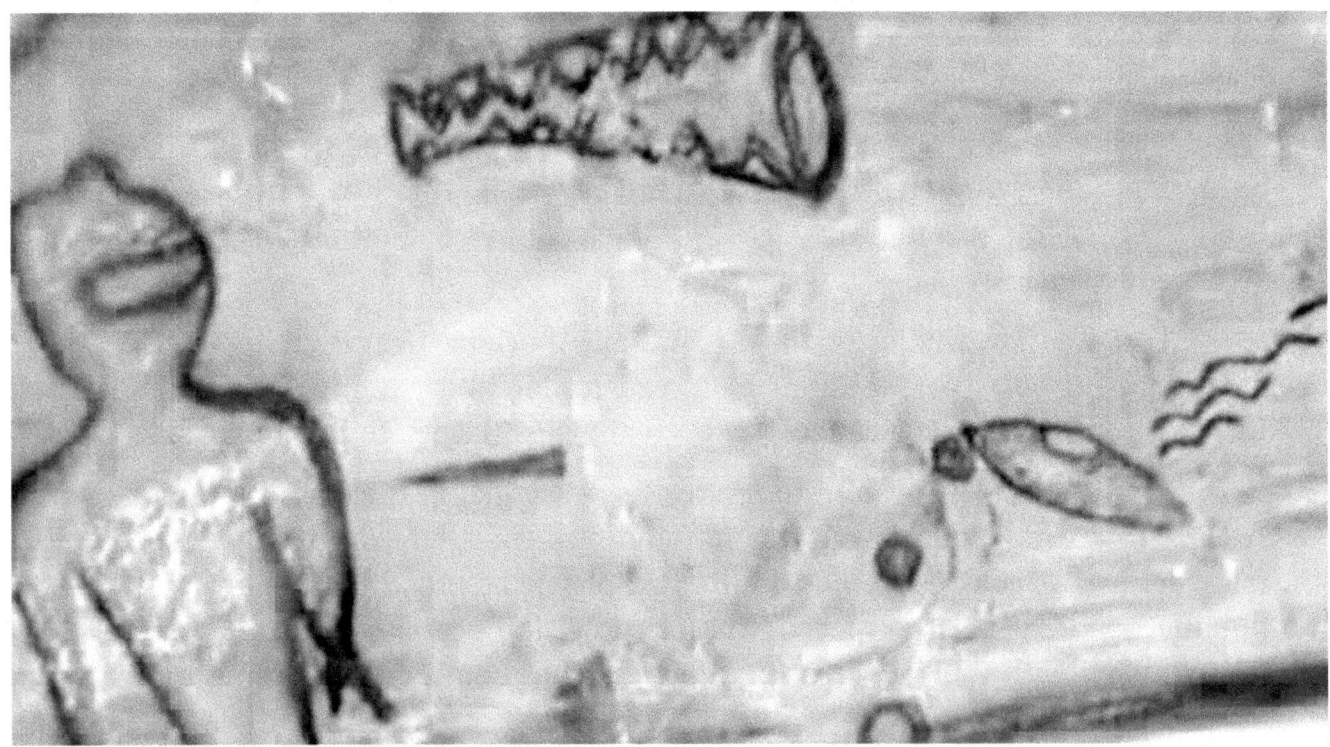

years, the sun turned the children's skin dark and they became the ancestors of the Aborigines.

Coptic Gnostic texts that were written around the first and second centuries CE contain passages that describe ancient encounters with alien-like beings called the Archons. A passage from *The First Apocalypse of James* (NHC V, 3) states: "A multitude of Archons may turn on you, thinking they can capture you. And in particular, three of them will seize you, those who pose as toll collectors. Not only do they demand toll, but they take away souls by theft. They are not entirely alien, for they are from the Fallen Sophia, the female divinity who produced them when she brought the human race down from the Source, the realm of the Pre-Existent One. So they are not entirely alien, but they are our kin."

It is interesting to note that the actions of the Gnostic Archons bear a close resemblance to modern reports of UFO abductions and the mysterious Men-In-Black, who supposedly travel in threes and pose as authority figures.

Agobard of Lyons, a bishop in 9th century France, wrote about the various "superstitions" he encountered among the peasantry. One such tale was that small, dark-skinned beings ("slyphs" or air elementals) traveling in sky-sailing ships were stealing farmers' crops and abducting people.

Agobard heard the rumor that four of these sylphs had been captured when the anchor of their sky ship became lodged on the belfry of a church. The captured creatures, who apparently could speak French, claimed to be from "Magonia," a land high up in the clouds. These four beings were stoned to death by an angry mob and their bodies thrown into a local lime pit. Agobard dismissed the rumors because they contradict the Bible, which has no mention of an aerial kingdom called Magonia.

SPACE BROTHERS AND HAIRY DWARFS

It was not until the 20th century that unexplained aerial objects received worldwide attention and were given a name, UFOs, or flying saucers. Starting in the late 1940s, the first investigators became convinced early on that UFOs were extraterrestrial spacecraft. Not surprisingly, the phenomenon quickly seemed to adapt to this belief structure. Books like Major Donald Keyhoe's "*The Flying Saucers Are Real*," (1950), which argued that the Air Force knew flying saucers

UFO Repeaters! Seeing Is Believing - The Camera Doesn't Lie!

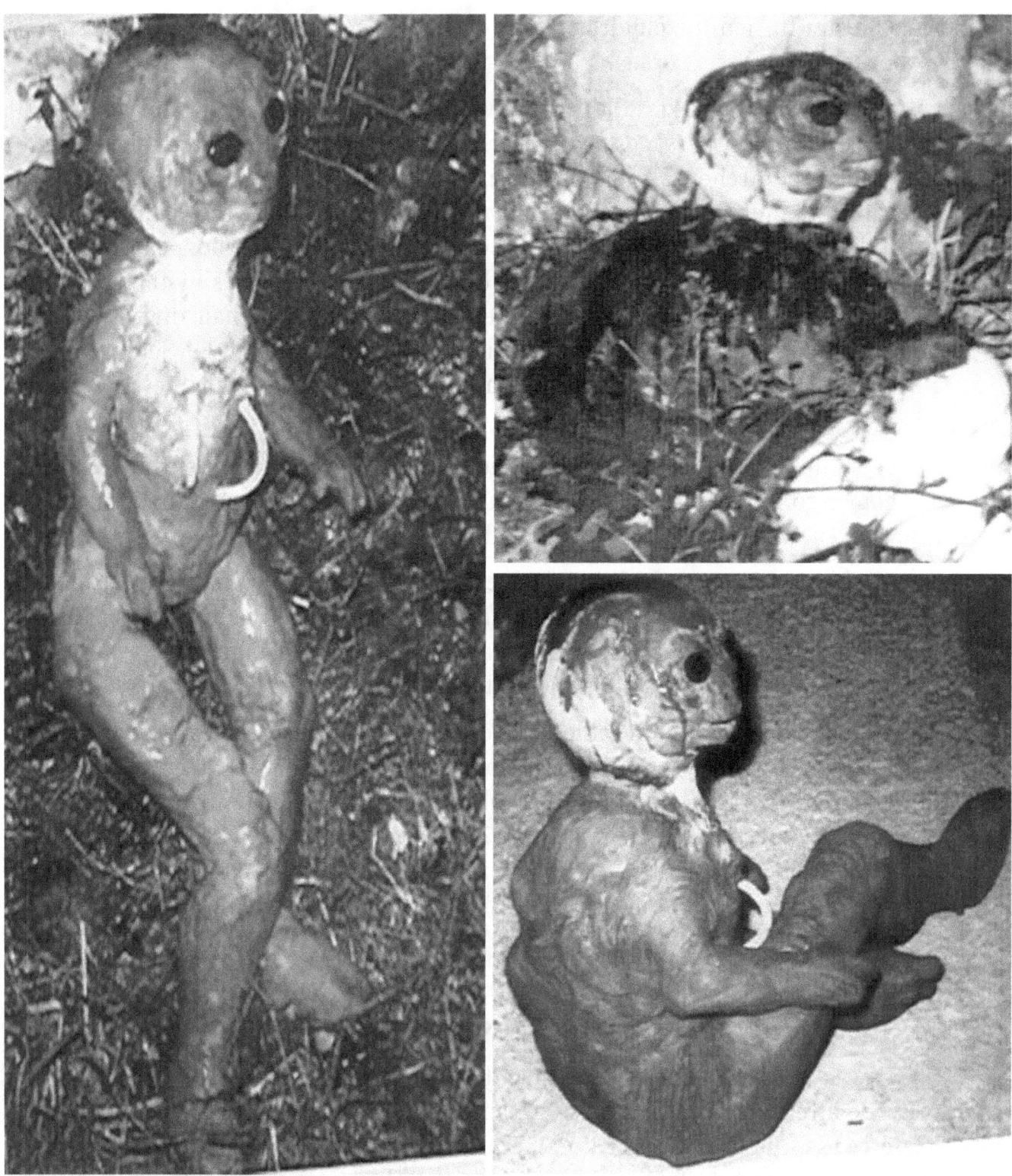

This weird creature was photographed between May and September, 1993, by 23-year-old Filiberto Caponi from Pretare d'Arquata, Italy. No UFOs were reported in association with this strange incident.

were extraterrestrial, quickly reinforced public opinion that UFOs were not of this Earth.

It is difficult to resist the siren call of the extraterrestrial hypothesis. From the very beginning, strange beings have been seen in association with UFOs. On July 23, 1947, in Bauru, Brazil, a Brazilian survey worker, Jose C. Higgins, and his crew saw a large "Saturn"-shaped object land and disgorge three seven-foot tall entities. These beings were dressed in transparent suits inflated like "rubber bags." All three creatures were bald with large round eyes, no facial hair, and legs longer in proportion than a human.

In August of 1947, Professor R. L. Johannis, while on a hike near Friuli, Italy, came across a large "lens"-shaped object perched vertically on a rocky ledge. Nearby were two "boys," or so Johannis thought. When the professor shouted at the "boys" about the strange craft, they shot him with what he described as a "smoke-ray." Johannis experienced an electric shock that laid him out flat on the ground, unable to move but still conscious.

When the two beings approached, he could tell that they were not boys but strange humanoids. The two creatures were about three feet tall with "earthy-green skin," long straight noses and large, protruding eyes that were the color of two "well-ripened yellow-green plums." Their hands had eight fingers, four on each side, making a claw rather than a normal hand.

The two beings left Johannis to climb back into the saucer, which removed itself from the ledge and silently disappeared. It wasn't until three hours later that Johannis felt strong enough to get up and return to the inn where he was staying. At the time Johannis, had never heard of "flying saucers," so he thought he had seen some experimental airship of the allied forces.

Many UFO sightings in the early 1950s reported structured machines that performed amazing aerial maneuvers beyond what conventional, earthly aircraft of the day could do. As well, when the UFOs actually landed, the creatures coming out acted just like what we expected from astronauts from another planet. They wore futuristic looking spacesuits with helmets and took soil, rock, water, and fauna samples before reentering their craft and zipping away.

Not unexpectedly, the 1950s saw the beginnings of the "contactee movement" when the UFOnauts got tired of simply collecting dirt and began to actually initiate conversations with the shocked witnesses alongside lonely

UFO Repeaters! Seeing Is Believing - The Camera Doesn't Lie!

In 1957, twenty-three-year old Brazilian farmer Antonio Vilas-Boas was abducted by small beings and taken inside a landed craft that looked like "a large elongated egg."

country roads. From that point, the UFOs stopped being a strange sky phenomenon and instead became a strange social phenomenon.

The poster boys of the early contactee movement were men like California's George Adamski and New Jersey's Howard Menger. Their space people were tall, usually blond and fair skinned, and claimed to be from planets right in our own solar system, Mars and Venus being the favorite choices.

The Space Brothers, as they became known, were here to help us mend our evil ways, especially our use of atomic weapons, which threatened the balance of the entire solar system. Most of these stories only further muddied the waters surrounding the UFO mystery. They also contributed to the impression that UFOlogy was populated by nothing more than nuts and crackpots who were out to make a buck off of the gullible. This is a stigma that still surrounds serious UFO research even today.

However, just when it seemed as if an easy explanation for UFOs had presented itself, the phenomenon revealed that there was more going on than angels from outer space and that the blond space brothers were not the only show in town.

In 1979, researchers from MUFON's Humanoid Study Group compiled a long list of more than 1,600 different UFO entity incidents. Contrary to the popular belief that sightings of UFO beings are generally rare, researchers found that many of the reports are well-documented, firsthand investigations involving credible witnesses.

THE FRENCH INVASION

The first major flap of UFO occupant sightings occurred during the French UFO wave of 1954. UFOs had been seen en masse all over Europe and South America that year, with the wave reaching its peak in Western Europe. Numerous reports of UFO landings and occupant sightings were gathered by several investigators, including Jacques Vallee and Aimé Michel.

On September 10, 1954, at 10:30 P.M., 34-year-old Marius Dewilde went outside of his home in Quarouble, France, to investigate why his dog was barking. He noticed a dark shape on a nearby railroad track, and coming towards him from the object were two strange beings about three-feet high and dressed in "diving suits."

UFO Repeaters! Seeing Is Believing - The Camera Doesn't Lie!

Height - 2½ to 3½ ft.

Sex - No indication.

Ears swept back; extended quite a bit above crown of head.

Eyes yellow center, white ring; about 6" apart; glowing.

Mouth a thin line; but not sure that there was a mouth.

Body powerful above waist, muscles clearly seen. Below waist thin and spindly, almost no shape to legs - sticklike.

Hands oversize, talons 2" or 3" long; webbing between fingers, starting about a knuckle above talons.

Feet not seen (or not noted).

Head almost round; bald; same color as body.

Nose - None; one man stated very strongly that there was none.

Neck - none.

Knuckles and fingers not counted.

Sketch of one of the Kelly-Hopkinsville, Kentucky "Goblins" that terrorized a family on August 21, 1955, after a UFO was seen to land nearby.

Dewilde rushed towards the small beings to try and capture one, when, unexpectedly, a bright, green light spouted from the dark object and dazzled him. The man instinctively closed his eyes and tried to run away, but his legs refused to move. Suddenly, Dewilde found he could move again and discovered that both the strange creatures and the dark craft had vanished.

For an article written by Vallee entitled "The pattern behind the UFO landings," Vallee researched two hundred UFO and occupant sightings out of thousands reported in 1954. Out of the two hundred cases, one hundred and eighteen involved UFOs that had landed. From these one hundred and eighteen reports, forty-two involved descriptions of the "pilots" of these crafts. The descriptions always involved beings which were near-human in appearance, sometimes absolutely human.

The "human" operators were always said to be of "European type" with few variations. In at least eight instances, the creatures were described as dwarfs whose faces and bodies were covered with hair. These bizarre groups of UFO creatures became especially predominant in South American sightings.

In the early morning hours of November 28, 1954, two truck drivers from Caracas, Venezuela, Jose Ponce, and Gustavo Gonzales, were driving to Petare, about fifteen miles away from Caracas. Around 2:00 A.M., the men found their way blocked by a glowing, disc-shaped object about ten feet in diameter, which was hovering about six feet above the street.

Gonzales brought his truck to a stop, and both men got out and walked closer to the object. When they were about twenty-five feet from it, they discovered they were being approached by what appeared to be a very hairy, dwarf-like man. Gonzales impulsively grabbed the creature and lifted him off the ground, but the creature twisted out of the truck driver's grasp and gave Gonzales a shove that sent him sprawling backward.

Before Gonzales could regain his feet, the humanoid, whose eyes glowed in the headlights of the truck like yellow cats' eyes, leaped on the man and began to claw at him with webbed hands that had claws about an inch long. Gonzales later told police that he tried to fight back with a knife into the creature's shoulder, but the blade glanced off of the creature as if its shoulder were made of steel. At this point Jose Ponce panicked and ran to seek help from a nearby police station.

As Gonzales tried to fight off his strange attacker, another hairy little man jumped out of the glowing craft and pointed a small shiny tube at him. There was

UFO Repeaters! Seeing Is Believing - The Camera Doesn't Lie!

In Quarouble, France, on September 10, 1954, a metal worker, Marius DeWilde, came out of his house and saw a dark object on the railroad tracks, then saw two dwarfs walking toward it. When he tried to stop them, he was paralyzed by a strong orange light beam. The creatures were under three-feet tall, bulky, and wore dark "diving" suits.

a brilliant beam of light, which blinded Gonzales for a moment, and he thought he was dead. But, when he could see again, the object was rising above the trees and quickly shot away.

Gonzales ran for the police station and showed up a couple of minutes after Ponce. At first, police thought the men were drunk or crazy. A doctor was brought in, who determined that both men were in a state of shock and that neither of them had been drinking. Gonzales was treated for a long, deep scratch down his left side, and later reports said that it eventually healed but left a permanent scar.

A few weeks later, on the night of December 16, 1954, three young men were driving on the outskirts of San Carlos, Venezuela, after a night out on the town. Jesus Paz asked his friends to stop the car so that he could relieve himself. Paz walked about 12 feet away from the parked car when he suddenly screamed and dropped down into the tall grass. His friends ran to his rescue and found him stunned and lying on the ground. A short distance away a small, hairy, manlike creature was running toward a shiny disc-like craft which was resting on the ground. The hairy dwarf disappeared inside of the object, which quickly rose off of the ground with a loud buzzing sound and vanished into the night sky.

Paz was rushed back to the city to the hospital, where doctors found that he was in a state of shock. Furthermore, the man had long deep scratches on his right side and downward across his spine, "like claw marks," the doctor said.

Paz told officials that he had walked around a bed of tall flowers when he almost stumbled over this short, hairy manlike creature that was examining the flowers. Paz tried to escape, but when he turned, the creature attacked him with its long talons, clawing and tearing his shirt and striking Paz on the back of the neck.

Several weeks later, Paz told a local reporter that his scratches had still not healed properly, remaining red and inflamed as the day when he was injured. After his initial interview, Paz refused to discuss his encounter and asked to be left alone.

THEY MIGHT BE GIANTS

On the opposite end of the scale are the UFO giants. Even though their reports are not nearly as numerous as the small humanoids, the UFO giants certainly are the most bizarre of the UFO occupants.

UFO Repeaters! Seeing Is Believing - The Camera Doesn't Lie!

During a UFO conference held on August 7-8, 1954, that featured three of the top "contactees" of the time, George Adamski, Truman Bethurum and Daniel Fry, this woman with her striking features, was photographed by Brazilian journalist João Martins. She identified herself as Dolores Barrios, a dress designer from Manhattan Beach, California.

João Martins did manage to ask Barrios a few questions: "- Are you or are you not Venusians? The woman, smiling, calmly replied: - No. - Why are you here? - Because we are interested in this subject. - Do you believe in flying saucers? - Yes. - Is it true that, as Mr. Adamski says, that they come from Venus? - Yes. They are from Venus."

The giants are the least humanlike of all reported entities, with sightings describing creatures seven to nine feet tall and an amazing diversity ranging from one-eyed Cyclops, beings with black-faces, bushy black hair, and, in some instances, with three unblinking eyes and large, round heads.

One amazing giant story was the account of a truck driver named Eugenio Douglas, who allegedly used a revolver to fight off three "shiny metal robots" some fifteen to twenty feet tall. This happened in Argentina on October 18, 1963. Douglas told police that he drove his truck into a ditch after a brilliant white light engulfed it near the town of Monte Maix. The light, he said, came from a twenty-five-foot disk parked in the middle of the road.

When he got out of his truck, Douglas was approached by three "indescribable beings" that tried to grab him. He managed to draw his pistol and fire several shots at the giants, who seemed unfazed by the bullets. Nevertheless, Douglas managed to get away and run toward town as the saucer lifted off of the road and made several passes at him. He said that each time he felt "a wave of terrible, suffocating heat." The police examiner later found that Douglas had suffered several unusual burns, unlike anything he had seen before.

Israel experienced a wave of UFO giant sightings in 1993. One such incident occurred during the early morning of April 20. Tsiporet Carmel stepped outside of her house and saw a large "silo-shaped" object in her back yard. Next to it, Tsiporet saw a seven-foot-tall being wearing metallic overalls. Its head was covered in what looked like a beekeeper's hat.

Tsiporet said, "Why don't you take off your hat so I can see your face?" The being answered her telepathically, "That's the way it is."

The giant then reentered the object, which vanished in a flash of light, leaving behind a large circle and shards of pure silicon in the yard as proof of the incident.

ENTER THE GRAYS

It's hard to pinpoint when the so-called "grays" first made their appearance. Several reports from the 1954 UFO wave described little creatures with large black eyes, but researchers have not found any substantial reports of the grays until the early 1970s.

Travis Walton claimed he saw small beings with large heads and big, dark eyes when he was abducted in 1975. Walton also said he saw three normal looking "humans" aboard the UFO, indicating that there were still some good old-fashioned aliens around.

The mid to late 70s saw an increase in UFO abduction reports. A majority of cases involved beings that appeared to be what we now refer to as the grays.

The movie, "Close Encounters of the Third Kind," portrayed its aliens as big-eyed, large-headed, gray creatures. So, even by 1977, this shape was already starting to become the cultural ideal of a typical extraterrestrial.

THE HOMOGENIZATION OF THE ALIEN

Today, unless someone has been living in a cave, anyone seeing a picture of a gray would identify it as a space alien. The grays have wormed their way into almost every part of our society. Television commercials portray grays frolicking at night over beers. Magazine ads show us grays coveting the newest line of sports sneakers. They are on tee shirts, bumper stickers, key chains, and anything else that could be used to sell a product. If these creatures do exist, they could conquer us simply by demanding royalty payments on all the merchandise sold using their image.

The grays seemed for awhile to be more a western hemisphere phenomenon. UFO occupant reports from other parts of the world still show a high diversity of entities. However, by the beginning of the 21st century, the gray alien meme had pretty much reached every corner of the planet. Many UFO groups will no longer accept UFO occupant reports unless it involves a gray, so, at least in the U.S., reports of beings other than grays have dwindled.

Like most other things in our society, the extraterrestrial has been homogenized down to the basic creature we all know and love. All differences have been eliminated to produce a simple, cuddly, big-eyed alien, fit for mom and dad and all the kids back home. But not me! I'll always remember the time when there were all kinds of different spacemen. I will tell my grandchildren that, when I was their age, I could pick from a dozen or more of the silly flying saucer folk.

We didn't have fancy-schmancy grays and we had to walk fifteen miles a day through waist-deep snow to see the flying saucers and their many different pilots. My grandkids will smile understandingly at me, hoping I'll soon fall back to sleep so they can continue to watch their gray alien cartoons and play their gray alien video games. I will go back to my happy dreams of space brothers, little hairy dwarfs and weird, glowing giants, wondering: where have all the spacemen gone?

Tim R. Swartz is the author of such books as: "The Lost Journals of Nikola Tesla", "Time Travel: Fact Not Fiction", and "America's Strange and Supernatural History". Available at Amazon.com

UFO Repeaters! Seeing Is Believing - The Camera Doesn't Lie!

Art By Carol Ann Rodriguez

Write Us For FREE Catalog

Send us your name and mailing address for our free catalog of interesting books and other items you won't find anywhere else in this world or any other!

Global Communications P.O.
Box 753
New Brunswick, NJ 08903

mrufo8@hotmail.com

www.conspiracyjournal.com

UFO Repeaters! Seeing Is Believing - The Camera Doesn't Lie!

BEWARE OF THE DERO
AND ESCAPE FROM THEIR CAVERN STRONGHOLD

REPRINT OF A RARE SERIES – THE HIDDEN WORLD
Featuring The Demented Works of Richard Shaver, Ray Palmer, And The Denizens Of The Inner Earth.

A must for conspiracy, UFO or horror buffs.

His stories caused a great sensation when published in the late 40s and 50s. The Dero, Richard Shaver lamented, were kidnapping surface-dwellers on a regular basis. They had appropriated sophisticated "ray" machines the great ancient races had left behind that made humans go stark raving mad. They spied on people and projected fermented thoughts and voices into their heads. And the Dero can be blamed for all misfortunes, small, personal and catastrophic.

12 VOLUMES IN THE SERIES NOW AVAILABLE
– Each Volume 200 or more large format pages.

( ) NO 1 – Tormented voices from the caves. The Home of the ancients. Below the Earth. Mantong, an ancient "unknown" language. The demented Dero wage war.

( ) NO 2 – Airplane crashes, train wrecks, celebrity deaths caused by underworld race. The Dark Cloud expands over earth as subsurface mutants, kidnap, torture and eat humans.

( ) NO 3 – Mandark – the story of the Messiah as told in the caves. Underground rail system to heal. Death Rays from the Inner Earth.

( ) NO 4 – Reality of the Sathanas. The forbidden playground of the Underworld. The madness of Richard Shaver – was he really in the caves?

( ) NO 5 – Deeds of the Elder Race. The occult explanation. The true sorceress and ladies of the Cavern World.

( ) NO 6 – Two torrid tales by Richard Shaver…Plus! Entering the secret vaults of the Elders. Learn of the beautiful female seducers who lure men to an untimely end.

( ) NO 7 – Complete stories by Shaver: Formula From the Underground and The Womb of the Titans. Also: Struggle of the Native Americans in the caves.

( ) NO 8 – Six stories by Shaver. How to get into the caves. Cult of the Witch Queen. How to build a space TV.

( ) NO 9 – Learning secrets of time and space. Is the Moon "deformed?" The oddities of gravity. Goddess of the Seven Stars!

( ) NO 10 – How to deal with voices inside your head. The ancient Telaug transmitters and telepathy – the same or in conflict? The plotters exposed by Shaver.

( ) NO 11 – Tunnels of the Titans by Vincent Gaddis. America's mysterious race of Indian Giants by Chief Sequoyah. Seeing in the dark by an MD. Letters File PLUS a lost article.

( ) NO 13 (issue 12 NOT available) – Clarifying the Shaver Mystery by Jim Wentworth. Shaver on Inertia. Inside Mount Lassen. Medieval Illicit by Shaver. The SECRET Shaver-Palmer letter file.

FREE BONUS: Order 3 books get BONUS CD interview with Shaver and Palmer and Long John Nebel. Order all books and get CD and 200 page hair-raiser SHAVER'S CHILLING TALES ($20 value).

ORDER YOUR COPIES TODAY!
Each volume just $25.00 –
Entire Set of 12 volumes of
the HIDDEN WORLD -
$210.00 + $15.00 S/H

Timothy G Beckley, Box 753
New Brunswick, NJ 08903

TWO REMARKABLY EERIE WORKS
BY WILLIAM HAMILTON III

Bill Hamilton is one of the most famous and longest serving American UFO researchers. He worked as a Senior Programmer-Analyst at UCLA, and has degrees in psychology, physics and Information Technology. From 1961 until 1965, he worked in the U. S. Air Force Security Service.

( ) COSMIC TOP SECRET: AMERICA'S SECRET UFO PROGRAM
America's classified anti-gravity and teleportation programs. Underground and underwater bases revealed. Secret reptilian agenda. **Large format, 310 pages—$32.00**

( ) TIME TRAVEL NOW — WORM HOLES, ANTI MATTER, THE REALITY OF OTHER DIMENSIONS! Here is the latest scientific as well as metaphysical findings on a topic that has long fascinated the public. Added material includes *SELF HELP GUIDE TO TIME TRAVEL* with Commander X, former military intelligence operative. This virtual course on Time Travel includes two special hour long CDs—**$32.00**

SPECIAL: 2 BOOKS - 2 AUDIO CD'S $49.00 + $6 S/H

Timothy Beckley · Box 753
New Brunswick, NJ 08903

THE WONDER BOOK OF ALL AGES!
SPECIAL RAY PALMER EDITION!
1250 Pages, 2 Volumes.
Illustrations.
Most Complete Edition

A New Cosmology! Delivered thru spirit intervention in 1870 in upstate NY to a practicing dentist. Details the sacred history of earth for the past 24,000 years beginning with submersion of Pan in the Pacific.

Tells about Einstein's theories. War in space. Who manages the earth. The glory of gods and goddesses. The truth about flying saucers.

A profound work deserving of serious attention.

Our special price $85.00 + $10 S/H.
Mailed directly from the printer
due to weight of seven pounds.

Timothy Beckley · Box 753
New Brunswick, NJ 08903
Mrufo8@hotmail.com for PayPal

Check Out All Our Books At Amazon. com

UFO Repeaters! Seeing Is Believing - The Camera Doesn't Lie!

EXPLORE OUR OVER 200 PRINTED BOOKS AT AMAZON.COM

EXPLORE THE BIZARRE, THE UNEXPLAINED... THE MYSTERIOUS!

UFOS, TIME TRAVEL, THE PARANORMAL, FORTEAN, OCCULT, INNER EARTH, CRYPTOIDS, CONSPIRACIES AND MORE

OUR AUTHORS INCLUDE: TIMOTHY GREEN BECKLEY — MARIA D'ANDREA — DRAGONSTAR — T. LOBSANG RAMPA — BRAD STEIGER — RICHARD SHAVER — WM ALEXANDER ORIBELLO — COMMANDER X — GEORGE ADAMSKI — GEORGE HUNT WILLIAMSON — TIM SWARTZ — NICK REDFERN — SEAN CASTEEL

Important Titles (Print & Kindle): UFOs From Undersea; Plans For Time Travel Machines; Subterranean Worlds Inside Earth; The Controllers; The Dulce Wars; The Missing Diary of Admiral Byrd; UFOs: Nazi Secret Weapons. 175 ADDITIONAL TITLES. For a comprehensive list, type Inner Light – Global Communications or Timothy Green Beckley at Amazon (US or UK). Also at www.FishPond.com.au.

Get our free CONSPIRACY JOURNAL newsletter— mrufo8@hotmail.com

TAP INTO THE MAGICK OF THE PYRAMIDS
THIS BOOK INCLUDES TEN OF THE MOST MAGICAL GOOD LUCK TALISMANS AND AMULETS FROM THE POWERFUL HIGH PRIESTS OF ANCIENT EGYPT

THE PYRAMIDS SPEAK
Ancient Mysteries Revealed Of Great Benefit To Modern Mankind

FIRST TO CAST SPELLS

A great deal of mystery has been associated with the pyramids of Egypt. For centuries there has been unprecedented debate as to how the massive blocks – each weighing several tons – were actually lifted into place, reaching right to the heavens and ending with a perfectly placed capstone. And while the pyramids have often been associated with mummification, the truth is that the pyramids were not really intended to be tombs.

In about 350 BC King Nectanebo found the power of occult magick to his liking. When his kingdom was threatened he would fight his enemies with wax figures animating these "robots" with the breath of life, using a ritual taken directly from the Book of the Dead, which was a stone ledger containing the world's most powerful incantations.

MANY QUESTIONS ANSWERED – BENEFIT TO ALL!

** Does A Time Capsule Rest Under The Great Pyramid? – ** Will The Cross Jesus Was Crucified On Be Found Beneath The Sands of Egypt? – ** Did Space Ships Use The Pyramids To Recharge So They Could Return Home? – ** Did The Ancients Realize That The Shape of The Pyramid Itself Was Very Powerful? – ** Why Has The Fact That Pyramids Have Been Found All Over The Planet Been Withheld From The Public?

FREE BONUS!!! ORDER THE PYRAMIDS SPEAK NOW AND YOUR BOOK WILL CONTAIN A MINATURE PYRAMID "KIT" TO COPY WHICH IS BELIEVED TO HAVE MAGICAL POWERS YOU CAN TAP INTO. ONE, TWO, THREE!

Order THE PYRAMIDS SPEAK - $21.00 + $5 S/H

( ) Also Available: SECRETS OF EGYPTIAN SPELL CASTING Amulets, Talismans, and Magical Lifeforms. Here are the spells of the great Egyptian pharaohs and their occult magicians. Even Moses is said to have followed in their footsteps and adapted their mystical formulas. Unlock the Occult Wisdom Of Antiquity And Experience The Awesome Miracle Of Egyptian Magic, Known To Be The Most Powerful Of ALL Time! Authored by the head of the British Museum of Antiquities.

270 large size pages—ISBN 1892062712—$24.00

SPECIAL BOTH BOOKS $39.95 + $5 S/H

Timothy G. Beckley· Box 753· New Brunswick, NJ 08903 · Mrufo8@hotmail.com (We can provide a PayPal invoice)
FREE DVD WITH ORDERS OF $30+: Beyond the Paranormal With Paul and Ben Eno and Guest, Tim Beckley

UFO Repeaters! Seeing is Believing - The Camera Doesn't Lie!
UFO Repeaters! Seeing Is Believing - The Camera Doesn't Lie!

NO NEED TO BE PARANOID – ITS JUST ANOTHER CONSPIRACY! DEEPEST, DARKEST SECRETS REVEALED

DIARY OF A CONSPIRACY SALESMAN
Who was Bill Cooper??? Was he a true patriot? A tough survivalist? Or simply a fanatic? Some knew him as a UFO "expert" (having claimed insider information on the government's actual knowledge of extraterrestrials living amongst us)...A conspiracy theorist...a former Navy Intelligence operative...and the person the President once called "the most dangerous man on American airwaves." Here is the INSIDE STORY as told by fellow patriot and government whistle blower Commander X.
Large Format, 136 pages, ISBN:1892062305—$15.00

DEAD MEN TALKING
Exposing The New World Order Conspiracy And The Evil Agenda Of The Brotherhood Of The Illuminati. The volume covers the full spectrum of HIGHLY CONFIDENTIALLY, SUPER SECRET, TOTALLY SUPPRESSED information that is available only on a NEED TO KNOW. ** —The Secret Brotherhood And The Mind Control Agenda ** — The Brotherhood and The Manipulation of Society ** — The Round Table ** — Royal Institute of International Affairs ** — Council On Foreign Relations ** — The Bilderberger Group ** — The Trilateral Commission ** – House of Rothchild ** – The Rockefeller Empire ** – Dr Henry Kissinger.
Large Format, 238 pages, ISBN: 1606110225—$18.95

FIGHTING THE FEDERAL RESERVE
MAVERICK? MADMAN? TRAITOR? SUPER PATRIOT? Congressman Louis T McFadden was the man who took on the Federal Reserve and was nearly assassinated . McFadden used "buzz words" similar to those bandied about by conservative talk show hosts today — words like "foreign influences" — "alien conspiracies" — and "subterranean corridors of power." But keep in mind, the Congressman was NOT referring to some imminent extraterrestrial invasion, but instead was attempting to alert the American public to the evils of the Federal Reserve and a parasitic banking system which sought, in a deliberate and calculated way, to destroy America. Here are his most important papers, detailing what he saw as a massive CONSPIRACY involving FRAUD and TREASONOUS ACTIONS that was formulated by power-hungry, evil individuals, along with the additional contemporary thinking of Senator Ron Paul.
7 x 10, 604 pages, ISBN:1606111035—$21.95

WALL STREET BANKSTERS

WARNING! THIS BOOK IS CONSIDERED HIGHLY DANGEROUS TO YOUR MENTAL STATE ** Exposes A World of Treachery – Answers the Questions: WHO ARE THE MASTERMINDS BEHIND WORLD DOMINATION? – WHO ACTUALLY MANAGES THE FLOW OF PAPER MONEY AND CONTROLS COMMERCE AND THE BANKING SYSTEM? . . . WHO — IF ANYONE — PROFITS FROM WAR? – For the first time names are given, and organizations exposed. Some have called this the most DANGEROUS book ever written, but why? Discover who financed the Russian revolution and why WW I and WW II did NOT have to happen!
Large Format, 384 pages, ISBN: 1606110268—$21.95

INCREDIBLE TECHNOLOGIES OF THE NEW WORLD ORDER
UFOs - Tesla - Area 51. Go inside Area 51. Learn of the latest developments in Tesla Technology, Free Energy and the Ultra Top-Secret HAARP Project. Learn the mind-blowing truth about the infamous Philadelphia Experiment and see how during World War II mankind first discovered the secrets of teleportation and time travel. Discover how Nikola Tesla, a man who was born in the 19th century, discovered the science behind anti-gravity and the Particle Beam Death Ray!
Large Format, 144 pages ISBN: 0938294385 $14.00

SUPER SPECIAL: ALL 8 CONSPIRACY BOOKS JUST $132.00 + $12.00 S/H

MIND CONTROL FOR THE MASSES

**DON'T BE A VICTIM OF:
MIND CONTROL, BRAIN WASHING,
LONG DISTANCE PSYCHOLOGICAL TORMENT
OR MENTAL EAVES DROPPING.**

Everything In TWO Banned Books
( ) # 1 – MATRIX OF THE MIND—Is someone watching us through our TV set? Is our phone bugged 24/7? – How about the mysterious satellite that passes over twice a day? Includes the mind control of model Candy Jones. Large format, 260 pages, $24.00.
( ) # 2 – MIND STALKERS—MIND CONTROL OF THE MASSES—False flags, ELF Waves, drugs, mental manipulation, behavior modification. Large format, 164 pages, $18.95.
Order both for $36 + $5 S/H and get a free conspiracy DVD.
3 Copies each book $100.00 + $8 S/H
Timothy Beckley · Box 753 · New Brunswick, NJ 08903
Mrufo8@hotmail.com for PayPal

**BANNED IN 22 COUNTRIES!
Book & CD Set
UFOS NAZI SECRET WEAPONS**
The most controversial work of its type. The author claims he has been a political prisoner for the last 20 years due to the publication of his censored book. Were Foo Fighters and German Made Flying Disks created by Nazi scientists and were they brought to the USA after the war, resulting with the crash at Roswell, NM?

Large Format. New Low Price: $21.95 + $5 S/H
196 pages, ISBN: 1606111167
BONUS CD FOR MAIL ORDER CUSTOMERS ONLY!

**Timothy Green Beckley
Box 753 · New Brunswick, NJ 08903**

Researchers Promote Use Of The Crystal Power Rod As A Modern Day WISH MACHINE

THE CRYSTAL POWER ROD AS A "WISH MACHINE"
Also Known Widely As The COSMIC GENERATOR this device is believed to have originated in Atlantis and supposedly operates with energy generated by the operator's mind, amplified by emotions, feelings, desires. Once amplified, these "wishes" can be projected over vast distances to influence others.

WISH MACHINES – MIND MACHINES
They come in various forms and are known as Radionics, Ociloclasts, or Hieronymous Machines, Detector Rods, Symbolic Machines or, put most simply, Black Boxes regardless of their appearance.

SUPER SECRET DOSSIER INCLUDED WITH YOUR POWER ROD
Your Crystal Power Rod (may vary slightly from illustration) and Mind Machine Study Guide is sold as a unit for $85.00 + $5.00 S/H and is obtainable from:
**Timothy Beckley · Box 753
New Brunswick, NJ 08903**

FROM EXOTIC DANCER AND RUSS MEYER VIXEN TO THE QUEEN OF SEDONA. EXCLUSIVE INTERVIEW WITH RAVEN DE LA CROIX ON YOUTUBE.COM

Subscribe for FREE to Mr UFO's Secret Files and click on interview (new ones added regularly)

www.ingramcontent.com/pod-product-compliance
Lightning Source LLC
Chambersburg PA
CBHW080533170426
43195CB00016B/2546

9 781606 111918